UNTOUCHABILITY AND THE LAW "THE GROUND REALITY"

UNTOUCHABILITY AND THE LAW
"THE GROUND REALITY"

K.D. Purane

Foreword by:
Rajendra Vora

GYAN

GYAN PUBLISHING HOUSE
NEW DELHI-110002

UNTOUCHABILITY AND THE LAW "THE GROUND REALITY"

(Law, Political Science, Sociology)

ISBN: 81-212-0652-9

Published in 2000 in India by
Gyan Publishing House
5, Ansari Road,
New Delhi-110 002

Laser Typesetting at: Power Photocomposers, New Delhi-110 002
Printed at: Mehra Offset Printers, Delhi-110 092.

Contents

Foreword

Dr. K.D. Purnane's work on the Implementation of Protection of Civil Rights Act of 1976, is first of its kind and therefore, invites attention of not only scholars in the area, but also the social activists in the field of Human Rights, especially of the Dalits. This work is a reminder to the fact that the legal protection alone is not sufficient for the Dalits. They will have to organize themselves and prepare for a sustained protest rather than mishandling the legal instrument for their short-term political gains. The dominant groups will have to come to terms with the reality by throwing away the feudal shackles. I am happy to note that Dr Purane's work which discusses these issues with the help of hard data is now being published in the form of a book for the benefit of a wider audience.

14th January 2000

Dr. Rajendra Vora
Head,
Department of Political Science and
Public Administration
University of Pune

Preface

Untouchability is a typical Indian problem. It has many sides. The Government of India has been trying to bring untouchability to nought, by passing various laws such as Prevention of Atrocities Act, 1989 and Protection of Civil Rights Act, 1976. The interpretations of such acts differ from the points of view of the untouchables and touchables.

This author happens to be a student of Political Science and Law. Hence, this interdisciplinary faculty is used by him to view the practical side of these laws.

In Maharashtra alone, there were many cases of violation of PCR Act, This writer attempts to findout the facts regarding the use and misuse of the Act, and his background as a teacher of Political Science and as a student of Law helps him to study the practical "Politics". In a sense, it is a unique contribution to the studies of politics. Ahmednagar district in Maharashtra is the area of study. The court-cases regarding the violation of PCR Act and PAA Act are studied from different angles. This book is an objective analysis of such cases.

I hope, the readers will find it a useful guideline to solve the problem of casteism at the national level. It deserves a patient and objective approach.

K.D. Purane

1

Survey of the Literature on Hindu Society and Untouchability

Survey of the Literature

Western scholars have observed that a traditional society is usually heterogeneous and complex. It is characterised by the principles of pollution and purity but if an attempt is made for the integration and upliftment of the Scheduled Castes in such a society, it is viewed as a peaceful revolution.

According to M. Glen and Sipra Bose Johnson, "Among the multitude of difficult tasks facing the new nation of India in 1947 none was more challenging than the integration of the most deprived 15 per cent of its population, the untouchables, into an equal partnership in the merging modern republic."[1]

It was of the leadership of Dr. B.R. Ambedkar that created increased political awareness among the Scheduled Castes in Maharashtra in general and the Mahar community, to which Dr. B.R. Ambedkar himself belonged, in particular.

The Problem, Nature and Background of Karjat Taluka

There are local conflicts and struggles for power among different groups in villages. Generally it is found that persons of a Scheduled Caste are used by one group in the village against the other, in their conflict or struggle for power. In Karjat Taluka, it was found that since 1976 there have been a few cases registered under the Protection of Civil Rights Act. Some cobblers were used as an instrument in local conflicts. In other cases the Mahars misused the Protection of Civil Rights Act for their own interest. An attempt has been made to study the nature and significance of Karjat Taluka, where efforts towards social integration were made and where considerable social harmony prevailed among all the villagers.

The Caste Composition

Karjat Taluka in Ahmednagar District is a case in point. It is a small taluka in Wastern Maharashtra which is prone to drought. The caste composition in Karjat Taluka is shown in Table 1.1.

Table 1.1: Castewise Population in Karjat Taluka[2]

Sr. No.	*Total*	*Males*	*Females*	*Total*
1.	Population	95076	89255	184331
2.	SC Population	13421	12622	26043
3.	ST Population	1140	1089	2229

Efforts Towards Social Interaction from 1960

Before 1960 there were separate wells for drinking water even among the Scheduled Castes. But since 1960 there has been one well for drinking water for all castes in every village. This was the result of efforts made by the village leaders. Karjat was a typical taluka in Maharashtra, dominated by Brahmins and Marathas, till 1960. There was cultural domination of the Brahmins. However the non-Brahmin leadership in Karjat Taluka was mainly responsible for creating social harmony in the village community, including the Scheduled Castes, immediately after 1960. Leaders like Ravasaheb Patil, Divanji Zarkar, Dr. Saptarshi, E. B. Nimbalkar, Bapusaheb Deshmukh, etc., encouraged the Scheduled Castes to come forward along with caste Hindus. The practice of providing separate tea cups to the Scheduled Castes at the common tea time in the Panchayat Samiti meetings and festivals and other public ceremonies in the villages was common before 1960. Ravasaheb Patil and Babasaheb Deshmukh and A.B. Nimbalkar carried forward the tradition of social harmony in the villages of the taluka.

Harmony among the village people prevailed up to 1976. The members who were elected to Grampanchayat and Panchayat Samiti, Director Boards of Banks, Cooperative Societies, etc. belonged to different castes including the Scheduled Castes. There was one common well for drinking water for all the communities in the villages: on the other hand many caste Hindus participated in the birth centenary of Dr. B.R. Ambedkar. All of them collected a common fund for the celebrations. Long processions were organized in the villages and people from all castes participated in them.

After the processions, a community meal was arranged in which all people participated, irrespective of their castes.

Religious books used to be read in temples and all people including the Scheduled Castes attended the rituals in the taluka. The people of the Scheduled Castes would beat the drums, enter the temples and even lift the palanquin and 'chabina'. No effort was made by the caste Hindus to show that the Scheduled Castes were the untouchables. Everyone came together for worshipping, festivals, singing bhajans, hymns, and distrubution of 'Sherni' in the fair. People mixed with each other freely and enjoyed the rituals and festivals without any social tension in the villages. It was felt that on no occasion and at no place the Scheduled Castes were discriminated against under the Protection of Civil Rights Act.

In 1981 a case was registered by Rangnath Udmale, in the office of Judicial Magistrate First Class Karjat Ahmednagar District. The procession of God Bhairavnath could not take place in the Babhulgaon village owing to a procession being taken out in celebration of the birth centenary of Dr. B.R. Ambedkar. However social harmony prevailed inspite of the registered case.

A study of Protection of Civil Rights Act and the cases under the Atrocities Act are being examined in this book. Inspite of the harmonious relationship in the taluka, attempts were made by some Scheduled Castes to register cases under the Protection of Civil Rights Act and Prevention of Atrocities Act. It is interesting to note the kinds of social, economic and political conditions that might have led to the registration of cases. An attempt would be made to study the motivation of these people while registering the cases. Hence, this study proposes to analyse the success and failure of these Acts in the Karjat Taluka of Ahmednagar District. There is harmony among all castes in this Taluka but there were a number of cases regarding atrocities which look place between 1978 and 1992. An attempt is made to study these cases in order to depict injustice done to the Scheduled Castes and Scheduled Tribes.

So far no study has been made about the injustice experienced by these people in Karjat Taluka. The book aims to analyse the issue of civil rights granted to Scheduled Castes and Scheduled Tribes by the Government.

Methods of Data Collection

There are different approaches in social science research in this regard.

They are:

1. Historical approach,
2. Case study approach,
3. Descriptive approach, and
4. Experimental approach.

The case study approach has been applied in this study. A case study approach for research is a rather recent development. It involves a deeper investigation of a single unit, which may be an individual, a family, an institution, a district, a community or any single event selected for intensive examination. This approach has been developed essentially as a problem-studying technique and also as a suggestive device for improvements in various dimensions of the cases under examination.

According to P.V. Young, "A comprehensive study of a social unit, be that unit a person, a group, a social institution, cultural group or even an entire community is called a case study".[3] According to Goode and Halt, "It is an approach which views any social unit as a whole. It is a way of organizing social data so as to preserve the unitary character of the social object being studied".[4]

A case study is that form of qualitative analysis involving the careful and complete observation of a person, a situation or an institution. It is an inclusive and intensive study of an individual in which the investigator brings to bear all his skills and methods or a systematic gathering of enough information about a person to permit one to understand how he or she functions as a unit of society.

This approach to research may be based on a given hypothesis or on any established conclusion but the study itself may help in developing a well-founded hypothesis for further investigation. This approach to research is, therefore, an open and objective examination of a particular unit with a view to develop a hypothesis for further research. The case study approach is also flexible in character as a researcher has complete independence in approaching the problem from any angle that he considers desirable and fruitful. As compared to historical approach, therefore, this approach does not suffer from rigidity of the historical data.

From this viewpoint therefore, it was thought that a case study approach would be useful. This is a study of various cases registered under the Protection of Civil Rights Act and Prevention of Atrocities Act, 1989 against the particular background of Karjat Taluka, Ahmednagar District. This kind of study is a beginning and needs investigation in depth.

The methodology to be used for the collection of data would be both from primary as well as secondary sources.

Personal Experience of the Researcher

The researcher comes from Karjat Taluka itself. He had, therefore, an advantage in collecting qualitative data about the taluka, including currents, cross-currents and undercurrents in the taluka. The researcher was a party to various important developments in the village and taluka. He had free access to all the castes in the villages. He took initiative in creating social harmony in the villages. He could seek the participation of many Scheduled Caste persons. He had an empirical knowledge of cases which were registered under the Protection of Civil Rights Act and Prevention of Atrocities Act. However, this kind of involved attitude and participation in taluka activities could create a bias against the Scheduled Castes. Therefore, efforts were deliberately made to study objectively, empirically, and an involved but neutral attitude. The researcher also relied on his participatory behaviour for empirical data collection.

Court Judgements

Fortunately the copies of court judgements were available for this study, because of the researcher's friendly relations with all the villagers and advocates. The copies of court judgements could be secured from the accused as well as from the plaintiff.

Interviews

Village leaders, judges, police inspectors, advocates, social workers, party leaders, Tahsildars, Deputy Collectors, Deputy Superintendents of Police, Block Development Officers, and concerned people in villages of Karjat Taluka were contacted for interviews. There were different experiences while conducting these interviews. The judges, police inspectors, head constables, Tahsildars and Deputy Collectors spoke openly about the cases. However, as they were government servants, they refused to give any authentic information and preferred to remain anonymous. The village leaders, social workers, like Govind Bhai Shroff, Sankarrao Kharat, discussed the problem in depth and with involvement.

The researcher could get an interdisciplinary perspective of this study only because of these interviews.

Information from Police Department (only cases resulted in compromise among many)

For the sake of this study, information from the police department was necessary so far as legal matters were concerned. The role of the police is very important as the results of the cases depend on how the police present them in the court. However, the police department willingly gave the necessary information, their views and experiences and also discussed the Protection of Civil Rights Act and Prevention of Atrocities Act and their implementation in general. Since they knew the researcher well, they hid nothing from him. This information proved to be very essential for this study.

Analysis of the Data

Data analysis is done after collection of data by methods like measurement of attitudes, scaling techniques, content analysis, document analysis, etc.

After the study of the cases, an attempt was made to interview village leaders and prominent persons like Govind Bhai Shroff, Sankarrao Kharat, Dr. Bhalchandra Phadke, Dr. Y.D. Phadke (from Aurangabad, Poona and Mumbai) respectively.

The comparative study of court judgements, information provided by the police department and information sought from the interviews was then analysed. A clear cut picture of the Atrocities Act, and implemention of Protection of Civil Rights Act in Karjat Taluka could be evolved after the above methods of data collection.

Thus the following chapters would deal with the steps taken by the Government in presenting atrocities against the Scheduled Castes and Scheduled Tribes.

Somna Ry

The present chapter emphasises on the survey of literature in Karjat Taluka of Ahmednagar District. The problem, nature and background of Karjat Taluka are highlighted. The efforts made by the social reformers in the taluka are discussed thoroughly. Various methods of data collection are discussed. It also analyses the data collected by the researcher.

References

1. Johnson Glen and Sipra Bose, 'Social Mobility among Untouchables' in Gupta G.R. (ed) *Chosion and Conflict in Modern India,* Vikas Publishing House Pvt. Ltd. New Delhi, 1978, 60-61.

2. Source. Primary Census Abstract 1991. Office of the Registrar General and Census Commissioner, Ministry of Home affairs, New Delhi, India.

3. Young P.V., *Scientific Social Surveys and Research*, Asia Publishing House, Bombay, 1961, 247 (2).

4. Goode and Hatt, *Methods in Social Research,*. New Delhi, Mac. Graw-Hill, International Books Company, 1932 , 33.

2

Nature of Hindu Society and Untouchability

The caste system in Indian society has long been a topic of study by Indian and foreign scholars. The recent writings of foreign researchers like Senart, Nesfield, Siz. H. Risley and Indian researchers like Dr. Ketkar were accessible to Dr. Ambedkar. The concept of the caste system in India has been difficult to explain despite the laborious attempts of the researchers. The Indian society in its historical perspective was never racially integrated; so is it today. It was a complex entity of Aryan, Dravidian, Mongolian and Scythian races. This particular theorem was agreed upon by well known anthropologists and was also accepted by Dr. Ambedkar who, in his writings and speeches, has dealt exhaustively and pointedly with the evils of the caste system. The first writing of Dr. Ambedkar on the caste system can be seen in a paper[1] read at the Anthropology Seminar on May 9, 1910, at the Columbia University, New York.

Dr. Ambedkar first defines castes as given by Senart, Nesfield, Risley and Dr. Ketkar. "As long as caste in India does exist, Hindus will hardly intermarry or have any social intercourse with outsiders, and if Hindus migrate to other regions on earth, Indian caste would become a world problem".[2] Here Dr. Ketkar gives the following two characteristics of caste system :

1. Its membership is confined to those who are born in it.
2. Its members are forbidden to marry outsiders.

Origin of Caste and Caste System

The idea of pollution is a characteristic of the caste system, only in so far as caste has a religious flavour. The absence of messing with outsiders is not due to positive prohibition but is a natural result of caste, i.e. exclusiveness. The various races of India, occupying definite territories, have more or less fused into one another and do possess a cultural unity, which is the only criterion of a homogeneous population. This cultural unity reflects in what we call endogamy which is the only characteristic that is peculiar to caste.

Dr. Ambedkar calls Manu a 'Tyrant' and tackles *Manusmriti.* He shows that the caste system is a legal system maintained at the point of a bayonet. If it has survived it is due to prevention of the masses from the possession of arms and denying to the masses the right to property. Therefore, the caste system, far from being natural, is really an imposition by the ruling classes upon the downtrodden classes. The study of the caste problem by Dr. Ambedkar involves four main points :

1. Inspite of the composite make-up of the Hindu population, there is a deep cultural unity;
2. The caste is a parcelling into bits of a larger cultural unit;
3. There is one caste to start with; and
4. Classes have become castes through initiation and ex-communication.

The equation of the different classes to different parts of the body is not a matter of accident, it is deliberate. The part fixes the gradation of the class and the gradation in turn fixes the function of the class. A Brahmin is the custodian of knowledge and learning, a Kshatriya is known for fighting, a Vaishya for function of industry and trade, and a Shudra is placed last in the social order and is given the filthiest function, namely to serve as a menial.

"Chaturvarna" in its last development is of two kinds:

1. Creation of the fifth class after the Shudras, and
2. Separation of the Shudra from the first three varnas. Brahmins, Kshatriyas and Vaishyas are "sacarnas" and the Shudras are "avarnas". The untouchables or Atishudras are classed as "avarnas".

To define a caste is harder than to give the derivation of the term. It is a collection of families or group of families bearing a common name claiming a common descent from a mythical ancestor, human or divine, professing to follow the same hereditary calling, and regarded by those who are competent to give an opinion as forming a single homogeneous community. Dr. Ambedkar goes on to add that the caste name is generally associated with a specific occupation and that a caste is almost invariably endogamous, but is further divided, as a rule, into a number of smaller circles each of which is endogamous, so that a Brahmin is not only restricted to marrying another Brahmin, but to marrying a woman of the same subdivision of Brahmins. This definition is open to question on the ground that descent from a mythical ancestor is claimed by the "gotra" and the internal exogamous division of the endogamous caste, than by the caste as a whole. Further, although the endogamous subdividion of a caste is a genuine and common feature of the institution, it is doubtful if the unqualified Brahmin can rightly be used as of the same caste at all. It is probably too vague to be of value because though the Brahmin belongs to one of the four original "varnas" or "colours" into which Rigvedic society was divided, a "varna" is very far from being the same thing as a caste. The Hindu word for caste is "jati" or "jat".

The division into various castes is the most significant system of social stratification in Hindu society. A good deal has been written by way of defining the complicated and unique institution of caste. Generally individual authors lay undue emphasis on one element or attach too much importance to one point in tracing the origin of the caste system and its ramifications such as race (Rislay), tribes (Ibbeston, Ghurye), occupation (Nesfield).[3] Whereas the general Hindu feeling about the caste system is that it has been established as a divine ordinance or at least with divine approval.[4]

The factors which led to the addition, fission and fusion of castes are conquest, migration, emulation, isolation, separation, occupational specialization, conversion and sectarianism, and the incorporation of tribal groups. This society permitted some individual mobility within these communities as well as the slower movements of whole communities.

The important features of castes in Maharashtra according to Irawati Karve are as follows:[5]

1. Castes are endogamous groups.
2. Castes are restricted to certain areas.
3. Castes have a certain traditional behaviour pattern which is

enforced in many cases by a "Caste council" made up of a number of respected elders in a caste.

4. Castes live together with other castes without mingling except on certain occasions. The intercourse between castes is peripheral or tangential.

5. A caste generally has a hereditary occupation, which is, however, not exclusive to it.

6. Castes are arranged in an hierarchical order.

Inspite of this rigidity in the caste system, instances of transformation of one caste into another are not rare today and were not rare in the past. New castes arose because of change in occupation, migration from one place to another and debasement or purification of customs.[6] According to M.N. Srinivas, "While the traditional system allowed individual caste to move up and down, the system itself remained unaltered." In other words, there was only positional change, not a structural one.[7] "Moreover, while a caste struggled for a higher position for itself in the local hierarchy, it resented the efforts of others in particular, the lower caste, to move up."[8]

Change in Hindu Society

In the early Vedic times, different members of the same family used to undertake different occupations of Chaturvarna (four classes) according to their inclination and abilities. Every member of the family enjoyed the liberty to adopt any profession he liked best. It is said that in Vedic times all men were equal and there was no trace of untouchability as we see it today. According to *Rigveda* no man was considered too high or too low in the society. But this healthy spirit of equality resulted, in course of time, to the tradition bound caste system and to the institution of untouchability which divided the Hindus, warped their thinking and eroded the structure of the community. Traditionally, each caste came to be associated with a profession, administration, trade or manual labour, and developed a high degree of exclusiveness among the professional classes. Depending on the nature of one's work, certain lowest sections of the community came to be regarded as untouchables and were kept more or less segregated even within villages. By practising untouchability, the upper castes kept them at a distance, and gave them a subordinate place within the system. "These were the people who were considered to be of very low caste since they had been traditionally engaged in occupations like shifting of night soil and treatment of hides and skins of animals which were considered "unclean" by the upper caste Hindus. Mahatma Gandhi referred to these people as Harijans or "Children of God."[9]

Nature of Untouchability

Untouchability means pollution by the touch of persons born in a particular caste or family. It is generally seen that this practice of untouchability is peculiar to Hindu society.

Dr. Ambedkar in his book, *The Untouchables, Who are They?*, discussed the origin of untouchability. He starts with the proposition that, "The Hindu civilization could hardly be called a civilization. It is a diabolical contrivance to suppress and enslave humanity."[10] Along with the development of the notion of defilement, primitive society had developed certain purificatory media and purificatory ceremonies for dispelling impurity. Primitive society had another method to get rid of impurity. This was to transfer it to another person. Therefore, it can be concluded that there are no people, primitive or ancient, who did not entertain the notion of pollution."[11]

"Untouchables", as a name generally applied to persons in the lowest classes of Hindu society, is of relatively recent origin. It first appeared in print in 1909.[12] The word is a literal translation of the Hindi word "Achhut". The Webster's dictionary vividly describes "untouchables" as a member of a large hereditary group in India having traditional Hindu belief and quality of defiling by contact the persons, food or drink of a member of a higher caste, and formerly being strictly degraded and restricted to menial work."[13]

From its very inception, the term has been hated, as it amounted to a degrading appellation for the people concerned. Notwithstanding, the use of the term has sometimes been advocated for psychological and political reasons; for instance B.S. Murty while recording his opinion on the merit of various expressions observed, "Perhaps the best of these is untouchable as it will remind him of his fallen state by a constant sting."[14] Similarly, Dr. Ambedkar used the term in the titles of his various books to highlight the degrading position of the people and to arouse sympathy for their political rights. His Highness Gaikwad of Baroda who took a deep interest in the matter, also advocated the term for its clarity.[15] To him the words "depressed classes" which had just begun to appear and "lower castes" were not satisfactory as they were too elastic. However, the word has now disappeared from ordinary parlance following widespread education and constitutional provisions.

It is a fact that no one is an untouchable because of his birth or because he follows a particular profession, which he does by honest living. Great thinkers and social workers like Raja Rammohan Roy, Dr. Ambedkar, Mahatma Phule, Mahatma Gandhi and others have all along expressed themselves against the practice of untouchability. The untouchability observed and practised in the society could be stated to be an act of inhumanity. It has no basis or religious theory. Religious principles which are broad and universal are one thing and customs which arise out of changing social conditions another.

Social reformers, religious preachers and other enlightened thinkers tried to dissuade people from following the evil practice of untouchability. It is common knowledge that the evil of untouchability has divided the society and impeded our progress as a nation.

Throughout Indian history, the evil of untouchability has been attacked by social and religious reformers, but it was largely through the provisions of the Constitution that the nation's conscience was awakened and the uplift of Scheduled Castes became a major issue in national life. The four orders of society as seen in the "Purushsukta" denote not only the origin of the classes but also the divine justification of the order of society.

According to Dr. Ghurye, special rights for the higher classes and disabilities for the lower ones were almost a universal feature of a class society.[16] It is, however, not only through legal measures that the evil of untouchability is being tackled, but efforts to erase it from the minds of the people have been made by focussing their attention on the degrading effects of social segregation and the injustice of social inequality. People are being systematically educated in this respect and made to realize that untouchability is a crime on social, moral and economic grounds. As a welfare state is wedded to socialistic ideals, the Government has now assumed greater responsibility for the well being of the Scheduled Castes. It is committed to the removal of all traditional disabilities that have stood in the way of their betterment and progress.

"The most distinctive feature of the Hindu culture was the religious elementary. Religion was interwoven with the Hindu system of law. The social basis of civilization was the joint family, the village community and the caste system. The last was regarded as divine ordained and has religious sanctions."

Thus untouchability is a corollary of the caste institution. It did not arise out of any personal fault or idiosyncracy on the part of an individual. Practically it was an attitude on the part of caste Hindus. A spirit of social aggression underlines this attitude. Doctrinally they were not part of Hindu society, while (existentially) they were an integral part of the local communities. In fact, exploitation or slavery was not unknown to any society in the past because economic needs in different forms were present in all countries. However, untouchability was a unique problem that was confronted only in India.

In modern times, there is a socio-political awakening among the untouchables also. An attempt is made to explain the same in the following pages.

Attempts by Social Reformers

After bringing out the nature of untouchability, the attempt is to show the social reform movements in detail. Energetic efforts to free the Hindu society from the evil system of untouchability were going on since the time of the Buddha (500 B.C.). He initiated them into his new religion. The ideological and spiritual attempts to abolish untouchability and establish social equality were going on for centuries. Chakradhar, Ramanand, Kabir, Chaitanya, Ekanath, Tukaram, Rohidas, Chokhamela and other 'saints' succeeded to a great extent in establishing spiritual equality.

Bhakti Cult (12th to 17th Century)

The Bhakti movement represented the Maharashtrian version of traditional cultural revolt. It survives to date. The Varkari Bhakti cult succeeded only after a period of coexistence of orthodoxy with radical movement. It was a religious awakening in Maharashtra. This movement represented a fundamental cultural revolt against the caste system, challenging its underlying principles and holding up ideals of a different social order in which equality of castes and equality of women were crucial.

This movement became popular even in rural areas. It reduced the intensity of casteism and brought about regional commonsense and solidarity. The Bhakti cult was an attack on ritualism which had prevented the growth of real Hinduism. This movement cherished certain spiritual and secular values. Vithoba (the name of the God) of Pandharpur became the common God of all castes including the untouchables. However, this movement was not without its limitations. It never tried to break the framework of four "varnas". The saints accepted inequality in society.

People sang together, participated in *bhajans* together, worshipped the same deity, made pilgrimages to the same temple but kept the caste injunctions with regard to the taking of food and water and endogamy. In her article, 'On the Road', Irawati Karve points out that all those people went to Pandharpur separately.

Dr. B.R. Ambedkar acknowledges the political significance of the Bhakti cult when he says that the political revolution led by Shivaji was preceded by the religious and social reforms brought about by the saints of Maharashtra.[17] Gail Omvedt aptly describes the Varkari cult when she says, "The Varkari cult in fact, contained conflicting trends within itself, representing both, a large element of compromise with caste orthodoxy and an anticaste equilibrium impulse.[18]

It was quite obvious that this kind of movement could bring very little change in the socio-economic condition of the untouchables, because the movement was not revolutionary in nature. On the contrary, the concepts of purity and impurity were becoming very rigid in villages, and the condition of the untouchables worse. The rulers recruited the untouchables in Army, but gave them separate and unequal treatment. Dr. B.R. Ambedkar described the painful situations of the untouchables under the Peshwa (post-Shivaji) rule. According to him at the time "the untouchable was not allowed to use the public streets if a Hindu was coming along, lest he should pollute the Hindu by his shadow. The untouchable was required to have a black wrist or on his neck a band as a sign or a mark to prevent the Hindus from getting themselves polluted by his touch through his mistake. In Poona, the capital of the Peshwas, the untouchable was required to carry, strung from his waist, a broom to sweep away from behind, the dust he trod on, lest a Hindu walking on the same should be polluted. In Poona, the untouchable was required to carry an earthen pot, hung upon his back wherever he went, holding his spit lest his spit falling on earth should pollute a Hindu who might unknowingly happen to tread on it.[19]

British Period

In the early British period, Raja Rammohan Roy, Dadoba Pandurang, G.D. Deshmukh and Vishnubhuva Barahmachari spoke against inequality in Hinduism and supported the cause of the lower castes and women. However, owing to the lack of organizational support, their preaching had a little effect on society.

In modern times Jotiba Phule spoke and worked for the untouchables. He was a man of action who belonged to a lower caste, *mali* (gardener). In fact, his ideas and the principles which he taught were not new, but what was significant was that he started a school for girls (1848), another school for the untouchables (1854) and founded the "Satyashodhak Samaj" (Society for the search of truth) in 1873. He organized non-Brahmin sections in Poona and challenged the supremacy of the Brahmins. His activities laid the foundation for the non-Brahmin movement in Maharashtra.[20]

In the opinion of Gail Omvedt, "Phule's greatest contribution was laid in his vigorous cultural revolutionary stand, his drive for equality and rationality, and in the creation of an organization, the Satyashodhak Samaj which would carry on agitation for social and religious reform at a mass level.[21]

Whatever limitations Phule had, it is undoubtedly clear that the spirit of his movement is still alive in modern Maharashtra, especially among the lower and the untouchable castes which carry with them his name with a great pride. The untouchables in Maharashtra take inspiration from him and respect him next only to Dr. Ambedkar. Even Dr. Ambedkar took inspiration from Jotiba Phule.[22]

Lokmanya Tilak (1856-1920)

Lokmanya Tilak was of the opinion that unless political freedom was achieved, social reform was meaningless. A caste eradication meeting was convened under the chairmanship of Vithal Ramji Shinde in 1878. Tilak gave a speech in which he declared that "even if God stood in the line of advocating caste system, I would not accept it".[23] In short, he strongly opposed the caste system in India.

Sayajirao Gaikwad (1893-1938)

The Maharaja of Baroda was a progressive ruler. He gave financial assistance to Dr. Ambedkar when the latter went to the USA in 1913. The Maharaja wanted to raise the status of the untouchables and by imparting them education and employment, he made certain attempts in that direction. It is significant that he appointed Dr. Ambedkar as his Military Secretary.[24]

V.D. Savarkar (1863-1966)

He was basically a political revolutionary from Ratnagiri. Owing to the British government's restriction on his activities, he began to take interest in social problems, especially untouchability. As he was an extreme rationalist, he criticized the orthodox methods and ritualism in Hinduism. However, he was for Hinduism and worked hard to reform it, neglecting the economic and social dimensions of the problem of untouchability. But his criticism of orthodox Hindu religion and the orthodox Brahamins helped to soften the intensity of untouchability in Maharashtra.

Raja Shahu Chhatrapati (1874-1922)

The Prince of Kolhapur State, Raja Shahu Chhatrapati took inspiration from Jotiba Phule and founded Satyashodhak Samaj (1912) in Kolhapur. He criticized "Chaturvarna", casteism and untouchability. He gave employment to Mahars, a dominant untouchable caste in Maharashtra, in different posts and brought the system of "Mahar Watan" to an end, put a stop to "Balutedari" and "Veth bigari" systems and gave equal rights to the untouchables in his State.

V.R. Shinde (1873-1944)

Popularly known as "Karmaveer", Shinde was a man of foresight. It was he who first raised the issue of untouchability at the national level and asked the Indian National Congress to pass a resolution to that effect. As a result, in 1977, the Congress adopted a resolution on the abolition of untouchability in Calcutta. He dealt with "Problem of Indian Untouchability", in which he categorically stated that the untouchables are the original inhabitants and rulers of Maharashtra and they were conquered by Marathas.[25] He founded the "Depressed Class Mission" for the untouchables in 1903.

S.M. Mate (1886-1957)

He founded the "Asprushyata Nivarak Mandal" (Society for the removal of untouchability) in 1917 in Poona. He used to visit the colonies of untouchables and started a school for them. He specifically pointed out and criticized references to untouchability in the Hindu religious books. Obviously the Brahmins hated him and called him "Mahar Mate".[26]

M.K. Gandhi (1869-1948)

M.K. Gandhi was a class by himself. He was a charismatic leader of India. By virtue of his many-sided personality, he defied classification. He was religious by nature and justified "Chaturvarna". He believed that it was the responsibility of the caste Hindus to undo the wrong done to the untouchables. He organized the "Harijan Sevak Sangh" in February 1933 and started publication of the weekly *Harijan* which became a most important journal and the forum through which he propagated his ideas on political and social reforms. Shortly afterwards, he decided to arrange marriages between caste Hindus and Harijans (untouchables).

After Independence, various measures were taken for uplifting the untouchables and the practice of untouchability was abolished by law. Scheduled Caste literary figures gave much of the credit for this change to Mahatma Gandhi.[27]

There were certainly many social reformers who tried their best to uplift the untouchables. Mention may be made of P. S. Sane alias Sane Guruji (1899-1950), the "Saint" Gadge Baba (1876-1957) and others. Sane Guruji advocated temple entry for the untouchables and when it was denied, he went on a fast at Pandharpur. He was sensitive and a humanist at heart. Gadge Baba, through the traditional method of "Kirtan" (discourse on religious matters), preached and practised equality and always advocated a secular and a tolerant view of life.

Efforts Made by the Untouchables Themselves

The Mahars, 'Mangs' and Chamars constitute the bulk of the untouchables in Maharashtra. "Bhangi" is numerically a very small community residing only in urban areas. The rest of the untouchables are small groups of Dhor, Mochi, Holar, etc. In Maharashtra, the Mahar caste is a relatively advanced caste among the untouchables, and moreover it has an altogether different part from other untouchables like Mangs and Chamars.

According to Dr. Ambedkar, "The Britishers became the rulers of India with the help of the Scheduled Castes who were called the untouchables by their own countrymen. They had no alternative but to join the British Army and earn their livelihood." With the advent of the British rule the Mangs and Chamars carried on their tasks in modern life. But the Mahars lost their significance when the post, courts and the police replaced them. Even before the arrival of the British, the Mahars had an escape from traditional work at the time of Shivaji as guards in the hill, forts and soldiers in the artillery. It is fairly clear that they had their own units in the armies of the Peshwas. But it is from the records of their service in the British Army that the Mahars contend that they are a martial race. A military monument at Koregaon near Poona served as a focal point in the legend of Mahar heroism, and a number of Mahar gatherings have been held at its foot.[29]

In 1892, the British rulers liquidated the Mahar Regiment and stopped the recruitment of Mahars. In 1894, Gopalbaba Walankar, a Kokani military man, attempted to submit a petition againt this, but failed because the retired Mahar soldiers refused to sign the petition.

In 1920, Shivram Janaba Kamble and Subhedar Bahadur Gangaram Krishnaji (Captain in British India Army) sent a sophisticated document of petition by the conference of Deccan Mahars. Though there is no record of the answer to this petition, their attempts show that the petition spoke for the Mahars, Mangs and Chamars. At the end of the first world war, the 11th Mahar Regiment was raised and disbanded shortly.

Meanwhile there were observed attempts of "Sanskritization" on the part of untouchables including the Mahars. G.D. Walankar wanted to replace Brahmins by Joshies (Mahar priests). K.B. Sansods and G.A. Gawai joined the Prarthana Samaj in 1910. In the late 1920's, the Mahars of Bombay attempted to participate in the public worship of Ganapati. By that time Dr. Ambedkar had entered into socio-political areas and in 1924 he became the president of the Managing Board of the Bahiskrit Hitakarini Sabha. This institution was established to look after the welfare of the Scheduled Castes. Primarily, his attempts were to Sankritize the untouchables. The Amravati satyragraha in 1927, the Parvati temple entry satyragraha (Poona) in 1929-30 and the five-year- long satyragraha for temple entry at Nasik that ended in 1935 are well known in this respect.[30]

Gandhi-Ambedkar Rift

From then onwards Dr. Ambedkar changed his strategy and avoided direct confrontation with the caste Hindus. With the beginning of representative government in India, he decided to use political means in order to uplift the Scheduled Castes.

In 1932, the British Prime Minster Macdonald announced the Government's constitutional proposal which included the Communal Award, by which the depressed classes were granted the separate electorates sought by Dr. Ambedkar and the caste Hindus. Dr. Ambedkar finally gave up the demand for separate electorates. The number of seats reserved for his community in the legislature was increased from 71 to 148.[31] This agreement is known as the "Poona Pact" and was later incorporated in the Government of India Act of 1935. Both the parties were unhappy with this pact. So this resulted in widening the gap between Gandhi and Dr. Ambedkar. Dr. Ambedkar finally decided to adopt different means. In 1935, he announced his intention to change his religion, at Yevala near Nasik, and to establish a political party called the Independent Labour Party in 1936 for broader support. He declared that even though he had been born a Hindu, he would not die a Hindu. The announcement of the conversion alienated the depressed classes other than the Mahars.

The Independent Labour Party, established by Dr. Ambedkar in 1936, was open to all. After the creation of Pakistan in 1947, the possibility of obtaining separate electorates for Scheduled Castes had been eliminated. Dr. Ambedkar continued to be a member of the Constituent Assembly after Independence, even though he was initially elected by the co-operative efforts of the Scheduled Castes and the Muslim League in Bengal. In August 1947, Dr. Ambedkar was named Law Minister in the first Cabinet of India, even while retaining his position as Chairman of the Committee responsible for drafting a constitution for the new nation.

Dr. Ambedkar joined the Government for the following reasons:

1. The offer was without any conditions, and,
2. One could serve the interests of the Scheduled Castes better within the Government than from without. Now Dr. Ambedkar advised his followers to forget the past and place the country above their community. He also asked the Scheduled Castes to forget their past difference with the Congress.[32]

Dr. Ambedkar concentrated his energies on conversion to Buddhism. Even in independent India, he felt frustrated and on October 14,1956, led the Mahars of Maharashtra to conversion. The step towards conversion was a reaction born out of frustration. Some hold the view that if Nehru had allowed the Hindu Code Bill to pass in Parliament, things would have been different. Dr. Ambedkar had a sense of fulfilment when he was converted and at that time he recalled his first announcement of conversion at Yevala near Nasik in 1935. Inspite of Dr. Ambedkar's intentions for conversion, the RPI movements remained mainly confined to the Mahars. He died on December 6, 1956, two months after setting the conversion movement, without giving an idea of a new political party in action or making plans for the development of either. After the death of Dr. Ambedkar, there was a struggle for power in the Scheduled Castes movement. Obviously, the lack of able leadership led to the disintegration of the movement.

In 1957, the Scheduled Caste Federation campaigned in the election with the Samyukta Maharashtra Samiti. The Scheduled Castes Federation won nineteen Assembly seats and six Lok Sabha seats.

The Republican Party of India (RPI) was formally organized after the elections in October 1957. In 1959, there was an open conflict in the RPI. This struggle for power resulted in the reduction of RPI seats in later election. In fact, the struggle for power had already started when Dr. Ambedkar was alive. In 1954, Dr. Ambedkar had categorically and conspicuously blamed his second rank for internal rivalry in the party. This power politics in the RPI put the Scheduled Caste community to loss and the Scheduled Caste movement lost its vigour.

Inspite of the facilities given to the Scheduled Castes by the Constitution, they remained backward. In India, various problems like insult, injustice, poverty, unemployment everywhere, particularly in the villages, gave birth to a new, young, energetic but angry organization of the Scheduled Caste youth, the Dalit Panthers. Namdeo Dhasal and Raja Dhale became the popular leaders among the Scheduled Caste youth.

The Dalit Panthers criticized the Hindu society, the Government and the RPI leadership. Suddenly a wave of enthusiasm swept among the Scheduled Castes. But it had no concrete socio-economic and political programme of its own. Only an anti-establishment stance could produce no results. The political parties from Congress and Communists rushed to some of the influential leaders. So the "Panthers" went the way of the RPI. A power struggle started in it and the leaders went on giving an ideological justification for it. Actually, today the "Panther" leaders are not even on talking terms. The Scheduled Caste movement once again remained leaderless.[33]

The contribution made by the above social reformers showed that the Hindu society was modernizing very slowly. The modern social and political thinkers from Maharasahtra came forward and helped a great deal to abolish the caste system. Prominent persons like G.B. Sardar, Baba Adhav, Tarkateerth Laxmanshastri Joshi, Bhalchandra Phadke, Y.D. Phadke, and Govindbhai Shrof, came forward and tried and have been trying to remove the evils of the caste system even today.

Maharashtra also gave birth to a number of Dalit leaders who tried to remove casteism in Maharashtra. Leaders like Namdeo Dhasal, Daya Pawar, Shankasrrao Kharat,. Raja Dhale, G.P. Pradhan, Laxman Mane, J.R. Kamble, Gangadhar Panthawane, Namdev Vatkar and others have tried to remove the caste system in their own ways. But the pace of modernization is not satisfactory, because our approach to modernization is based on tradition. We have assumed that change is necessary but continuity is essential.

Condition of Scheduled Castes in Maharashtra

In the beginning of the 19th century there was an impact of the varna system on the social conditions of Maharashtra. The varna system was deeply rooted in the social life of the people. The poisonous tree of caste system was growing day by day. The society was divided into various factions. The practice of discrimination by caste system was in vogue. Therefore, the caste system became very rigid. Every caste was given a different status. A person who broke the laws of the caste system was severely punished.

It was during Peshwa rule that the caste domination of Brahmins was in vogue. The other castes were treated as inferior. There was also the political domination by this class. They thought that the people of the lower castes were born for serving them. In short, this particular community dominated the lower castes. On the other hand, the condition of the lower castes became very critical. The upper caste people treated the lower castes badly. They had no political rights to exercise. The Scheduled Castes were not allowed to use water from public wells, lakes and ghats. Their condition was more horrible than that of slaves. In brief, the attempts made by the soical reformers and the Government to abolish untouchability and the caste system did not yield much results. It was no doubt the beginning of creating a new social order in India.

This chapter traces the origin and growth of the demeaning caste system in India. It also outlines the religio-historical background and the four-fold structure of this typically Indian phenomenon. The chapter also highlights the attempts made by the social reformers to condemn and abolish the practice of untouchability in Hindu society. Social reformers like Sayajirao Gaikwad, Jotiba Phule, Dr. B.R. Ambedkar, Shivram Janaba Kamble, Gopalbuva Valangkar, Shri Shahu Maharaj tried to eradicate the caste system. In order to eradicate the caste system in India, the great saints of the Bhakti cults and some Britishers made attempts in this direction. The untouchables themselves also were at the forefront in removing the stigma. The present chapter also highlights the socio-economic condition of the Scheduled Castes in Maharashtra. However, casteism holds place in the Indian society. The makers of the Indian Constitution thought to make a legislation for abolishing the practice of untouchability.

References

1. Dr. Ambedkar B.R. Writings and speeches. *Caste in India: TheirMechanism, Genesis and Development.* Indian Antiquary: A Journal of Oriental Research, Vol. I RVI, May 1917, Total pp. 520. 81-95.
2. Dr. Ketkar S.V. *The History of Caste in India* Rawat Publication: Jaipur, 1919, Reprint p. 4.
3. Dr. Kane P.V. "History of Hindu Dharmshastras" Vol. II, Part I, Poona : Bhandarkar Oriental Research Institute, Poona, 1974, p. 19.
4. Hutton J.H. *Caste in India, its Nature, Function and Origins* Bombay Oxford University Press, 1969, 4th edition reprints, 1973, 1977, p. 170.
5. Karve Irawati *Hindu Society: An Interpretation* Deshmukh Parakashan Poona: Deccan College Post-graduate and Research Institute, 2nd edition, 1968, p. 16.
6. Bose N.K. *The Structure of Hindu Society* Orient Longman, New Delhi, 1975, p. 166.
7. Srinivas M.N. *Social Change in Modern India* Orient Longman, New Delhi (Indian Edition) 1972, p. 93.
8. *Ibid*, p. 92
9. Gandhiji's symbolic language comprises a study in itself. A glance at the origin of his key terms, "Harijan" may be a good example of his use of words.
10. Dr. Ambedkar B.R. "The Untouchable who were they and why they became untouchables", Bharatiya Buddha Shiksha Parishad, Second ed (1969), Gonda, U.P, Preface, p. 8.
11. *Ibid,* p. 8.
12. Galanter Marc "The Abolition of Disabilities, Untouchability and Law" in J. Michael Mahar (ed), *The Untouchables in Contemporary India*, Tuscon, 1972, p. 243.
13. Webster, Third New International Dictionary by William Collins-Word Public Company, USA, Vol.3, 1966, p. 2513.
14. Murthy B.S. *Depressed and Oppressed* S. Chand & Co. (Pvt.) Ltd, New Delhi, 1972, p. 167.
15. His Highness the Gaikwad of Baroda, "Depressed Class of India" *Indian Review,* Dec. 1969, reproduced. The Depressed Classes of India, New Delhi, 1977.
16. Dr. Gharye G.S. *Caste and Class in India* The Popular Book Depot, Bombay, 1961, p. 182.

17. Dr. Ambedkar B.R. *Annhilation of Caste* The Bharat Bhushan Press, Bombay, 1945, p. 44.
18. Gail Omvedt *Cultural Revolt in a Colonial Society* Scientific Socialist Education Trust, Bombay, 1976, p. 54.
19. *Ibid,* p. 44.
20. Padhye, Prabhakar and Tikekar S.R. "Aaj Kalcha Maharashtra" Vaicharik Pragati (Marathi), Bharat Gaurav Granthmala, Bombay, 1935, p. 167.
21. Gail Omvedt *ibid* p. 121.
22. Vaidya, Prabhakar, "Mahatma Phuley Ani Tyanchi Parampara" (Marathi), Lokvanagamaya Graha, Bombay, 1976, p. 116.
23. Shinde V.R. "Bhartiya Asprushyatecha Prasar" (Marathi) Maharashtra Shasan. Samaj Kalayan, Bombay, 1976, p. 152.
24. Rajshekariah A.M. B.R. Ambedkar *The Politics of Emancipation* Sindhu Publication Pvt. Ltd, Bombay, 1971, p. 10.
25. *Ibid,* p. 165.
26. Dr. Kharat Shankarrao *Dr. Babasaheb Ambedkaranche Dharmantar* (Marathi), Thokal Prakashan, Pune, 1966, p. 15.
27. Das Bhagwan, *Thus Spoke Ambedkar*, Bhim Patrika Publication, Jallunder city, 1969, p. 44.
28. *Relloit* Elemor, "Learning the use of political means" in Kothari Rajni (ed), *Caste in Indian Politics*, Orient Longman,(2nd edition), Delhi, 1973, p. 32.
29. Panthavane Gangadhar *Vidrbhache Pani Petale Ahe,* Vijay Publication, Nagpur, 1976, p. 33.
30. Smith D.E. *India as a Secular State*, Princeton University Press, New Jersey (USA), 1963, p. 494.
31. *Relloit* Elemor, "Learning the use of political means" in Kothari Rajni (ed), *Caste in Indian Politics,* Orient Longman (2nd edition), Delhi, 1973, p. 56.
32. Dr. Kharat Shankarrao *Babasaheb Ambedkarachi Patre*, Thokal Prakashan, Pune, 1966, p. 349.
33. Gajare M.F. (Ed) *Dr. Ambedkaranchi Bhashane*, Ashok Prakashan, Nagpur, 1976, pp. 106-107.

3

Philosophy of the Constitution of India and the Need for Legislation

It is believed that untouchability was practised in India since Manu's times. How far it was justified at that time could be a debatable point. But no one would justify untouchability on any ground in the present society. Many saints and social reformers started preaching against the practice of untouchability centuries ago but the abolition of untouchability by legislation was attempted for the first time in the fourth decade of this century, when popular governments assumed power in the respective States which were known as provinces under British India under the Government of India Act 1935. Such Acts were enacted in a few States but they did not aim at the complete abolition of untouchability. They made some enabling provisions in an attempt to give entry to the backward classes into the temples.

It is significant that during the days of the national struggle for Independence under the leadership of Mahatma Gandhi, the removal of social disabilities was an integral part of the constructive programmes launched to ameliorate the poor and the downtrodden. It is a widely acclaimed and a well known fact that Mahatma Gandhi always used to stress the relevance and importance of this issue to build a harmonious nation. On the eve of Independence, many Acts were enacted by various provinces and States for the removal of social disabilities. Among these the "Temple Entry Proclamation" issued by the Maharaja of Travancore in 1936 deserves a special mention. The content of the proclamation is an essay on statesmanship, religious tolerance and wisdom, and warrants to be reproduced verbatim.

Need of Legislation

Isolated Government action to protect the lower castes from disabilities may be found as early as the mid-nineteenth century. As reform activity on behalf of and political activity by untouchables multiplied, resolutions and orders confirming the right of untouchables to equal use of governmental facilities, schools and wells, were passed in Bombay and Madras, as well as in some of the progressive Princely States. In 1923, the Bombay Legislative Council resolved that the untouchables be allowed to use all public watering places; wells, schools, dispensaries etc.[1]

It was only after Mahatma Gandhi's fast, (1932), in opposition to the Communal Award provision of separate electorates for untouchables that the Congress leaders were willing to countenance the positive use of law for providing various facilities to the untouchables.[2] As a result, between 1932 and 1936 a number of temple entry and anti-disabilities bills were introduced in the Central Legislative Assembly and in the Madras and Bombay legislatures.

In 1938, the Madras Legislatur passed the first comprehensive and penal Act to remove social disabilities, making it an offence to discriminate against untouchables not only in regard to publicity-supported facilities such as roads, wells and transporation but also in regard to "any other secular institution" to which the general public was admitted including restaurants, hotels, shops, etc.[3]

In 1938, for the first time, British India Government intervened to secure the opening of temples to Scheduled Castes when Bombay and Madras Provinces passed Temple Entry Acts.[4] Madras again took the lead in enacting a comprehensive Temple Entry Act, making it a criminal offence for any person to prevent any Hindu from entering or worshipping at any temple. The British rulers in pre-Independence India never thought over the caste problem in India seriously. However, many saints and social reformers preached against the practice of untouchability centuries ago. It is worthwhile to remember that Acts passed by States were not aimed at abolishing untouchability completely.

After 1938 followed the Bombay Harijan (Removal of Social Disabilities) Act 1946 (Bombay Act No. X of 1947) which was passed by the Bombay[5] legislature for the removal of social disabilities of Harijans. The said Act was passed with the object of removing the social disabilities from which Harijans suffered with regard to the enjoyment of social and secular amenities of life. Section 3 of the Act declared custom, usage or law, for the time being in force, or the decree or order of a Court, or anything contained in any instrument, to the contrary, every place of public worship which is open to Hindus generally or to any section or class thereof shall be open to all sections and castes of Hindus, and no Hindu of whatsoever section or class, shall, in any manner be prevented, obstructed or discouraged from entering such a place of public worship, or from worshipping, offering prayers there, or performing any religious service therein in the like manner and to like extent as any other Hindu of whatsoever section or class may so enter, worship prayer or perform.[6]

Custom or usage to the contrary no Harijan shall, merely on the ground that he is a Scheduled Caste, be eligible for office under any authority constituted under any law or be prevented from enjoying the amenities described by clauses (b) (i) to (vii) thereof. The other section of this Act made suitable provisions to enforce statutory rights conferred on Scheduled Caste.

Following the Poona Pact, Mahatma Gandhi speeded up his campaign among caste Hindus to mitigate the evils of untouchability. It was in the course of this campaign to promote improvement and upliftment of the untouchables that he bestowed on them the new name "Harijan", meaning "Children of God", which he took from a poem by a saint in his native State Gujarat. The new name was intended to give dignity to the untouchables and to impress on caste Hindus the need to admit these unfortunates into the Hindu fold.[7] But due to the rift between Mahatma Gandhi and Dr. Ambedkar, very few among the Scheduled Castes liked to be called "Harijan". Nobody took it in the proper spirit. According to them, it just meant getting another name instead of a caste name, but a name that meant the same thing, i.e., untouchables. Therefore the followers of Dr. Ambedkar were rather more critical than other Scheduled Castes in their reaction to this term. Even though the Scheduled Castes did not like the term Harijan, it was freely used and is still being used by caste Hindus.

In practice, the untouchables commonly refer to themselves by their various "caste" or "community" name. The exception is that of the new generation of the Mahars of Maharashtra. They call themselves the New Buddhists and not Mahars. But this too was a common reminder of status. In the villages, the caste name itself is usually used by the caste Hindus as a derogatory expletive. The Constituent Assembly had appointed a number of important committees and sub-committees, besides the drafting committee. The minorities sub-committee was one of them. The mission of this sub-committee was to safeguard the interests of all minorities to their satisfaction. This committee consisted of Vallabhbhai Patel (Chairman), Jawaharlal Nehru, Rajendra Prasad, K.M. Munshi and Dr. B.R. Ambedkar.[8]

Dr. Ambedkar, as a leader of the Scheduled Castes, submitted an exhaustive note on political and social safeguards for the Scheduled Castes. By way of political safeguards he suggested the establishment of non-parliamentary irremovable executives both in the union and in the units. He pressed that the Scheduled Castes should have a minimum representation according to their population ratio in the legislatures, ministries, municipalities and local boards. Those representatives were to be elected through separate communal electorates. Dr. Ambedkar further suggested that the Scheduled Castes should have a minimum share of the posts in the various public services in proportion to their population.[9]

On the social side, Dr. Ambedkar was specially concerned with what he called social boycott. He suggested stringent punishment for social boycott and for promoting, instigating or threatening social boycott. For the amelioration of the condition of the Scheduled Castes, he suggested provisions of funds in the budgets of the Union and State Governments for higher education, secondary education, and for education abroad of members of this community, the settlement of the Scheduled Castes in separate villages (dropped later on), and the setting up of a settlement commission for this purpose. Jagjivan Ram, a prominent leader of the Scheduled Castes, supported these suggestions. He also argued for special ameliorative measures like Housing Board to allot suitable plots and provide good houses.[10]

Presenting the draft of the Constitution to the Assembly, Dr. Ambedkar, referring to the articles on safeguards for minorities, observed that all the minorities including the Scheduled Castes have loyally accepted the rule of the majority which is basically a communal majority and not a political majority. He further stated that whether the minorities will continue or vanish must depend upon the habit of the majority to discriminate against the minority. The advisory committees of the Constituent Assembly accepted the reservation for Scheduled Castes and Tribes only due to their peculiar position, for a period of ten years. Dr Ambedkar wanted it for a longer period. Voting for the abolition of communal reservation after ten years was practically unanimous.[11]

After Independence and proclamation of the Constitution, the list of Scheduled Castes in India was notified by the President, in accordance with the provisions of Articles 366 and 341 of the Constitution. Article 366 of the Constitution gives the meaning of the word "Scheduled Castes". Scheduled Castes means such castes, races or tribes or parts of groups within sub-castes, races or tribes as are deemed under Article 341 to be Scheduled Castes for the purpose of this Constitution.

The President together with the Governor can specify the castes, races, tribes in States and Union Territories. Parliament may by law include or exclude from the list of Scheduled Castes specified in a notification issued under clause (i) any caste, race or tribe or part of group within any caste, race or tribe but save as aforesaid a notification issued under the said clause shall not be varied by any subsequent notification.

The Constitution has provided facilities and privileges for the people belonging to Scheduled Castes and Scheduled Tribes. It was done with a view to ensure social progress to those sections of our people who were kept under conditions of backwardness in all spheres of life due to some historic reasons. Therefore, the President of India has been empowered under the Constitution to issue orders specifying the castes or tribes for the purpose of facilities and privileges granted under the Constitution and Parliament has been given the authority to amend such orders by enactments.

In the light of this, the President had issued the Constitution (Scheduled Castes) Order 1950 and Constitution (Scheduled Tribes) Order 1950, so the list of Scheduled Castes is now contained in the Constitution (Scheduled Castes) order, 1950 as amended from time to time. Thus, it is clear that Scheduled Castes shall have the same meaning as clause 24 of Article 366 of the Constitution and "Harijan" means a member of a caste, race or tribe deemed to be a Scheduled Caste under the Government of India (Scheduled Castes) order.

Provisions in the Constitution

The new Indian Constitution abolished untouchability with a stroke of the pen through Artricle 17. "Untouchability is abolished and its practice in any form is forbidden. The enforcement of any disability arising out of "Untouchability" shall be an offence punishable in accordance with law".[12]

Parliament is authorized to make a law prescribing the punishment for this offence (Article 35) and in the exercise of this power, Parliament enacted the Untouchability (Offence) Act, 1955.

The Constitution goes beyond that; it refused to recognize not only "untouchability" but also discrimination based on caste, race, religion, sex, or place of birth (Article 15).[14] Article 19 (5) says that the Scheduled Castes have every right to purchase property anywhere and also to settle down and carry out any trade or business in the way they like and there shall be no restrictions on their legal occupations and movements.[15] Article

25 provides, "The Hindu religious institutions of a public character will be thrown open to all classes and sections of Hindus".[16] In the provisions of Article 29 of the Constitution, it was stated that admission to a Scheduled Caste student to a State run, managed or assisted educational institution shall not be denied on the basis of caste, creed or religion.[17] By Articles 330 and 334, seats have been reserved for the Scheduled Caste candidates in the State legislatures and also in Parliament.[18] Article 16 and Article 335 provide for the obligation of the State to consider their claims in the making of appointments to public services and reservation for them in case of inadequate representation.[19] Articles 164 and 338 and the fifth Schedule to the Constitution say that for looking after their interests and welfare, special officers will be appointed and special departments will be opened.[20]

Basically, the Indian Constitution does not recognize any religion or caste. It aims at creating equality among all Indians. But by providing special treatment to the Scheduled Castes, the Constitution hopes to help them effectively to come to the level of the caste Hindus. In other words, this is a protective discrimination to create equality. This was all together a new approach to the problem. Initially, the Government wanted to restore justice, liberty, equality, status for all opportunity and fraternity, by peaceful means.

After Independence

The makers of the Constitution held that the Government should hold fast to those policies that would achieve maximum economic development and social justice within the framework of representative institutions and national unity with equality. Since the Scheduled Castes were socially and economically backward, the new Government thought that a special and substantial assistance should be given to them so that in course of time, they could rise to the standard and status of the caste Hindus.

The only target was to achieve integration of the Scheduled Castes and to reduce the gulf between them and the caste Hindus by making special efforts. So, it was decided to fight the evil of untouchability by a mixture of legislative action, suitable educational measures and socio-economic reforms.

Article 340 of the Constitution laid down the provision for the appointment of a commission to investigate the conditions and difficulties of the socially and educationally backward classes within the territory of India and to make recommendations to remove the difficulties.

However, inspite of all these provisions, the Constitution does not define "untouchability". Neither is it clear what constitutes its practice in any form or a disability arising out of untouchability.

Kaka Kalelkar Commission

The first Backward Classes Commission was set up by a presidential order on January 1, 1953, under Article 340 of the Constitution of India and it submitted its report on March 30, 1955. Prime Minister Jawaharlal Nehru laid a copy of the report with a memorandum of action taken before the houses of Parliament on September 3, 1956. The Commission also prepared a list of 2399 backward castes or communities for the entire country, 837 of these were classified as "most backward". The Registrar General and Census Commissioner of India assisted the Commission in making population projection of 1930 backward castes or communities.[21]

The Untouchability (Offences) Act, 1955

The second step taken by the government was to enact the Untouchability (Offences) Act, 1955. Accordingly, Parliament is empowered to make a law prescribing punishment for practising untouchability. The Untouchability (Offences) Bill 1954, was later adopted as the Untouchability (Offences) Act, 1955. The Bill was referred to the Joint Select Committee in September 1954. Finally, the Act was passed by Parliament on May 2, 1955, and received the assent of the President on May 8, 1955. The Act came into force from June 1, 1955. The Act declares certain acts as offences, when done on the ground of "untouchability" and prescribes punishments for:

1. Refusing admission to any person to public institutions.
2. Preventing any person from worshipping in any public temple.
3. Disability of access to any shop, source of water, place of services, etc.

Under the provisions of this Act, it is an offence to not permit a person to enter any religious or public place or draw water from a common well or tank on account of untouchability. Denying entry on the basis of caste to any restaurant, educational institution, hospital or even dharmasala has been declared an offence. This Act made it an offence to enforce occupational profession and trade disabilities.

The Act says that it is an offence to refuse to sell goods or services to a Harijan, only on account of his being a Harijan. It says that molesting, injuring or annoying a person organizing a boycott of or taking any part in the ex-communication of a person who has exercised the rights accorded to him as a result of the abolition of untouchability, are offences. Further, the Act provided that the imposition of disabilities is made a crime punishable by a fine up to Rs. 5001, or imprisonment for a period of six months, or both.[22] Higher penalties have been prescribed for subsequent offences. The onus of proving innocence has been thrown on the accused. The offences under this Act are cognizable and compoundable.

The Act contains one further novel and notable feature. It provides that where any of the forbidden practices is committed in relation to a member of a Scheduled Caste, the Court shall presume, unless the contrary is proved, that such act was committed on the ground of "untouchability".[23] In other words, the burden of the proof lies on the accused and not with the prosecution.

However, this Act of 1955 does not define the term "untouchability". It seeks to make some general provisions punishing certain kinds of historically prevalent practice and patterns of behaviour. The definitions given here only relate to places where the practice of untouchability might be resorted to viz. hotel, place of public entertainment, place of public worship, and shop. An explanation was added to Section 10 making a public servant who wilfully neglects investigation of an offence, liable for punishments as an abettor. Section 15 A was added, casting duty on the State Government to ensure that the rights accruing on account of the abolition of untouchability be availed of by the concerned persons. Section 7 A was added making unlawful compulsory labour on the ground of untouchability an offence. Time alone will decide whether the loopholes have been effectively plugged.

This Act has been in the statute book since 1955. The law is aimed at the abolition of untouchability through legislation alone. Mass growth of awareness of the necessity of eradication of untouchability is necessary to achieve the high moral goal set in the Constitution. For some members of any society, time works slowly and moral growth is a slow process. Atrocities against untouchables are exposed every day in the news. The implemention of the provisions of the Protection of Civil Rights Act has, therefore, become almost a daily affair.

The experience of implemention of the Untouchability (Offences) Act 1955, showed that there were certain loopholes which made the proper implementation of the Act difficult. The offences were compoundable and no minimum punishments were provided. Very few cases were filed in courts and out of those cases many were compounded, and in a very small number of cases which ended in conviction, light sentences were awarded. Therefore, with the object of plugging the loopholes and making the penal provisions more stringent, a bill ultimately became the Untouchability (Offences) Amendment and Miscellaneous Provisions Act 1976. By this amending Act, amendments were made from Section 3 to 7 A by which minimum punishments were prescribed and the discretion of the Court to award punishment of less than one month and a fine of less than one hundred rupees for conviction under Section 3 to 7, and imprisonment for less than three months and a fine of less than one hundred rupees for offences under section 7 A was taken away. Section 16 A was added, making the provision of the probation of Offenders Act, 1958, applicable to any person above the age of 14 years and who is found guilty of having committed any offence punishable under this Act.

L. Elayaperumal committee 1965 (The Committee on Untouchability)

The Government of India (Department of Social Security) constituted a committee in pursuance of the recommendation made by the Central Advisory Board for Harijan Welfare, under the Chairmanship of L. Elayaperumal, on April 27 1965, to study inter alia "the various aspects of untouchability; in particular, the working of the Untouchability (Offences) Act 1955, and the restrictions, if any, imposed on the entry of Harijans into public places of worship and to suggest remedial measures".[24]

The Committee took almost four years to submit its report. The observations of the Elayaperumal Committee were that (a) we constrained to point out that during the course of our tours, we came to know that copies of the Act were not even available at many of the district offices and that many Government officials had no knowledge of the provisions of the Act" and (b) "the fact that the said Act is not properly and effectively working is clear from the report of the Commissioner of Scheduled Castes and Scheduled Tribes and also from the information collected by the Committee" answer adequately the terms of reference of the committee relating to the working of the Untouchability (Offences) Act 1955.

We speak of democracy, equality, etc. but even today we find that about 8 crores of downtrodden people in our country are deprived of real freedom and equality. Even today we find that members of the Scheduled Castes and Tribes and the Adivasis are living as untouchables and like second class citizens, and at many places they are treated worse than animals. They are deprived of the fundamental rights that are available to other Indian citizens. In villages, members of these communities are prohibited to draw water from the common ponds and wells. In many places they are prohibited to visit temples or places of public worship. It is not enough that the problem is left to be tackled by the Ministry of Education and Social Welfare alone. We will have to review this from different angles, i.e., socially, economically and politically. All departments like planning, finance, etc., should be aware of this problem and the lot of backward classes of people.[25]

This is a regrettable condition of the so-called untouchables in our country. For this purpose mere legislation is not enough. We had already passed legislation against such offences as far back as 1955. But even today, after 50 years of freedom and inspite of all these legislations, untouchability is still prevalent. The Elayaperumal Committee says the problem of untouchability is, therefore, inseparably linked with the question of caste system and the social set up based on that. It is an indisputable fact that the caste system is the dominating social force in this country. Hence, any attempt to remove untouchability without striking at the root of the caste system is simply like treating the outward symptoms of a disease or drawing a line on the surface of water. Untouchability cannot be abolished in this country unless the social order is changed by establishing new values, and for this purpose the values based on the Hindu religion must be changed first.[26]

The people of the higher castes should come forward to help in its removal from the roots. There is a need to create social consciousness among the members of higher castes to tackle the problem. They should change their outlook otherwise this problem is not likely to be solved.[27]

Weakness in the Untouchability (Offences) Act 1955

The weak points of the Untouchability Act can be enumerated as follows:

1. The Act forbids the denial of facilities and services on grounds of untouchability. But it is necessary to prove that the denial of facilities and services is preceded by specific intention. It is difficult to obtain convictions since states of mind are difficult to prove.[28]
2. The Act is equivalent in its coverage of facilities which are used by the public but are not technically "Public".[29]

3. The offences under this Act are treated as compounded, e.g., they can be settled by a compromise between the parties concerned. This provision reduces the effectiveness of the Act because the Scheduled Caste person has to live in a village, where he or she is in minority, and the caste Hindus, by exercising undue pressure or threat, see that a "compromise" is reached.

"Untouchability" is abolished and its practice in any form is forbidden. The enforcement of any disability arising out of untouchability shall be an offence punishable in accordance with law.

The complete abolition of untouchability was one of the visions of Mahatma Gandhi in his concept of "Ramrajya". The Untouchability (Offences) Act adopts the Gandhian ideal without any qualification. "Untouchability", however, is not defined in the Constitution, presuming that it is known to all.

Justice Sreenivasa Rao observed that the subject matter of Article 17 is not untouchability in its literal or ideological sense but the practice as it had developed historically in this country. In the Act also, the use of the word "untouchability" refers to the meaning of the term in the context of the historical development of the practice and does not contend its literal meaning. A literal construction of the term would include persons who are treated as untouchables either temporarily or otherwise for various reasons, such as their suffering from an epidemic or contagious disease or on account of special observance such as are associated with birth or due to special boycott resulting from caste or other disputes.

Section 2 (D) Place of Public Worship

A place of public worship means a "temple" or a place by whatever designation known, dedicated to, or used by the Hindu community, or any section thereof, as a place of religious worship. Worship means such religious service as the bulk of the worshippers may participate or offer in a temple and includes the right to bathe in tanks adjacent to the temple, subject to such rules and regulations as may be made under this Act.

Section 2 (D) place of public worship, Denomination. The word "Denomination" has been defined to mean a collection of individuals elapsed together under the same name, religious sect or a body having a common faith and organization designated by a distinctive name. It contemplates not only a religious denomination but also a section thereof. Hence, the Hindu includes any division, subdivision, caste, subcaste, sect or denomination whatsoever of Hindus.

The Back Cash: Adverse Effects of Protective Discrimination

Scholars like Dushkin, Zalliet,[30] Galenter[31] are, on the whole, favourable to the policy of protective discrimination, while Harold Issacs[32] thinks that it has created a separate class. But most of them have taken a note of the adverse side effects of this policy. It is to be noted that these side effects are serious.

Two observations can be made about the policy of protective discrimination; firstly, among the caste Hindus, there is a bitter teaching that this policy adversely affects the requirements of merit and that it impedes the legitimate chances of caste Hindus. The caste Hindus think that this is nothing but the appeasement of the Scheduled Castes at the cost of the former.

Secondly, the Scheduled Castes, especially the salaried Scheduled Castes, have created a vested interest in backwardness. It was observed that Scheduled Caste couples got taxable salaries and wanted scholarships for their children in colleges. In Maharashtra, this tendency was clearly discarded among the educated Mahars, the new Buddhists. The caste Hindus are very critical of this vested interest in backwardness. It may be noted that it was one of the reasons behind the recent violent caste conflicts in Maharashtra. The caste Hindus accuse these New Buddhists as "Sarkari Brahmins" i.e., Government-created Brahmins.

Resolution re-welfare of Scheduled Castes and Scheduled Tribes moved and debated in the Rajya Sabha in 1976

Shri Gian Chand Totu (Himachal Pradesh): Sir, I beg to move the following Resolution:

> "This House is of opinion that the various organizations and departments set up by the Centre and the States for the welfare of the Scheduled Castes and Scheduled Tribes have not been able to make the desired impact on the socio-economic development of the persons belonging to these classes in spite of the huge financial grants made available to them and recommends that government should take immediate steps to abolish all these organizations and departments and utilize the funds thus saved for awarding scholarships to the needy school and college students belonging to Scheduled Castes and Scheduled Tribes and by providing new schools and colleges near their homes."

Sir, I would like to give a little clarification about the last few words in my Resolution. "By providing new schools and colleges near their homes". I do not mean that these schools and colleges have to be provided exclusively for the Scheduled Castes and Scheduled Tribes. I only say that schools and colleges, wherever these facilities are not available, should be made available to them.

Sir, it was twenty-nine years ago that we achieved independence. That great man, Mahatma Gandhi, who got us this freedom, uttered many slogans. One slogan was that there should be food for everybody, a home for everybody and clothes for everybody. Lakhs of our countrymen sacrificed all their comforts for achieving the India of their dreams. We did get our independence, Sir, and some of our dreams were realised. But most of our dreams have not been realised and one reason for this is that we do not have cost consciousness in our country. I agree that we had scant resources, but even those scant resources had not been put to the right use and, therefore, the desired results were not there. The demand was for more staff and more departments, forgetting that more staff and more departments would again tell on our funds which were scant and, therefore, we will not be able to achieve our aims.

Then there was another situation in our country. Because we were slaves for a long time, we wanted to have freedom. And so, our leaders gave a call to the country to condemn the then established government. Had our leaders not given that slogan, we would not have achieved freedom. So, we started criticising that government. But, even after we achieved our independence, unfortunately that trend continued in the country—of, criticising the government day in and day out.

There is another aspect of our national life and that is individualism. If you look at our history, you will find that our tradition is such that we stress too much on individualism. We would clean our homes and put the dirt and rubbish on the streets. It is because of this individualism that our great religion, Hinduism, got the caste system and even other great religions, whether it is Islam or Christianity, also picked it up and classes were created among them also. Now, Sir, these two distinct features of Indian life—slavery for centuries together and individualism—played havoc with our lives. If we go back by one year in the highest democratic institution in the country—Parliament—most of its time was taken up by the demands of individuals or a group of individuals, and even those sections of the society which call themselves progressives, were most of the time clamouring for individual rights or the rights of a group of individuals. The situation came in the country when individual rights were getting overriding consideration over national interests and, therefore, our country started going towards an abyss: I need not narrate all that. It culminated in the railway strike. The purpose of the leaders was something different and the aims given were something else.

Thanks to the emergency, a sense of discipline came, a sense of realism came. We began to realise that apart from our rights there are certain obligations also, and that realisation has prompted me to bring this Resolution before this House. It is my humble effort to bring to the notice of the House and through it to the notice of the country, the state of affairs of one of our aspects, and that is the administration. During the emergency so many steps have been taken and so many things have been achieved, but I do not think we have been able to change the administration—the colonial administration—through which all of our policies have to be handled.

Sir, I will just now dissect the report of the Commissioner for Scheduled Castes and Scheduled Tribes. I must make it clear that I do not mean any individual criticism, nor do I know who the Commissioner is. My criticism is only about the system that we have evolved.

Sir, regarding the welfare of the Scheduled Castes and the Scheduled Tribes and other backward classes, the important Central and Centrally sponsored programmes under the Backward Classes scheme are as follows:

Post-matric scholarships. Now I have looked into the figures given in the report, which show that about 3 lakh Scheduled Caste students and about 60,000 Scheduled Tribe students have been given scholarships. Now, if I see, on an average how many students are there and how many of them can be there, I can easily say that the number would be more than 50 lakhs. After 29 years of independence, with our budgets soaring so high, we have not been able to provide scholarships for all the students of Scheduled Castes and Scheduled Tribes.

The second activity is the 'Girls' hostel'. During the year under review, we have provided only 25 lakhs and 40 lakhs for the girls' hostels which would hardly suffice. If the cost of one room is taken as Rs 5000, a hostel of 20 rooms would cost Rs. one lakh. So in this country with such a huge population, if you just create hostels for 200 students or 300 students, is it going to touch the fringe of our problems?

Then, Sir, we are spending so much on research, evaluation and development projects. I fail to appreciate, when we accept that 50 per cent of our population is below poverty line, what is the research to be done. The research is not needed when most of the people do not get food, they do not get clothing, they do not have enough space. So, under the limited resources we have to spend those sums on these researches. These researches are done at a particular development of the country. That infrastructure we have not been able to create, nor will we be able to create if we go on spending in the way we are spending.

Then, there is 'cooperation'. I will just show, later on, as to what our physical achievement is in the field of cooperation.

Then, Sir, 'aid to voluntary organisations of all-India character'. On Annexure I, the names of various institutions have been given, to whom 75 lakhs of rupees in a year are do-led out. In this connection, I remember an old story. I was an MLA in the erstwhile PEPSU State—PEPSU, i.e. Patiala and some other districts. There, in my own district of Simla, a high-powered committee of Adam Jati came to look to the conditions of the Scheduled Tribes. Well, I come from a middle-class business family. My father was an employee in the Government of India. But he resigned in 1919 and set up a small business. So, I was a little cost conscious. I was then wondering how all these people came from Delhi. They came in big cars, had very sumptuous lunch and what was the purpose of all that. If you dissect some of the organisations—I do not know any of the organisation, nor do I know any of the individuals running these organisations—I am sure, you will find so much of wastage. And what is the proportion of expenditure which you take from these organisations? It is 10 per cent or 20 per cent but this sum of 35 lakhs of rupees is purely meant for their administrative purposes. So, Hon. Members can realise that Rs. 35 lakhs have been given for a year to certain institutions for keeping their central offices only.

Now, Sir, there are Welfare Departments of States. I happened twice to be an MLA, first in the PSPSU and then in PUNJAB, and I distinctly remember that in my district there were 20 to 30 sanctions for house building loans of Rs. 200 each, and each loanee would spends Rs. 200 to Rs. 300 in chasing the MLA, then they would spend another Rs. 200-300 in chasing the District Welfare Officer and ultimately when he used to get Rs. 2,000, some amount would be taken away by the accountant because he was disbursing the amount; every man thought that even if he was getting Rs. 1000 it was sufficient for him because he was getting it without doing anything. Now, in a population of many thousands, if 20 or 30 people do get these loans, it is not sufficient. If, after 20 or 30 years of independence, this is our achievement, that we are able to give loans of Rs. 2000 each to 20 families in a district, it is highly unsatisfactory. The whole stress in our administrative structure has been to expand it. Parkinson's law applies to the Indian administrative structure very aptly. I have great regard for the Indian Administration because 30 per cent of it do work very hard, and it is because of that 30 per cent that the whole administrative machinery is running but here I am talking of the system as such where the trend is to expand. This is one of the normal activities. Then other activities have also been brought in. As the Report says: The functions of the State Welfare Department are: "Provision of land and land development scheme..." I think it applies equally to the backward classes or to the classes whom we call "have-nots". Then it is mentioned: 'Subsidy for cottage industries, cooperation, supply of agricultural implements, etc. and supply of poultry, sheep, pigs and goats, etc. Medical facilities, drinking water supply schemes...." Now, how are these to be different from the normal activities of the government? If we go on creating departments for this section of the society or for that section of the society, then the whole amount would be spent on the establishment itself. I am sure if you dissect—and I will show this to you later on—you will find that 50 to 70 per cent of the amount is spent on the establishment itself.

Now, Sir, this Report of the Commissioner for Scheduled Castes and Scheduled Tribes is for the year 1973-74. I must admit that I have not been able to go through the whole report, but I did see some chapters and I also dare say that, though I am quite an optimist, after looking into those chapters I became pessimist. Chapter in and chapter out there is demand for more staff and more offices. When you look to the achievements during the last 29 years, they are very depressing. Now, regarding education, in CLASS 9 and above, while the percentage in the corresponding age of other communities is 23, in the case of Scheduled Castes and Scheduled Tribes it is only 11. Even with spending all these funds, 50 per cent of the Scheduled Caste and Scheduled Tribe students have still not the opportunities to go to the schools—and I am sure they do not have the opportunities mainly because of economic reasons.

Then, Sir, the Report says something about hostels. Andhra Pradesh has 467 hostels, Bihar has 90 hostels and Gujarat has 150 hostels. Now, assuming that in each hostel there are about 100 students, how much population have they been able to cater in the present state of affairs? I believe, they have not been able to cater to more than 5 per cent of the population.

And there is another interesting figure. Gujarat Tribal Development Corporation, Ahmedabad was given a total fund of Rs. 5.83 lakhs, out of which pay and allowances and advances come to Rs. 1.55 lakhs, stationery etc. comes to Rs. 0.75 lakh.... honorarium and TA to Chairman, sitting fees and TA to Directors come to 0.26 lakhs and purchase of vehicles, petrol and repairs to vehicles amount to Rs. 0.67 lakhs. The cost of dead stock office equipment and furniture comes to Rs. 0.56 lakhs. Loans and grants which have been distributed come to Rs. 2.04 lakhs. For distributing loans and grants amounting to Rs. 2.40 lakhs you have spent more than Rs. 3 lakhs on the establishment itself. If you look to the cost of giving loans by the LIC or the banks or the government expenses relating to petrol and repairs to vehicles amount would not be more than 2 to 3 per cent. But here more than 70 per cent of the expenditure is on the establishment. I am sure that by the time it comes to realising the loans, 90 per cent of the establishment cost would be spent. And this much amount has been spent only in giving the loans. But if inspectors have to be kept when the loans are given, you can very well realise how much more it would have cost.

Then there is the statement showing progress of schemes undertaken by various State Governments/Union Territory Administrations to promote the agricultural practices of Scheduled Caste persons in the State Sector programmes of Fourth Plan. In Andhra Pradesh there are 250 beneficiaries.

It has a population of 2 to 3 crores. And I do not think that the labour and the money you are spending in compiling this report would be worth while for such a small thing. Maharashtra has 400 persons and Punjab has 32 persons. This gives an idea of the activities.

I would like to bring to the notice of the House the statement showing expenditure incurred from 1969-70 to 1973-74 and physical targets achieved on the schemes of cooperation for Scheduled Castes in the State Sector. Assam has been able to raise only 50 societies; Kerala has been able to raise only 3 societies. These are not exceptional cases these are the general cases, and I am quoting from their own Report.

I go to housing, one of their other activities. In Kerala they have been able to give loans and subsidies in respect of 68 houses. In Andhra Pradesh they have been able to give loans and subsidies to 1100 individuals, and in Haryana to 638. When our population runs into crores, how are these figures of 10s and 100s going to satisfy this 20 per cent segment of our population? And if you include the backward people also, that segment would easily come to 30 per cent.

I would like to draw your attention to another statement showing allocations made, expenditure incurred and physical targets achieved on the Housing Schemes of Scheduled Tribe persons in the State Sector Programme of Fourth Five Year Plan. We are proud of the fact that Kerala has given loans for two houses in a single year. Figures about some of the states are not available. Figure for West Bengal is available. It has given loans and subsidies for 204 houses.

Incidentally, I saw another Report of the Social Welfare Department. I do not know—there is a fashion with all our departments to go on increasing their activities, but the funds do not increase. With new activities, new staff comes and ultimately 60 or 70 or 80 per cent of the funds which Parliament earmarks for these activities go towards the cost of the establishment itself.

The Social Welfare Department includes the Child Development Division, Nutrition and Relief Projects Division, Women's Welfare Division, Handicapped Welfare Division, Social Security and Defence Division, Planning, Research, Evaluation and Monitoring Division, etc. And when I see these divisions of whether it is the integrated child welfare service or creches for children or welfare of destitute children—I find that they have not been able rule to cater to more than one per cent of the population in the last 29 years. Now, will ever any time arise when we will be able to cater to the majority of our population? I have got figures here. Well, one record is there which is impressive and that impressive record is that they have been able to send ten delegations out of India with the scanty resources that they had. Sir, again they give grants. They have given grants of Rs. 11 lakhs to various organisations. Where the organisations are able to show an expenditure of 10 to 20 per cent, 80 per cent of the funds would be given to them as grants. And this reminds me of another story. I was an MLA in Punjab and I attended one function which was organised by one of the important MLA. That MLA was giving more importance to the Director of the Social Welfare Board than to the Minister himself. Then I became curious. I wanted to know why. Ultimately I found out that that MLA was running some institutions and was getting subsidies from the Social Welfare Board.

Sir, in the Report there is mention of untouchability. Even if all the funds of the Government of India are given, it will not be sufficient for removing untouchability. About two years ago there was a bye-election in my state. I was on a tour during that election. A few carpenters and ironsmiths came to me. They said they wanted government jobs. I asked, "Why do you want government jobs? You are doing well in your profession." They replied "In government jobs we will not have to work hard." So government jobs in the countryside have become synonymous with no work. Sir, our elders, our leaders gave the right of voting to all the sections of the society. This untouchability is, by and large a political issue. It is not an administrative issue. There is some confusion in the Report itself. The Commissioner will excuse me if I say that this whole set-up is just a post office. They do not have any executive power. Whatever they monitor, they bring it to the notice of the Parliament, they bring it to the notice of the government. It is the government or it is the Parliament which gives directions. And I have tried to show the way the money is being spent at the moment, and how they have not been able to cater to a sizable sector of the society. Now, Sir, in the first four Five Year Plan, there has been a total expenditure of Rs. 450 crores. In the Fifth Five Year Plan, there is an outlay of Rs. 455 crores. I am sorry, I go back to untouchability.

In my own area I see that the prosperous Harijans can enter any house. It is only the poor people who cannot go. So this untouchability cannot go unless you improve the economic condition of the Harijans. When you talk of harassment, when you talk of atrocities, this harassment and these atrocities are not directed against the Harijans only. They are directed against the down-trodden, the have-nots of the society. And this would continue. Whatever effort you may make is not going to remove it. What is going to remove it is their economic betterment. You have bring those people at par with the rest of the society. I have tried to show from the figures provided by the government itself that we have not been able, and we will not be able in the next 50 years at the present pace to achieve our aim. Whatever funds you may allot to them, 70 to 80 per cent would be spent on the establishment. Therefore, I would like to draw the attention of the House and, through the House of the country to need for devising suitable ways and means and methods so that there can be maximum benefit to these classes for whom these funds are allotted and there is minimum expenditure on the administrative structure. Therefore, I have proposed certain things in this Resolution. I am sure if you take into account Rs. 450 or Rs. 455 crores which are provided and about Rs. 100 or Rs. 150 crores which will be available in the state sector, then you can concentrate on just one activity instead of 100 or 200 activities which are taken up by this department. Let that activity be anything—land, housing, drinking water or education. But let there be no favouritism, let there be no opportunism and let there be no nepotism. Whatever facility we can create should be made available to all the sections of society. If there are ten subsidies and hundred people claim them, then there will be nepotism and favouritism. Even these classes would not be backward in any way. If they are given equal opportunities which they have been denied so far, they will be on par with others. One way of giving them equal opportunities is to see that all children of school-going age go to school. As I showed from the figures, now 50 per cent of such children do not go to school, the main reason being economic condition. If government can divert all these funds only for giving scholarships to such children, then the problem will be solved. If there is no nearby school or college, you should provide them hostel expenses. If that is done, within 20 years the face of this country will be changed. If, instead of concentrating upon one activity, you squander this money on 100 or 50 or 200 schemes, then the present state of affairs would not improve. Now there is some realisation in the government and I see that the allocation for the Social Welfare Department which was Rs. 14 lakhs in 1974-75 has been reduced to Rs. 9.12 lakhs in 1975-76. But since the funds have been reduced, still the establishment costs will go up.

Mr. Deputy Chairman: You will have to wind up now.

Shri Gian Chand Totu: Sir, I have tried to dissect this report. I am sure if you analyse the working of other departments of the Government of India, there will be ways of saving Rs. 3,000 crores in the annual plan of the Centre and about Rs. 1,000 crores from the state sector. These 4,000 crores will be sufficient to provide water, electricity and roads in each village of India. That would bring socialism. We do not have the basic necessities of life. Our people in the villages do not have drinking water or roads. Without basic necessities, we talk of socialism and giving equal opportunities and creating infrastructure for other things. I am sure if we concentrate our attention on one important activity which I mentioned, and restrict our spending to this, then we can build up India of our dream.

The question was proposed.

Shri Bir Chandra Deb Burman (Tripura): Sir, I congratulate the mover of the Resolution. It requires courage to call a spade a spade. It is difficult to disclose facts as they are. In the present situation, we do not have the courage to disclose facts. In spite of our tall talks and huge expenditure of money, the conditions of Scheduled Castes and Tribes are just as they were before. That is the fact and it is also a fact that the money that has been given for the amelioration of their conditions has been taken away and is being taken away by the middlemen and the money does not go to those for whom it is actually meant and so, the situation is such that we must say what the fact is and he has been bold enough to say that all these organisations and departments should be abolished. I think that this resolution will make us realise that in the name of the amelioration of the economic conditions of the members of the Scheduled Castes and Scheduled Tribes we are spending crores of rupees and that their conditions have not actually been improved. Whenever there is a question of filling up the posts reserved for the Scheduled Castes and Scheduled Tribes, the same stereo typed answers are given that suitable candidates are not available. In spite of the lapse of 29 years since we achieved independence, the situation is the same. Who is responsible for that? Who is responsible for not making them suitable for jobs during the last 29 years or so? Crores and crores have been spent for making them educated and for making them suitable for such posts. If suitable candidates are not available, as has been said quite often, the government should make efforts to see that they become suitable. I say this because during the last 29 years, even a baby born at the time of our getting independence would have become a major and would have become suitable for any job. So, even after crores and crores of rupees have been spent it is surprising that we do not get suitable candidates for any post. But I know that these people have got the ability, these people have got the qualification also. But the only thing is that is taking is that we are not giving them enough scope. The Mover of this Resolution has spoken about the Report of the Commissioner for the Scheduled Castes and Scheduled Tribes. The Report is here and there is a warning given to us in this Report as has been given in the earlier Report. It is there on page 2 of the Report and I would like to quote:

"The reason for this state of affairs is not hard to find...."—This was mentioned in the earlier Report also—"It is the vast and distressing gap that exists between what we profess and what we practise. The sympathy that exists for these unfortunate communities in the minds of our national leaders does not percolate in the same intensity and sincerity to the leadership at the lower levels where there is a general absence of disciplined committed party workers and followers. On the other hand, those in the administration at various levels who are responsible for the implementation of welfare programmes and schemes do not work with due sense of commitment."

I lay emphasis on the last few words here. The Report says that those who are in the administration at the various levels and who are responsible for the implementation of welfare programmes and schemes do not work with due sense of commitment. Who is responsible for this? The people in the administration who are responsible for the implementation of the welfare programmes and other schemes do not work with a committed sense of responsibility and I do not know what the government is doing about it. How can the officers who man the administration violate this mandate of the government without fear of any punishment or without getting any punishment from the government? So, I think that this Resolution is only a warning and the warning is that if you do not understand the writing on the wall, if you still commit the same mistake that you committed during the last 29 years of our independence which is not a small period, you know what will happen. You say that these weaker sections are not suitable for certain jobs. Through nepotism they want to get hold of these white collared jobs today. But that will do no good to them in the long run. Keeping thousands of people unemployed and under-fed, keeping thousands of people deprived of their work and deprived of the responsibility of work, they think they will be able to monopolise these white collared jobs. As my friend said, government job means job without work. They think that only by procuring white collared jobs they will be able to maintain themselves. But that is not possible. The upsurge of unemployment throughout the country is adding weight to the problem that is before us. This meagre government job will not be able to help them. So, time has come when you have to share your bread along with your own brothers. If you do not, they will move whenever an occasion arise. So, time is a very, very great factor. Time waits for none, if we lag behind, time will kick us back.

Mr. Deputy Chairman Sir, I come from Tripura which is a very backward state. It was tribal dominated state. Fifty per cent of the population there was tribal population before Independence. With a huge upsurge of refugees, they became a minority. In 1974 in this House I have spoken of their condition. These tribal people have now come to the streets, working as day labourers. They are breaking stones, they are breaking concrete. You go to any village in Tripura, you will find that tribal men coming to the streets and working as day labourers. They are earning their bread through manual labour. But those who think that occupying government jobs they will survive, I think, they are living in a fool's paradise.

Mr. Deputy Chairman, Sir, I have just now got a letter from one of my students. He is a pre-medical student. He was trying to get adminision in a medical college. There are 37 seats allotted for this purpose. He told me that he had got an apprehension that he would not be admitted. I asked him: 'why do you fear?' You are the only tribal candidate. But now I learn that he has not got the chance. Through nepotism the only candidate, Scheduled tribe candidate, who has passed pre-medical examination, has not been admitted into a medical college. This is the way you are spending money for the welfare of weaker sections. This is an eye opener. Time will come when you will be awakened by some very, very rash, action. So, this Resolution which my friend has given in a very lucid expression, is nothing but an ultimatum. Be sure, by conscious, of your own act.

You are spending crores and crores of rupees on welfare activities. But this money is squandered in the midway. It does not go to the person for whom it is meant. If this sort of squandering of money in the name of Scheduled Castes and Scheduled Tribres goes on, a day will come when they will realise this thing and when they will come forward to have their own share. That day will be a very dangerous day. I will quote what Rabindra Nath Tagore said:

"Oh, my unfortunate countrymen,

To whom you are insulting, you are humiliating,

You will be at par with them through insult and humiliation

If you do not share your bread with all of them,

You will be crushed by the ashes of cremation ground."

I think the government will look at the writing on the wall and give sufficient attention to the spirit of the Resolution. Just spend your money for giving scholarships and you will see how many talented boys you will get in the course of years to man all these important portfolios. Even for the recruitment of Class IV and Class III employees, we find that candidates are not found suitable. We have heard the stereotyped explanation many times. That stereotyped explanation will not do. I want to conclude by supporting the Resolution. Those who are squandering government's money and playing with the lives of backward classes and backward people are digging their own graves. With this, I support this Resolution.

Shri K.K. Madhavan (Kerala): Sir, I oppose this Resolution with all the might at my command. Going through the Resolution, I find that the Hon. Member who has moved this Resolution finds fault with the organisations and the departments set up by the Central and the State Governments. He finds out the inadequacies in the functioning of these organisations and departments and rapidly comes to the conclusion that all these institutions and organisations should be abolished forthwith. For what? For utilizing the funds thus saved for awarding scholarship to the needy students from Scheduled Castes and Scheduled tribes and for providing new schools and colleges near their homes.

What does this mean, Sir? The Resolution on the face of it appears fairly good, but going deep into this it is bad.

Shri Krishnarao Narayan Dhulap (Maharashtra): Go by the intention, the spirit behind it.

Shri K.K. Madhavan: I think, the Hon. Member does not know that when there is something written, the meaning of the words written is more important than the spirit....

An Hon. Member: Spirit is important.

Shri K.K. Madhavan: No, no. Even with the best of intentions, one can go to hell. So, what is more important is the text. It is not a question of what he intends. We should go by the wording and by the sense which the wording of the Resolution carries. I was very carefully listening to his speech. He finds falt with the institutions, organisations and departments. He says that a lot of money is spent—probably, mis-spent—on this. On what? For giving housing, grants, giving education to the children, for giving assistance in industries and so many other things. But towards the operative part of the Resolution, while making a suggestion, he says that all this money should be channellised into only one purpose, and that is for giving scholarships and for starting schools and colleges near their homes. I do not understand why the hon'ble friend who is crying aloud and shedding tears against the misdeeds and the injustice done to the unfortunate people for centuries and ages fails to see that a well thought-out and comprehensive scheme is in operation, in however inadequate way it may be. Does he mean to say that the Harijans should not have housing grants, should not have houses? Does he mean to say that the Scheduled Castes and the Scheduled Tribes should not have some share in the industry? Does he mean to say that there should not be proper roads where there are concentrations of people belonging to the Scheduled Castes and Scheduled Tribes? I do not know what he means. But all that he says is that there is only one need and that is giving scholarships and providing schools and colleges near their homes. I think this is a stupid scheme. With all respect to the learned friend, I should say that it is a stupid proposal, because he does see reality.

Shri U.K. Lakshmana Gowda (Karnataka): It is very harsh.

Shri K.K. Madhavan: When harsh things are said, hard replies are needed. He does not see what the problems of the Scheduled Castes and the Scheduled Tribes are. I do not deny the necessity of education. Due emphasis should be laid on education. At the same time, one cannot close one's eyes to the other problems that face them. My Hon. friend himself was admitting that one of the main problems is economic backwardness. I say he has not understood the problem. It is not economic backwardness only. If economic backwardness is the only problem, then certainly there are other people also who are backward. But, fortunately, the framers of our Constitution and the moulders of our administrative system, however, imperfect they may be now, have rightly analysed the problem. The problem of the Scheduled Castes and Scheduled Tribes has different facets. That is why they have earmarked funds for housing, for industry, for co-operative institutions, for education, for drinking water facilities and for so many other things. My learned friend thinks that only by giving education to a few students and by establishing a few new schools and colleges in the vicinity of their homes all these problems will be solved. As a matter of fact, it is a multi-faceted problem which needs a multi-faceted programme. In India both the Central Government and the State Governments are alive to the situation and they have evolved a working programme, a comprehensive working programme for ameliorating the conditions of these backward people. I do not know what prompted out my friend to bring forward a Resolution like this. My only inference is that he has not seen the Scheduled Castes and the Scheduled Tribes in the right perspective. He has not lived among them. He does not know the sentiments of these people. He does not know the emotions of these people. He does not know the aspirations of these people. His is not the perspective of a social reformer. Evidently he is not a social reformer, as is patent from the words and tone of his speech. Hand he been social reformer he would certainly have come to the proper solution to this problem. I am not interested in his pedigree. I am not interested in his background of eduction. I am not interested in his birth and other things. This is a personal matter and I do not want to go into that. By whatever standards I measure him, seeing the content of the Resolution which he has placed before us, I have reason to think that he has not cared to see the conditions and such surroundings of these unfortunate people, the Scheduled Castes and the Scheduled Tribes. I can understand his saying that the administration is top-heavy. In that case it was his duty to give proper suggestions, healthy suggestions positive suggestions as to how the administration could be streamlined instead of recommending outright the abolition of all the institutions, departments and organisations. It is equally surprising, Sir, that from the other side also a sympathetic response has come in favour of the Resolution. Strangely, Sir, this is a matter where the reactionaries and the revolutionaries agree as against the Scheduled Castes and the Scheduled Tribes. If there is any inadequacy in an administration, if ought to be Tribes. If there is any inadequacy in an administration, it ought to be improved. My learned friends here do not say that certain other departments which are notorious for their imperfections and malpractices should be abolished. But they are very happy at that. But there is extra unanimity when there is a proposal to abolish all these institutions, departments and organisations which are positively meant for the welfare of the Scheduled Castes and the Scheduled Tribes. I do not understand this unanimity in spite of their political differences. All that I can infer is that the cultural background of these people is the same old one. In spite of the political differences, that they profess, they have the same feelings and they have the same psychological response to the problems of the Scheduled Castes and Scheduled tribes. Sir, it is time that this type of defective approach to the problem is put an end to. What is required is a positive programme the basis for which has been laid by the Father of the Nation, by Pandit Jawaharlal Nehru and by all our great leaders who knew the problem and who organised this welfare programme—both official as well as non-official.

Sir, I am not very happy. I am not satisfied that we have done all the things for them. I am not satisfied. I am dissatisfied because these are, as I said the other day, problems which have been created during centuries and ages and they cannot be wiped off in a day or two. It requires patience; it requires determination; it requires self-sacrifice. It was for this that Mahatma Gandhi said that everybody, every enlightened citizen in this country should be prepared to do something for these unfortunate people.

He ended the fast only on the promise by leaders of this country that they would take up the responsibility of removing the unfortunate condition of these people. The leaders gave an undertaking and it was only after that Mahatma Gandhi gave up his epic fast.

My learned friends do not see the importance, the human emotions behind, this huge problem. There may be differences between the leaders. But fortunately, with the exception of a few handful of people, the large majority of the thinking people in this country are agreed on the problem and the approach, that the problems of the Scheduled Castes and Scheduled Tribes are very big, multitudinous and complicated and that they ought to be solved by effective means. Unfortunately this attitude is wanting among some of our latest political leaders. They profess revolution, but their course is that of reaction. That is the paradox. The main requirement for approaching this problem is to have enlightened type of people organised in such a way that we can show to the world that we are dedicated to the cause of these people. The Resolution, I think, reminds me of Judas. A poor woman, Mary of Magdalene came to see Jesus. She brought appointment which she applied to his feet. But Judas came forward and said: "What a foolish woman! If she had instead of purchasing this ointment distributed this money to the poor people, hundreds of poor people could have been served and saved." Form the Resolution, and from the tone of the mover of the Resolution and of the persons who supported the Resolution, I feel that 'Judas-ism' has not totally disappeared from this country. Sir I oppose this Resolution.

Shri Krishnarao Narayan Dhulap: Mr. Vice-Chairman, Sir, I would like to express my views on the Resolution moved by Shri Gian Chand Totu. This Resolution can be divided into two parts. In the first part, the mover has expressed his anxiety and distress that the various organisations and departments set up by the government have not been able to deliver the goods. He feels that the various departments have not fulfilled the tasks entrusted to them in regard to the amelioration of the conditions of the Scheduled Castes and the Scheduled Tribes in this country. In the second part, he has demanded—I do not know whether out of frustration or anger—that all these organisations and departments which have been set up should be abolished and the—money thus saved should be utilised for giving scholarships to the Scheduled Caste and the Scheduled Tribe students and for establishing schools, and colleges nearer their homes. As far as the first part is concerned, I agree with him to a certain extent. About the operational part of this Resolution, Sir, I beg to differ from him.

My friend, the previous speaker, Mr. Madhavan, was very harsh with the mover of the Resolution. I request him to see the good behind the Resolution. The intention is that he wants the government to move briskly, expeditiously and see that what is promised to these downtrodden people is given to them as early as possible and these communities are brought on par with other communities in this country.

As far as setting up of schools and colleges near the homes of the Scheduled Castes and Scheduled Tribes is concerned, I would put forth a different suggestion the Hon. Minister should take note of . Only yesterday we discussed here the Report of the UGC. The new formula given by the UGC is 10+2+3. Upto the tenth standard there will be high schools everywhere in the country but the eleventh and twelfth standards will be restricted in the sense that either colleges will be asked to open those classes or some high schools will be given permission to run them. This will be a great handicap in the way of the education of the backward class students. In a tehsil there is likely to be only one high school having eleventh standard and those who are living in hilly tracts—Scheduled Tribe and Scheduled Caste students—and far-off villages will find it well-high impossible to attend the school which will be running the eleventh standard classes. So, you will be putting a seal on the education of the backward class students. Either they will have to traverse the ten or twelve miles from their home villages to the school, which is opened at the tehsil headquarters or their parents will have to make some arrangement for the children to stay in some house at the tehsil headquarters—which will be impossible for them taking into consideration the financial conditions of the parents of the Scheduled Castes and Scheduled Tribes students. So, this will be coming in the way of their education. To avoid this difficulty I would give a suggestion which the Hon. Minister should take note of and see that something is done. If anything is done then I think he mean business and wants to do something for the backward class students.

The suggestion is this: At every district headquarters there should be a hostel wherein the Scheduled Castes and Scheduled Tribes students should be admitted and given free boarding and lodging, and free education should be given to them in the institution opened for the Scheduled Castes and Scheduled Tribes students. Unless and until something of this type is done, I do not think in the near future we will be getting better type of students from these communities for the jobs which are reserved for them.

Now, what is happening? What do we see in the Reports of the Scheduled Castes and Scheduled Tribes Commissioner? Even on the floor of this House, whenever a question is asked, we get the reply that the youths who appeared before the selecting authority were not up to the mark; they were not fully qualified; they were not found suitable. So, these are the replies we generally hear on the floor of the House. There is no doubt that there is a privileged class in this country. The parents of the students are very rich. They can get all the facilities. So it is impossible for the students belonging to the Scheduled Castes and Scheduled Tribes to compete with those who are better-placed and get employment anywhere where there is competition and merit. So, we want that they should come up. All our energy should go in seeing that their lot is improved, they are given more and more facilities and more attention is paid to them so that they can come up to the level of the candidates coming from higher-up communities.

Secondly, after going through the Report of the Scheduled Castes and Scheduled Tribes Commissioner and after seeing the replies given by the Hon. Ministers on the floor of this House, I still feel that on paper there are schemes and schemes; moneys are provided but those who are there to deliver goods have no mind to do the work with which they are entrusted. There is a top-heavy expenditure but very little goes to the cause of the downtrodden people, to the students belonging to the downtrodden community. So, this should be checked. A survey should be conducted and scrupulously we should see that those who are coming from these communities are entrusted with this cause of the people belonging to the Scheduled Castes and the Scheduled Tribes. Sir, I come from a district where one-third of population is of Scheduled Tribes. There are so many co-operative societies being run. But they are not being run by the people belonging to the Scheduled Tribe but by the people who belong to a higher strata of society. So, whatever benefit is there, whatever profit accrues because of the co-operative movement goes in the pockets of those who are already and the replies given are that the affairs and the poor Adivasis are made to toil there day in and day out. They are hardly in a position to make both ends meet. This is how the top-heavy expenditure is made and this is how the middleman is eating away all the money. Everything goes to the department or organisation for betterment of the conditions of these higher-up people.

Sir, I have got two replies given by the Hon. Ministers on the floor of the House. During the emergency, urgency was to be the core of the whole activities of the government. And the relies given are that the Government is not having mind to see that urgently is there and the organisations which are entrusted with the work for the betterment of the conditions of these people, they are not doing their job. For example, I will read out some of the figures from the statement given by the Hon. Minister of Finance:

"Statement showing amounts outstanding as on 31st March, 1976, in respect of credit extended by nationalised banks to landless farmers who have been distributed land by State governments...."

So, because of the 20-point programme, these people, farmers, farm labourers, Scheduled Castes people, are given certain lands. But only giving of land is not going to solve their problems. They should have some inputs, they should have some agricultural implements, so that they can till the land and see that they get some yield. Now, what is the position? Sir, most of the areas of Andaman and Nicobar Islands, Arunachal Pradesh, Dadar and Nagar Haveli, Goa, Daman and Diu, Laccadive and Mizoram are habitated by Scheduled Castes people, but not a single rupee has been paid by any nationalised bank to these people. Same is the case with Manipur, Meghalaya, Nagaland where not a single rupee has been paid by way of loan or by way of help to the landless people who have been given land by the government under the 20-point programme for betterment of their lot. Then, in Jammu and Kashmir also—my friend Nizam-ud-Din is not here—not a single rupee has been paid. I do not know whether nationalised banks are there or not, but not a rupee has been paid in Jammu and Kashmir the State from which the honourable Minister of State for Home Affairs comes. Now, take a big State like Bihar. Bihar has been paid only Rs. 32,000. Such a huge amount has been paid to the landless farmers who have been allotted land by the government under the 20-

point programme: So far as Assam is concerned, they have been paid Rs. 1,47,000. But the actual figures are quite different because certain banks, e.g., the Punjab National Bank, which have given some amounts have said that these are the combined figures for all the States. As far as Himachal Pradesh is concerned one bank, the United Commercial Bank has given Rs. 1000 to the landless farmers in Himachal Pradesh. Another bank, the Punjab National Bank, has given Rs. 1.71 lakhs, but they have given that these are the combined figures for all the States. So, ultimately the Himachal Pradesh people might have not only Rs. 4000-5000. So this is the state of affairs. The same is the case with the surplus land which has been allotted under the 20-point programme because of the operation of the Land Ceiling Acts all over the country. Sir, hardly 3,98,000 persons were eligible to get land. And how much land were they given? 8,27,000 acres. That means about two acres of land were given to each farmer or landless labourer because of this emergency programme. So, this two-acre land with no money to improve the land, with no money to have inputs for the land, and no money to have agricultural implements, will be lying waste. Whatever scheme is there, it is only on paper. The actual thing is that seeing backwardness with our own eyes, we can say that the situation itself is very hopeless. Therefore, I would request the honourable Minister through you to apply his mind to the question of the whole organisation that has been set up for doing good to the downtrodden people, and if he finds after scrutiny that some of the organisations in States are eating up money the corruption should be rooted out, and if there is top heavy expenditure, it should be curtailed and something concrete and solid should be done. For that I will give only one suggestion that every district collector should be asked to enlist the names of those who are unemployed and semi-employed in the villages, particularly young men belonging to the Scheduled Castes and Scheduled Tribes. And whenever there is any opportunity, they should be first employed. In my district of Thana in Maharashtra which is highly industrialised in spite of the fact that it is has one-third Scheduled Tribe population, hardly any person is employed in the factories which are springing up like mushrooms. But these people are not employed for reasons best known to them. So my suggestion would be that whenever any factory comes up the collector of that district should see that whatever manual work is here for which no skill is required for posts like gardeners, peons etc. these people should be given preference and where skill is required, the youth belonging to the Schedule Castes and the Scheduled Tribes should be given training; depending upon the tyhpe of the factory coming up, before that, they should be given training and whenever a vacancy occurs they should be employed. Already, government departments are full; there are more employee than what is necessary. Only if somebody retires or dies is there any opportunity for someone to get a job, and there too influence also takes place. And these people who have got no influence whatsoever are left out.

With these words, I would request the Minister to take into consideration the suggestions made and also the intense feelings behind the moving of this Resolution.

Shri Narasingha Prasad Nanda (Orissa): Mr. Vice-Chairman, Sir, with utmost respect to the mover of the Resolution I must submit that it is misconceived. The problem has not been considered in depth. The magnitude of the problem of Scheduled Castes and the Scheduled Tribes has not been considered. It appears that Mr. Totu only wanted to express his anguish or, if I may say so, his displeasure at the manner some mistakes here and there he might have noticed in the working of the organisations and departments set up by the Centre and the States for the welfare of the Scheduled Castes and the Scheduled Tribes. Sir, I would very respectfully submit that this Resolution is completely misconceived. I do not want to use a strong language but it will be enough if I say that Mr. Totu has not at all taken into consideration our constitutional obligations for the Scheduled Castes and the Scheduled Tribes in this connection, Sir, I beg to refer to Article 46 of the Constitution. Part IV of the Constitution deals with the Directive Principles of State Policy. By merely reading some of these provisions of the Constitution, you will yourself come to the conclusion how misconceived this Resolution is. Article 46 reads:

> "The State shall promote with special care the educational and economic interests.... "

Each word of this Article is significant.

"...of the weaker sections of the people, and, in particular of the Scheduled Castes and the Scheduled Tribes, and shall protect them from social injustice and all forms of exploitation."

Then, Sir, I refer you to Articles 330 to 342 of the Constitution. They are in Part XVI of the Constitution. Kindly see the provisions contained in Articles 330 to 342. I would like to make a particular reference to Article 338. This article provide for the appointment of a commissioner or an officer who has to discharge certain functions. He has to safeguard the interests of the Scheduled Castes and the Scheduled Tribes. He has also to make a report to the President of India. These are certain constitutional obligations which have to be fulfilled by the government. I am not going into the details now far want of time. If we read these Articles, Articles 330 to 342, together with Article 46, we will find that there are certain constitutional obligations towards the members of the Scheduled Castes and the Scheduled Tribes which have to be fulfilled by the government. For the last two and a half decades Government have been making efforts in that direction. I would submit that the problems relating to the betterment of the conditions of the Scheduled Castes and the Scheduled Tribes are of a vast magnitude and they cover the whole gamut of their social and economic life. The commission established under the Constitution, has to deal with their educational problems. It has to see whether the members of the Scheduled Castes and the Scheduled Tribes are properly represented in the services. It should look into cases of atrocities and harassment. It has also to go into the extent of rural indebtedness among the Scheduled Castes and the Scheduled Tribes and how many of them are working as bonded labour. Then, this commission should also ensure their adequate representation in Parliament and in the State legislatures. The problems of the Scheduled Castes and Scheduled Tribes in relation to agriculture, housing, medical and public health and so on have also to be gone into. The administrative setup for this includes the Home Department, the Planning Commission and various other departments of the government. I am mentioning all this just to show the magnitude of the problems which are tackled by these institutions and organisations to which my friend, Mr Totu, referred in his Resolution and says that they should all be abolished. He wants that all the money which is now being spent for their cultural advancement, for their educational advancement, for their economic advancement and for their social upliftment should be spent only on education. The problems of the Scheduled Castes and the Scheduled Tribes cannot be solved merely by establishing a few schools here and there and educating their children. Apart from the administrative agencies, there are also a number of non-official agencies which are working for the welfare of the Scheduled Castes and the Scheduled Tribes. I do not know whether Mr. Totu has anything to say against these non-official institutions. But those non-official agencies, I think, are of a very representative character and those agencies have been functioning for not one, two, five or ten years; they have got their traditions, their sacrifices for the upliftment of the Scheduled Castes and Scheduled Tribes. To mention only a few, the All-India Harijan Sevak Sangh, the Bharatiya Depressed Classes League, the Harijan Sweepers Sevak Sangh, the Bharatiya Adimjati Sevak Sangh. The Ramakrishna Mission functions also for the Scheduled Castes and Scheduled Tribes. But my friend wants to abolish all these institutions. The Home Department will be abolished, the Special Commissioner for Scheduled Castes and Scheduled Tribes will be abolished, the Planning Commission will be abolished—the whole administrative set-up will be abolished. Then who will give this money to the Scheduled Castes and Scheduled Tribes for the establishment of schools and colleges? So, you see how illogical the approach is.

There must be a logical approach to everything. Sir, the Resolution may be well-intentioned. After all, here we are not sitting in judgment over the Resolution moved by Mr. Totu; we are not going into the intentions of Mr. Totu. But supposing the House agrees to this Resolution, it will take us to a position of complete absurdity—a position which is impossible to accept. Therefore, what I beg to submit is that the Resolution as moved by Mr. Totu is completely misconsidered. I am not going in the question of ideologies or the economic philosophy, the social philosophy, the political philosophy behind it. All those questions I am not going into. Purely taking the Resolution on its own merits I beg to submit that it is impossible to accept this Resolution because it will lead us to a position which can never be accepted by any man of ordinary prudence.

And certain points were made that in respect of some educational institutions some grant was made—and that grant was not too less compared with the expenses on the administrative set-up. I would submit regarding statistics there is a very interesting joke. Statistics never prove any point. Like the weather reports of the Meteorological Department, statistics always lead us to wrong conclusions. Once a teacher was going with his students. There was a flood in the river. He asked the students to stand in a line and measured them; he took the average height and asked the students to get into the river. And half the students were washed away because the Law of Averages did not work with them. My friend, Mr. Totu is putting a figure here, Mr. Dhulap quotes another figure from somewhere else and says nothing has been done. I would submit, this type of negative approach, this type of approach to try to prove a point to belittle whatever has been done during the last two and-a-half decades, I at least cannot agree with.

Sir, I do not want to take much of your time. I am going to conclude.

Shri Bhahmananda Panda (Orissa): Statistics are like the bathing suit of a lady—which reveals what is obvious and conceals what is vital.

Shri Narasingha Prasad Nanda: Statistics are never decisive; they are only indicative. Therefore, statistics do not prove a point.

Sir, I will conclude my speech on this Resolution with a remark of our great Prime Minister, Shrimati Indira Gandhi, She says:

'While I am fully conscious of the slowness of this work, I do not think we should belittle the progress which has been made in the last twenty years.'

'There is, for example, remarkable achievement in the field of education.' This is only an example she has given. Further she has said: 'We have today a large number of doctors, engineers, administrators and professors coming from these groups. Within a few years some of them will be in toe top rung of their professions. They have important positions in all the political parties and I have no doubt that they will hold a much larger number of such positions as times go out. In fact, I think that it is their active role in the legislatures and in the government which has done so much to wipe out many of the old prejudices. The growth of industries and urban communities is also helping in this progress. Yet we realise only too poignantly that much more needs to be done.'

In complete agreement with the Prime Minister, I would submit, Sir, that much more needs to be done but it does not mean that because there is headache, we should also cut off our head.

The Minister of State in the Ministry of Home Affairs, Department of Personnel and Administrative Reforms and Department of Parliamentary Affairs (Shri Om Mehta): Mr. Vice-Chairman, Sir, I am thinkful to Hon. Mr. Totu that he has brought this subject before the House and given me a chance to explain the position as to what has been done by the government during the last 25 years to remove the backwardness of this section of the society, i.e., the Scheduled Castes and the Scheduled Tribes. I am also thankful to other Hon. Members, particularly Khan Saheb, Mr. Verma, Mr. Nanda, Mr. Madhavan and others, who have in a way supported the government for all the work they have done during these past years and I will start with what Mr. Nanda said in his speech, quoting from the Prime Minister, that in this field a lot of work has been done, particularly in the field of education. Here the Hon. Mover of the Resolution has expressed the view that almost all the organisations in the States and at the Centre which are engaged for the past 25 years in the amelioration of the conditions of the Scheduled Castes and Scheduled Tribes, should be immediately closed down and all that fund should be diverted to the educational field. I do not belittle the part education has to play in removing the poverty, in taking the people to a better life but at the same time, I will like to bring to his notice that whatever has been done in this field is due to these organisations only, which have been busy, doing developmental work and other work, to see that those who have been exploited for centuries, those who could not get what due to them and were very poor, to bring them on par with others; they have done a lot for them in the past decade. Sir, I do not claim that we have done all that is desired or that could be done but I would not hesitate to say that the various measures taken have, in fact, made considerable impact and we have achieved notable success in our efforts. Sir, Article 46 of the Constitution enjoins upon the State the special duty to promote with special care the educational and economic interests of the weaker sections of the people, and, in particular, of the Scheduled Castes and the Scheduled Tribes, and to protect them from social injustice and all forms of exploitation. The responsibility of implementation of this Directive Principle of State Policy devolves on the Ministry of Home Affairs at the Centre and the Department of Harijan and Tribal Welfare in the States. As will be seen from the statement of expenditure, a considerable headway has been made in this direction through the agency of these organisations.

Sir, I will place before the House certain statistics. Though Mr. Panda may not agree with me that statistics are very essential for that, but still I will place these statistics before the House to show in brief what has been done in the last decade for the amelioration of these castes. Sir, in the Fourth Plan period, the whole expenditure for the development of Scheduled Castes and Scheduled Tribes and Other Backward Classes was Rs. 451.05 crores. Sir, at the time of the Fifth Five Year Plan, our Prime Minister thought that we must pay special attention to the development of these unfortunate people who have been exploited since centuries. Accordingly, the Fifth Five Year Plan provided a sum of Rs. 289 crores specifically for this community besides the provision for general sectors which is more than twice the outlay provided in the Fourth Plan. Out of this an amount of Rs. 119 crores has been provided in the Central sector and Rs. 170 crores in the State sector. Sir, in addition to this, the Fifth Plan provides Rs. 200 crores for the sub-plans in the tribal areas. Besides, this, Sir, we are giving scholarships which are called Post-Matric scholarships. For the information of the honourable Member, I must say that these scholarships are not given on a selective basis but are given to each and every student who is eligible to receive it—each and every student who goes to a college or to a university, if he is eligible, gets this scholarship. I must tell my honourable friend that in the beginning of the First Five Year Plan, the number of such students was only 2,200. Now, if he takes this year only, the number has gone up two-fold as compared to the last year. Only last year we rationalised the whole scheme and the amount now being paid is almost one and a half-times what they were being paid previously. The maximum which is paid as a scholarship or a stipend is Rs. 125 per month to a student from this community. In the first year of the Fifth Plan the expenditure was only Rs. 10 crores, but this year we will be spending around Rs. 13.62 crores only on scholarships which will be very beneficial to the students coming from these classes. Not only this. Only yesterday I have announced in this House that under the scheme of 10+2+3, we are going to give scholarships to all those students who have qualified up to 10th class and will be going into 11th class. There will be about 2,30,000 students who will be benefited by this in the remaining years of the Fifth Plan. You can imagine, Sir, the enormity of the expenditure we are incurring on higher education. It is only on higher education. I will come to the pre-Matric education later. It is only on the post-Matric education that we are spending so much and we are giving benefits to such a large number of students. About the pre-matric education I would like to say that 12 lakhs students belonging to the Scheduled Castes and Scheduled Tribes have received, stipend and other educational incentives during the first two years of the Fifth Five Year Plan for continuing studies in the middle and high schools. And the enrolment of the Scheduled Castes students for school education is expected to be 93 lakhs and 37.34 lakhs for the Scheduled Tribes in 1976-77.

Like this, the percentage of literacy has gone up, in the case of the Scheduled Castes and the Scheduled Tribes respectively, from 10.27 per cent and 8.54 per cent in 1961 to 14.71 per cent and 11.29 per cent in 1971. There has been an appreciable increase not only in the number of students, but literacy among the Scheduled Castes and Scheduled Tribes students has also increased. As you know, Sir, for the progress of any country or any community, the basic thing is that education should be provided; unless education is there, that community cannot progress.

My friend said that nothing has been done in respect of hostels. 633 girls' hostels have been set up for the Scheduled Castes girls during the entire plan period. Most of them are in the district headquarters so that those girls who live in the villages and want to have higher education can come and stay free in those hostels. In addition, a further 100 hostels for the Scheduled Castes girls will be set up during 1976-77. Like this, in the field of education, whatever is possible is being done. If we look to the total number of hostels which have been provided for the boys and girls, the number will be more than 4000, which will cover almost a good percentage of the districts in the whole country.

Now, I will come to the employment figures. Some points have been raised about the employment of the Scheduled Castes and the Scheduled Tribes. Sir, about the services where their representation was negligible, I wish to point out the IAS, the IPS whatever quota has been fixed by the Constitution has been filled. As he knows, the quota is 15 per cent for the Scheduled Caste and $7^1/_2$ per cent for the Scheduled Tribes, and up to this time, in the IAS, IPS and non-technical services of the Central Government, the quota of 15 per cent for the Scheduled Castes and $7^1/_2$ per cent for the Scheduled Tribes are filled up completely. And there is not a single year in which we have not fulfilled the prescribed quota. Sir, they will ask, what about the other offices? In the other categories of government service also we have tried to do it. Last time, when I was speaking on the Report of the Commissioner for the Scheduled Castes and Scheduled Tribes, I gave figures showing how we are trying to improve, so that the quota which has been fixed is full subscribed. I would like to say that in 1965 the total number of officers in Class I was 318. In 1975 it has gone up to 1197. So, my friend will see that in the last 10 years, there has been 400 per cent increase in the number of Class I officers.

In Class II, the number in 1965 was 864. In 1975 it has gone up to 2,639. In Class III, the total number in 1965 was 96,114. Now it is 1,74,025. In Class IV, excluding sweepers, the number in 1965 was 2,1,073. Now it has gone up to 2,30,811. The percentage is 18.64 for the Scheduled Castes. So, Sir, against the quota of 15 per cent, in Class IV we have 18.64 per cent belonging to the Scheduled Castes, excluding sweepers and those who are engaged in unclean work. Similarly in the case of the Scheduled Tribes also, the total number of posts filled by them in Class I in 1965 was 52. But in 1975 it is 219. So, like this there is appreciable increase in other classes also. I will not like to take up the time of the House in giving the figures but I will only like to say that we have taken several steps to implement these schemes. We have not only given scholarships but we have sent our boys to the foreign countries also. We have given them stipends and scholarships so that they could go to the foreign countries and learn there and get higher education. And most of them have returned and have given benefit to the country. Like this whatever has been possible has been done. In the technical field where not many students are coming forward, there also we are trying to give them some pre-technical training so that they could go into the technical services. In the Industrial Training Institutes also, we have got seats reserved for them. There are 366 Industrial Training Institutes all over the country in which an appropriate number of seats is reserved for these communities and suitable stipends are given to them. In 1975-76 alone more than 20,000 Scheduled Castes and Scheduled Tribes youth were given professional and vocational training in various trades in these institutions. The Central Government has also been awarding national overse as scholarships to the Scheduled Castes and Scheduled Tribes, denotified nomadic and semi-nomadic tribes and other economically backward students. Under this scheme 21 scholarships are awarded every year, 11 to the Scheduled Castes, six to the Scheduled Tribes, one to denotified nomadic and semi-nomadic tribes and so on. They are being sent to higher levels also in engineering, technology, medicine, agriculture, and other subjects. Till the end of 1974-75, 218 persons of these classes have benefited under this scheme.

Sir, as you know, the 20-point programme announced by the Prime Minister is there and most of it is for the benefit of the weaker sections of the society; and the Scheduled Castes and Scheduled Tribes form the majority of them. So most of the schemes like land to the landless house to the houseless and abolition of rural indebtedness and bonded labour system in some sections of the society. And in one year we have done a lot in this field also. Under the 20-point economic programme, over 63 lakhs person have been provided with house sites, the majority of whom belong to the Scheduled Castes and Scheduled Tribes. Some States have undertaken programmes for construction of houses on these house sites. He was quoting some figures. I do not know from where he got them. He said that only two houses were constructed in Kerala. Shri Madhavan who comes from Kerala and my other friends from that State know that there is a very ambitious programme of constructing one lakh houses in Kerala. I do not know whether the Kerala Government have fulfilled it. But at least 50 per cent of those houses were constructed and were given to the people who are economically backward.

Shri K.K. Madhavan: I would like to give information that 50 per cent of those houses are for Scheduled Castes.

Shri Om Mehta: Nearly four lakhs houses have been constructed so far under this scheme and a large number of beneficiaries belong to Scheduled Castes and Scheduled Tribes. In addition, the Housing Corporation set up in various States are actively involved in assisting backward classes in this regard. It was said that money is being spent on training and research. Unless you have training and research, you cannot find out the causes of poverty or how to remove it. These tribal institutes are being set up in the country only for that purpose so that they will know the causes of backward and poverty and will take steps to remove them. Not only that, for tribal areas, and special programme has been made. Last year in the Fifth Five Year Plan for the first time from the Central grant about Rs. 200 crores have been kept for tribal areas. Special sub-plans are being prepared for tribal areas. In 18 States these sub-plans will be prepared for areas where there is a substantial tribal population. So far sub-plans for 10 States have been finalised and it is expected that for the remaining 8 States, these will be finalised by the end of the year. These sub-plans will go a long way in ameliorating the conditions of the tribal population. We have decided that all areas where the tribal population consists of 50 per cent will have tribal plans. Apart from the sum of Rs. 200 crores, we are providing money from the general sector also. Earlier the money which was kept for the development of these areas and for the Scheduled Castes and Scheduled Tribes was being diverted to other fields. Now we have issued special orders through a new account-procedure that such money should not be diverted for anything else and should be spent for this very purpose. Otherwise there will be audit objections. We have also see to it that for services in the tribal areas, priority will be given to tribal boys. For instance, for services in the police and Forest Department, tribal boys will be given preference. Sir, you come from Orissa. You know the tribal problems there. In other areas also these poor people are exploited. For instance, people from Bastar area will know the problems of tribals there. Now we have said that vending of liquor should not be there because the contractors used to fleece them, take money from them and harass and exploit them. We have issued instructions to all the States that the excise policy for the tribal areas should be changed and there should not be any vending of liquor in these areas. If at all liquor has to be there, it should be through the government controlled shops. We have also said that the tribals who brew their own liquor should be allowed to do so. And, Sir, no checks should be put on them. So, this is the new Excise policy which has been decided now then in respect of forest wealth also which these people were collecting for centuries and selling, we have said that there should be no exploitation because the contractors used to exploit these people in this sphere also. They used to exploit these tribals and we have said, for the first time, that there should be no middlemen and that this sort of exploitation of the tribals by the contractors should not be there. We have said that these things should be directly purchased by the governments or by the co-operatives and the governments should directly purchase these products by fixing their prices also so that there is no exploitation.

Then, Sir, we come to the question of liquidation of the indebtedness of these people. This scheme is also mainly for the Scheduled Tribes people though it is for the Scheduled Castes and Scheduled Tribes people. It is mainly for the Scheduled Tribes people, who, being mostly illiterate are by and large exploited more by the people. We have also said that the lands of the tribals which have been taken away from them should be got back and returned to them because the exploiters by hook or by crook take advantage of the illiteracy of these people and deprive these tribals of their lands. Now, laws are being passed against alienation of the lands of the tribals so that the lands which have been taken away from them by these exploiters would be given back to them. So, Sir, whatever is possible has been done and is being done and I am sure that when all the steps are taken very soon a time will come when the differences between the Scheduled Castes and the Scheduled Tribes on the one hand and the other classes on the other will not be there. It has been said that no much is being done. Today, Sir, we have seen to it that the Scheduled Castes and the Scheduled Tribes get their due representation, whether it is in the Ministry of Shrimati Indira Gandhi or whether it is some other forum or organisation, and, for the first time, Sir, the Ministry headed by our Prime Minister, Shrimati Indira Gandhi, contains two Ministers who are tribals—one from Orissa and other from the Bastar region of Madhya Pradesh. Like this, Sir, whatever is possible is being done.

The honourable Mover of this Resolution made a very interesting point that whatever money is being given is spent more on the departments which are looking after the welfare of these backward classes. Sir, for the information of the honourable Member and for the information of the whole House, I must say that the overall expenditure on the establishment at the Centre is about one per cent of the total outlay and at the States level it is about fifteen per cent in non-plan and 71 per cent in the plan. So, for his information I must say that whatever we have spent and we are spending is much less and the rest of it is being spent for developmental purposes only. I do not say that there might not be any corruption. It is possible that some funds are diverted or are not utilised properly or that other malpractices are there because of the illiteracy and backwardness of these people. But by and large, most of the money that has been allotted to these sectors is being spent only on those sectors and it is not as if the money is being spent on the administration only.

I think I have covered most of the points which were raised except the one which was mentioned by Shri K.N. Dhulap who said that educational and job training facilities are not being provided to the Scheduled Castes and Scheduled Tribes people in order to enable them to get employment. The Apprentices Act, 1961, as amended, provides that the States should extend job training facilities to the Scheduled Castes and Scheduled Tribes people in the various States. It is estimated that 20,000 Scheduled Castes and Scheduled Tribes trainees are being trained in the Industrial Training Institutes in the country every year. Moreover, there are at present six Training-cum-Guidance Centres for the Scheduled Castes and Scheduled Tribes, 11 Centres for training for the State Services, 2 Centres for training for Engineering Services and 4 Centres for training for Class III Services. Over 450 persons were appointed to the IAS and IPS, posts so far through the six All-India Training-Centres. One hundred Scheduled Castes and Scheduled Tribes persons have been appointed in IAS and IPS, etc. During last two years.

The other point that was raised by Mr. Dhulap was that the financial provisions for Scheduled Castes by the nationalised banks are inadequate. Sir, in addition to the provision by nationalised banks under special schemes, Finance Development Corporation have been set up for Scheduled Castes in Assam, Andhra Pradesh, Haryana, Kerala, Karnataka, Punjab Rajasthan, Tamil Nadu and Uttar Pradesh. These Corporations provide financial assistance to Scheduled Caste persons under several economic uplift programmes. Sir, the next Resolution is about agriculture and Mr. Shinde will be replying to that Resolution. He will also say that in the general sector also there are schemes, irrespective of caste or creed, and there also the Scheduled Castes are getting benefits of these schemes in addition to the schemes which are specifically meant for the Scheduled Castes and Scheduled Tribes.

Thank you, Sir.

Shri Gian Chand Totu: Mr. Vice-Chairman, Sir, I am grateful to the Hon. Members who have taken note of my Resolution and spoke on it. Sir I would like to remove some of the misgivings. Neither by Resolution nor I said that Government has not done anything. On the contrary, I am very much conscious of the advances made by the Government, particularly in the last one year. And I would like to draw the attention of the House to the wording of my Resolution also where I only said:

> "... have not been able to make the desired impact ...."

References

1. Galenter, Marc "Untouchability and the law" in J.Michael Mahar (ed), *The Untouchables in Contemporary India,* Tuscon (Arizona, The University of Arizona, Press) USA, 1972, p. 237.
2. *Ibid,* p. 238.
3. *Ibid,* p. 239.
4. *Ibid,* p. 240.
5. The Bombay Harijan Temple Entry Act, 1947 (Bombay Act XXV of 1947).
6. The Bombay Hindu Places of Public Worship (Entry Authorization).
7. Issacs Harold *India's Ex-untouchables,* Asia Publishing House, Bombay, 1965, p. 39.
8. Siva Rao B. *The Framing of India's Constitution,* The Indian Institute of Public Adminstration, New Delhi, 1968, p. 766.
9. *Ibid,* p. 748.
10. *Ibid*, p. 649.
11. *Ibid,* p. 769.
12. Basu D.D. *Introduction to the Constitution of India*, Z.17 Calcutta, 1971, p. 81 (S.C. Sarkar)
13. *Ibid*, p. 81.
14. *Ibid*, p. 78.
15. *India 1976,* page 103, Research and Reference Division, Ministry of Information and Broadcasting, Government of India.
16. *Ibid*, p. 103.
17. *Ibid*, p. 103.
18. *Ibid*, p. 103.
19. *Ibid*, p. 103.
20. *Ibid*, p. 104.
21. Kalelkar Commission March 30, 1950 App. I Volume II preface.
22. Galenter Marc *Ibid,* Arizona, The University of Arizona Press, USA, 1972, p. 242.
23. *Ibid*, p. 242.
24. The Committee on Untouchability, R. Elayaperumal Committee (M.P.) Govt. of India, 1965, April 27.
25. Lok Sabha Debates, Vol. No. 50, Col. No. 155 to 244, Lok Sabha Secretariat, New Delhi, May 23, 1972, Col. No. 155.

26. *Ibid,* Col. No. 158.
27. *Ibid,* Col .No. 159, 161.
28. Dubey, S.N. "Administration of Social Welfare Programme" Secretariat Maharashtra Govt. Bombay, 1973, p. 29.
29. *Ibid,* p. 30.
30. Zelliot, Eleanor "Gandhi and Ambedkar", in Mahar Michael J. (ed): *The Untouchables in Contemporary India,* Tuscon,1972, pp. 69-95.
31. Galenter Marc. *Ibid,* Arizona, The University of Arizona Press, 1972, 227, 314.
32. Issacs Harold, *Ibid,* Asia Publishing House, Bombay, pp. 65, 70, 1965.

4

History of the Protection of Civil Rights Act, 1976

When the Constitution of India was framed, a provision was adopted in Article 17 which provides as below.

Article 17 which makes the practice of untouchability an offence must be read with Act 35 (a) (ii) which confers upon Parliament the exclusive power to make laws prescribing punishment for those acts, which are declared to be offences under part III including Section 17. In the exercise of the powers, conferred by Article 35, Parliament has enacted the Untouchability (Offences) Act, 1955.

Broadly, it prohibited enforcement of any religious disability in any religious places like temples, and social disabilities in public place like shops, restaurants, etc. It assured the untouchables the same rights as any other person in the enjoyment and use of wells, water tap, public conveniences and cremation grounds, educational institutions, hotels and hospitals. Any act which prevents an untouchable from enjoying these rights is made punishable. The present Act came into force on June 1, 1955.[1] The Act had no doubt some statutory effect, but the cancer of untouchability was not completely eradicated.

Ever since the Untouchability (Offences) Act, 1955 came into force, there has been criticism both inside and outside the Parliament that the Act is not serving the purpose for which it was enacted. It was pointed out that punishments awarded under the Act were too few and inadequate. In view of these criticisms, the Government of India appointed a committee under the chairmanship of R. Elayaperumal to examine, amongst other things, the problem of untouchability with reference to the working of the Untouchability (Offences) Act, 1955 and to make recommendations to the Government for its amendment. A Bill to amend the Untouchability

(Offences) Amendment and Miscellaneous Provision Bill 1972, was introduced in the Lok Sabha in April 1972. Later on the Bill was referred to a joint committee of both the Houses of Parliament which submitted its report in February 1974. It was passed by Parliament in the monsoon session of 1976 and assented to by the President on September 13, 1976.

The crucial issues regarding offences connected to untouchability were discussed via the aforesaid Bill and portions of the debates are reproduced below.

Untouchability (Offences) Amendment and Miscellaneous Provisions Bill: Debates in the Lok Sabha on May 22, 1972

Prof. S. Nurul Hasan: I have already moved that the Bill to amend the Untouchability (Offences) Act, 1955 and further to amend the Representation of the People Act, 1951, be taken into consideration.

This is a very simple but important Bill. The House would recall that in 1955, the Untouchability Offences Act was passed to give effect to the solemn declaration contained in the Constitution in Article 17, according to which untouchability stood abolished. But inadequacies were felt in the existing Act and many Hon. Members, in Parliament as well as others pointed out those inadequacies. The government, therefore, decided to refer this matter as well as other matters to the Committee on Untouchability, Educational and Economic Development of Scheduled Castes, set up under the chairmanship of Shri Elayaperumal in 1965. The Elayaperumal Committee studied the problem of untouchability as well as the functioning or the working of the Untouchability Act, 1955 in detail, and made a number of recommendations. The purpose of those recommendations was to plug some of the existing loopholes and to make the penal provisions more stringent. Most of these recommendations have been accepted by government.

There has been only one modification and I shall explain each of the major provisions of the Bill.

First of all is the question of amendment relating to the raising of the quantum of punishment under the Act. The second is making offences under the Act non-compoundable. Thirdly, bringing within the definition of 'place of public worship' privately-owned temples used as places of public worship and disqualifying persons convicted under the Act from contesting elections to the Central and State legislatures. Lastly, the utterances of public personalities justifying untouchability whether on historical or philosophical grounds are also proposed to be brought within the purview of the law.

I am placing for the consideration of the House a small change government have made in the Bill from the recommendations of the Elayaperumal Committee. The Committee had recommended that in the case of the first offence, it should be punished by imprisonment of not less than 3 months but upto 6 months and also fine of not less than Rs. 50 but upto Rs. 200. While government naturally agree that the punishment must be deterrent, it has been felt that if the-punishment for the first offence is quite so deterrent, there may be a tendency on the part of courts to acquit the accused on the basis of some doubt or the other. Therefore, government have proposed that in the case of the first offence the punishment may not be less than one month but upto six months—the maximum remains the same and the fine must be not less than Rs. 50, as was also recommended by the Committee, but upto Rs. 200, also in accordance with the Committee's recommendation. Hence the only difference is that in the case of the first offence, the minimum punishment recommended by the Committee as 3 months has been changed to 1 month in the Bill. I would like however to make it clear at the very beginning that government do not wish to adopt any very rigid attitude in the matter and if it is the general feeling of the House that we should accept the Elayaperumal Committee's recommendation *in toto*, I would be prepared to do so.

I would request the House to give this matter expeditious consideration because the whole matter has been gone into in great detail by the Elayaperumal Committee. The report of the Committee was submitted in 1969 and for reasons best known to the House, it has not been possible for government to bring forward legislation amending this very important Act. I move.

Mr. Speaker: Motion moved:

"That the Bill to amend the Untouchability (Offences) Act 1955 and further to amend the Representation of the People Act, 1951, be taken into consideration."

***Shri Krishna Chandra Halder** (Ausgram): Mr. Speaker, Sir, I would like to speak in Bengali.

I, on behalf, of my party rise to support this Bill. Sir, we are going to celebrate the silver jubilee of our independence but the cases of offences of untouchability are very much prevalent even today. Untouchability has been proclaimed an offence in Article 17 of the Constitution. In pursuance of the provisions of Article 35 of the Constitution, the Untouchability (Offences) Act, 1955 was passed in this House. The Elayaperumal Committee was formed to study the offences committed under untouchability and to review the working of the Act. A discussion also had taken place in this House in 1970.

We speak of democracy, equality etc., but even today we find that about 8 crores of downtrodden people in our country are deprived of real freedom and equality. Even today we find that members of the Scheduled Castes and Scheduled Tribes and the Adivasis are living as untouchables and like second class citizens and at many places they are treated worse than animals. It has been stated in this House many times that the members of the Scheduled Castes, Scheduled Tribes, the Harijans etc., are deprived of the fundamental rights that are available to other Indian citizens. In villages members of these communities are prohibited to draw water from the common ponds or wells. In many places like Kerala etc., they are prohibited to worship in temples or places of public worship. It is not enough that the problem is left to be tackled by the Ministry of Education and Social Welfare alone. We will have to review this from different angles i.e., social, economic and political. All departments like Planning, Finance etc. should be alive to this problem and then only there can be some betterment in the lot of these backward classes of people. Major portion of these 8 crores of downtrodden people are either landless labourers or share croppers or they work as industrial labour in the urban industrial areas. We have discussed in this House the sad incident where 30 Adivasis were burnt alive in Purnea district of Bihar because they were involved in disputes over possession of land. This is the way how people of higher classes are committing atrocities on them. We have also discussed in this House the sale of Adivasi girls and women in Orissa who are our sisters. This is regrettable condition of the so-called untouchables in our country.

*The Original Speech as delivered in Bengali.

For this purpose mere legislation is not enough. We had already passed legislation against such offences as far back as 1955. But even today after 25 years of freedom and in spite of all these legislations, untouchability is prevalent. The Elavaperumal Committee says, I quote, "The problem of untouchability is, therefore, inseparably linked up with the question of caste system and the social set up based on that. It is an indisputable fact that the caste system is the dominating social force in this country. Hence any attempt to remove untouchability without striking at the root of the case system is simply to treat the outward symptoms of a disease or to draw a line on the surface of water. Untouchability cannot be abolished in this country unless the social order is changed by establishing new values, and for this purpose the values based on the Hindu religion must be changed first."

It further says: "A clear realisation of this fact on the part of the people is the pre-condition for any steps towards a social reconstruction resulting in the removal of untouchability for Scheduled Castes in this country". Therefore, Sir, today we will have to go to the roots of this malady to solve this problem. Because we have not yet been able to eradicate the malady of untouchability in our country. Our prestige in the eyes of the outside world has suffered a blow. In the *Patriot* newspaper of 11th September, 1971 it was published how the Harijans were treated in Hodal town in Gurgaon. The news item says, "The caste Hindus of Hodal town in Gurgaon district have been blocking all roads and streets leading to a Harijan locality in the town thus immobilising the residents completely for the last one month and have not been allowed to lodge a complaint with the authorities."

Sir, the aggrieved people were not even allowed to lodge a complaint with the authorities. The Registrar General of India has carried out a survey to some extent but the Committee has gone to the extent of saying: at page 46 they say: "However, the general impression which we gathered during our tours is that the figures, cannot be truly representative, which promoted the Committee to conduct a plot survey in one of the districts of UP." Therefore, Sir, this act should be given wide publicity to inform the people that practice of untouchability is an offence punishable under the law. Not only that, many officials in our police departments also are either ignorant or indifferent to this piece of legislation due to lack of sympathy and feelings for the backward classes of people. In that very report of the Committee it has been said, I quote, "As regards the provisions of the Act, the figures are unsatisfactory. It is a matter of great regret that out of 30 only 2 police officials could tell something about the provisions of the act (the Untouchability Offences Act.)" This is the situation in which we find ourselves. We will have to examine the problem from economic, social and political points of view. The ruling party speak about ideals of Mahatma Gandhi but in his birth place, Gujarat, at places like Porbandar, Rajkot etc., untouchability is prevalent and people of lower castes are looked down upon. This evil is in existence in Gujarat, Rajasthan, Uttar Pradesh, Tamil Nadu and various other States. I feel Sir, that more enactment of legislations is not adequate to counter and eradicate this evil. The people of higher castes should come forward to help its removal from the roots. There is need to create social consciousness among members of higher castes to tackle the problem. They should change their outlook otherwise this problem is not likely to be solved.

I would also like to recall, Sir, what Dr. Ambedkar, the author of our Constitution and a prominent leader of the people belonging to the Scheduled Castes and other backward classes, said in 1936. He said, "Democracy is not merely a form of government. It is primarily a mode of associated living of conjoint communicated experience. It is essentially an attitude of respect and reverence towards fellowmen. Any objection to liberty ? Few object to liberty in the sense of a right to face movement in the sense of a right to life and limb... Why not allow liberty to benefit by an effective and competent use of a person's power...? To object this kind of liberty is to perpetuate slavery. For slavery does not merely mean a legalised form of subjection. It means a state of society in which some men are forced to accept from others the purposes which control their conduct''.

Sir, even while supporting this Bill, I would like to refer to a news item that appeared in the Madras edition of the *Hindu* dated 22.4.1972. It says, "Mr. O.P.D. Salappa complained that private educational institutions were not entertaining Scheduled Castes students."

Sir, I only want to point out that Scheduled Castes students are prevented even from getting admission to schools in many parts of the country. Not only that Sir, an IAS Scheduled Caste Officer at Jaipur was allotted a quarter in an area habited by high caste people but he was not allowed to live there and was forced to shift to another residence in the Bhangi colony. This is the condition in which we are living. Sir, on the 16th February this year a news item appeared in the *Hindu* (Madras edition). It says "There are 10 temples in Kasargot area in Cannanore district which are barred to Harijans." Therefore, we see, Sir, that even now Harijans are debarred from entering and worshipping in temples in many places. It has also been seen at certain places that Harijan teachers though appointed by authorities were not allowed to conduct classes just because they were Harijans. They were relieved of their duties and were told not to come to the school but collect their pay when due. Sir, in section 7 of this amendment Bill it has been stated that "In section 8 of the Representation of the People Act, 1951, sub-section (1), after the words "The Indian Penal Code' the words, brackets and figures 'Or under the Untouchability Offences Act, 1956' shall be inserted."

Shri Krishna Chandra Halder: Sir, here mention have been made about the disqualifications of candidate for election to the legislatures either of the Centre or the State. I will suggest Sir, that if a person is found guilty of offence under the Untouchability Act, he should be debarred from voting rights for a period of six years. His name should be removed from the voters list for a period of six years. Our poet Tagore has said that "he, whom you have left behind, is pulling you back and retarding your progress." If such a big section of our population remained downtrodden and backward, the entire nation will remain backward. It can never progress. It has been said that "Man is the supreme and ultimate truth, there is nothing beyond Man." In this spirit Sir, I will appeal to all sections of people to come forward with open mind and help the cause of uplift of these downtrodden people. Those who have been denied human values and basic rights so long, should be welcomed in our folds and all their rights should be restored to them. With these words, Sir, I conclude my speech.

***Shri P. Venkatasubbaiah:** Sir, the Hon. Minister of Education has brought forward this Untouchability (Offences) Amendment and Miscellaneous Provisions Bill, 1972. When we discuss the subject pertaining to untouchability, we have to understand that there is a history behind this problem and that the future of Millions of destitute peoples

*The Original speech as delivered in Telegu.

who have for ages been neglected by society and are outside the pale of society. For the emancipation of these unfortunate peoples the Father of the Nation devoted his life and energies and formulated many schemes. Instead of being called the low caste people or the cobblers or scavengers, they have been christened as Harijans, children of God. Our history is replete with the heroic struggle launched on behalf of these people by various social welfare organisations and social workers. We cannot easily forget the historic Poona Fast undertaken by the Mahatma for securing to these unfortunate people social and economic justice. And we all know the memorable role played by Dr. Ambedkar in this struggle. But what is tragic is that in spite of 25 years of our independence and in spite of the work of these great leaders in this behalf, this social inequality and injustice is still in our midst.

We have heard with shame of the incidents in Kanchikacherla in Andhra Pradesh and in other places like Gujarat and Maharashtra. Only a few cases come to our notice through the newspapers but there will be many more which are not reported about the atrocities committed against these poor unfortunate people. These incidents go to show how deep-seated is the prejudice against these so-called untouchables in our body politic. So the question we should ask ourselves is whether through legislation we can eradicate this deep-routed malady. We assume that this prejudice is got evident in the cities. But as I said earlier this prejudice is in our blood. This is evident in our neglect of these people in the matter of allotment of house sites or even in the fundamental need of providing drinking water to them. On paper we have grandiose schemes for the betterment of their lot but for some reason we have so far not been able to translate these plans into tangible action. We have provided that adequate representation should be given to them on the Panchayati bodies, Zilla Parishads. But in point of fact, what is happening? The tenants of rich landlords or their stooges get elected to these bodies defeating the very purpose for which such reservations have been made for these backward classes. Because of the policy of the government there is a suspicion in the minds of the people whether instead of eradicating this social evil we are perpetuating it. For instance, you are allotting them house sites on the outskirts of the villages or towns leading to segregation of these low-caste people from the so-called high caste people. By confining them to these specified areas, you are shutting out the human and other channels of communication between these classes and the high caste people. Until you try to integrate these people socially with the other communities you will not wipe out the feeling of distinction between these two classes. And social justice will not be done by these unfortunate people. Till this integration takes place and till you secure to them a better status than now, untouchability does not stand the ghost of a chance of being eradicated and your plans and programmes will not succeed.

In the matter of providing them educational opportunities and in the matter of their marriage also, the social consciousness should be aroused. There should, in fact, come about a social revolution. Encourage inter-caste marriages with these people. Incentives like increased job opportunities for the persons contracting such marriages and for the off-spring of such union should be liberally offered, Sir, as matters stand now these people are discontented and disheartened. Even though reservation of jobs is there for them, people belonging to these classes are not appointed to these reserved posts on the plea that suitable and deserving persons of these communities are not forthcoming. Thus, they are denied even the small percentage of opportunities provided to them. This is the bare fact. This is happening every day everywhere—be it in the Railways or other government departments. If this is how we are going to accept them as our social partners we can know how far we have progressed in our society.

There are so many social welfare organisations and Harijan Sevak Sanghs. Government should encourage such social organisations. Not only in the public field but more so in the social field, the increasing need of non-official organisations is being felt and they should be encouraged by government.

Sir, 99 per cent of our agricultural labour or landless labour are Harijans. So government has to consider how best to improve the economic conditions of these people. They depend on the land they cultivate and in justice they should get all the surplus land that would be available after the ceilings of land are imposed. Otherwise there is the possibility of such lands being cornered by rich landlords. These landless Harijans will then be deprived of their rights and cheated out of their rights and due.

You may make the punishment for practising untouchability more and more stringent. But I would like to remind that this social scourge cannot be wished away by legislation only. Great leaders like Mahatma Gandhi and Dr. Ambedkar have given their lives for the eradication of this social evil a stigma on the fair name of our country. If social justice is to be done by these people, there should be a sea-change not only socially but even in the attitude of the government. In the matter of jobs, the Harijans should be posted as high officials like District Collectors. They should be provided jobs much more than the reserved quota for them. Then only there will be social transformation. Otherwise they would be deprived even of the rights guaranteed to them.

Sir, the progress of the plans and programmes meant for these backward classes has so far not been upto our expectations. Therefore, I request that a special committee should be appointed to go into the question of the implementation of these programmes and to identify the areas where there has been a shortfall in the targets. They should be empowered to evaluate the progress of these activities in each and every State.

With the problems of Harijans are closely connected those of the Adivasis in various parts of our country. These innocent people have also been neglected by us so far. As a result of this neglect, they have fallen a pray to the philosophy of violence. Whenever the neglected find that through democratic processes and constitutional methods they cannot enforce their rights, they enforce them through violent means, government should, therefore, see that these people are weaned away from the path of violence by restoring to them their rights and opportunities.

In conclusion I would reiterate that if we want to integrate these Harijans into the mainstream of our society, if we want to provide them social, political and economic equality, all of us, the government and social welfare organisations should work for them and towards this end. At least then we would have in part atoned for our past neglect of these Harijans, the children of God.

"The judge should study the character and age of the offender, his early breeding, his education and environment, the circumstances under which he committed the offence, the object with which he committed it and other factors. The object of doing so is to acquaint the judge with the exact nature of the circumstances so that he may give a punishment which suits the circumstances".

Mr. Speaker: Nine or ten minutes for each at the most. Sometimes Members grab some time and the next Member has to suffer because of that.

Shri J. M. Gowder (Nilgiris): Hon. Mr. Speaker, Sir, I am thankful to you for giving me an opportunity to say a few words on the Untouchability (Offences) Amendment and Miscellaneous Provision Bill, 1972 on behalf of my party, the Dravida Munnetra Kazhagam.

Sir, the provisions of the Untouchability (Offences) Act, 1955 are sought to be amended through this Bill. In spite of the fact that this amending Bill has been brought before this House after a lapse of so many years, still there are many lacunae and loopholes in the statute that are to be removed and plugged. In the legislation formulated by the Government which swear solemnly by the establishment of a secular state in the country you find the word 'religion'. Is this in consonance with the professions of the ruling party? This is what you come across in the original Act:

"Whoever on the ground of "untouchability" prevents any person—

(a) from entering any place or public worship which is open to other persons professing the same religion or belonging to the same religious denomination or any section thereof... .

If untouchability is practised in respect of a person professing the same religion, then there is penal provision under this Act. I am sure, Sir, you will agree with me that in a secular State the people belonging to different religions should have the freedom to worship wherever they want. For example, if a section of Hindu religious faith prevents another section from entering a place of public worship on the ground that that section belongs to Scheduled Castes, then the penal provision is attracted, as the practice of untouchability is an offence. If you extend this a little further, what happens if non-Christians or non-Muslims are prevented from entering the place of public worship of Christians and Muslims? This is not an offence. Only when such discrimination is practised with the express sanction of laws, the efficacious penal provisions for eradication of untouchability lose their intrinsic value. I have advanced this argument to show that if the government are keen to have the word 'religion' in such a legislation, then naturally there cannot be any possibility of having a secular state in the country. You will agree with me that religion is the bed-rock of casteism and bigotry that are bedevilling the entire country. Unless 'religion' is deprived of its legal backing, you cannot successfully implement any legislation for the removal of untouchability.

I have no hesitation in saying that the government are to be blamed for the perpetuation of untouchability in the country because they do not seem to plug the loopholes in the Act. These loopholes are the breeding ground for the practice of untouchability in the country. To whichever religious faith a place of public worship may belong, there should not be any practice of untouchability and here there is no need for mentioning 'religion', in the Act.

[Mr. Deputy Speaker *in the Chair*]

I am proud to say that the Tamil Nadu Government are occupying a premier place in the country so far as removal of untouchability is concerned. That is because the Government of Tamil Nadu have taken certain pioneering steps in this direction. For centuries the people belonging to a particular community could alone become the priests in the temples. This profession had been the exclusive perogative of a certain section of the society. Now, the DMK Government has passed an Act under which anyone can become the *archaka* (*priest*) in a temple. Even a Harijan can hope to become an *archaka* in a temple. You will agree with me, Sir, that this laudable legislation is worthy of emulation by other States and in fact the Central Government should give a lead in this direction. During the five-year period of administration the DMK Government have enacted such progressive measures. Now the Congress Party is in power at the Centre and also in most of the States. I do not think it will be impossible for the ruling party to enact such meaningful and progressive measures throughout the country. Similarly, in the matter of inter-caste marriages to which a reference was made by the speakers who preceded me, the Government of Tamil Nadu are awarding Gold Medals. The people contracting inter-caste marriages with Harijan community are given incentives and encouragement. I wonder why other State Government should not take the cue from the Tamil Nadu Government for the removal of untouchability. The Central Government seem to be concentrating all their energies in political manipulations and in political expediencies. The ruling party is more interested in winning elections and in toppling the Opposition Governments in the States than in implementing the Acts for the removal of untouchability and in encouraging inter-caste marriages with Harijan community. I would like to ask which of the Central Ministers is giving serious thought to remove untouchability and to provide ways and means for the upliftment of Scheduled Castes.

During 1968 the number of untouchability offences was 203. There were only 203 offences when the number of Scheduled Castes people is about 11 crores. Out of this, in 35 cases there was conviction and there was acquittal in 52 cases. In 39 cases, reconciliation was reached outside the court. 77 cases were reported to be pending. From this it is clear as to how many cases of offences are brought to the notice of the authorities. Firstly, the Harijan against whom this offence has been committed has no courage to approach a court. Secondly, he has no money to spend on such a case. Thirdly, after contesting a case against a caste Hindu, how is he going to live in the midst of a community predominated by caste-Hindus after the case is disposed of in his favour? The very fact that the Scheduled Castes are economically at the lowest rung of our society is resulting in the perpetuation of untouchability in our country. Even if a Central Minister belongs to the Scheduled Castes, he is not known by that factor. The power that is vested in him makes him known better throughout the country. Only when the economic status of the Harijans and the Scheduled Castes is improved, these people will gain respect in the society, I would like to know what concrete steps have been taken for their economic upliftment. The father of our nation, Mahatma Gandhi, two and half decades ago gave the clarion call to the nation that untouchability should be done with immediately. What has been done by the government to translate his vision into action? I am sorry to repeat that the energies of the government are getting dissipated in other directions, but not in the removal of untouchability.

I commend this amending Bill which seeks to enhance the punishment. But, what steps have been taken to give free legal aid to the Harijans who are the target of such offences? It is common knowledge that these people have no resources to fight in a court of a law. Unless they are given free legal aid, how are they going to take advantage of the provisions of this

Act? If the government want to implement this Act vigorously, there must be a provision in this very Act, giving free legal aid to the Harijans and the Scheduled Castes, who are the harassed victims of other sections of our society. The Elayaperumal Committee has made many valuable suggestions. The Hon. Minister himself stated that though this committee had recommended three months of imprisonment the government have brought it down to one month in this amending Bill, as if the practice of untouchability is coming to an end in our country.

I regret to point out that this Act has not yet been made available in regional languages. The police, the magistrates and the revenue officers are not fully acquainted with the provisions of this Act. They are the people to implement this Act: I would like to suggest that in the syllabus of the training schools for Police, for Magistrates and for Revenue Officers, the Untouchability Offences Act should get a prominent place so that the concerned people get an intimate knowledge about the provisions.

You know, Sir, that it is impossible for the Harijans to go to a First-Class Magistrate's court situated far away from their place. They have neither conveyance facility nor they have money to spend on such visits. I would suggest that mobile courts should be established throughout the country for the purpose of implementing this Act vigorously. I would also like to point out that adequate protection should be given to the people belonging to Scheduled Castes and Harijan community, who take courage in their hands to report such offences committed by caste Hindus. I would also stress the need for raising the standard of living of these people, which will ensure them a place of honour in our society and not the place of exploitation. The government cannot eradicate untouchability solely with the assistance of this Act providing punishment.

I came across a report that in Chandigarh there are separate dharamshalas and cremation grounds for Scheduled Castes people. While they live they are ill-treated, harassed and victimised. But after their death also, they should be burnt or buried in a separate cremation ground. I would like to know why this kind of a thing should not be made an offence under this Act. I would ask of the Minister as to what action has been taken by the government against the people like Puri Shankaracharya who want to perpetuate untouchability in the country.

Mr. Deputy-Speaker: This is provided for in the Bill by which such things will be taken care of.

Shri J.M. Gowder: What happened to the case against Puri Shankaracharya? Before I conclude, I would appeal to the Hon. Minister that the lacunae and the loopholes in the legislation meant for the removal of untouchability are removed. This kind of amending Bill should not be taken advantage of by the ruling party to get the votes of Scheduled Castes people. The provisions of the Bill should be implemented mainly in the interest of removing untouchability and in the interest of uplifting the economic interests of people belonging to Scheduled Castes.

Mr. Deputy-Speaker: Have you read the Bill?

Shri Shivnath Singh: Yes, Sir, I have read it, I have gone through it thoroughly.

Mr. Deputy-Speaker: You are talking of inter-caste marriage and things like that.

Shri Shivnath Singh: I am going to the root cause.

Mr. Deputy-Speaker: What you say is something different from what is provided in the Bill.

Mr. Deputy-Speaker: He is yet to make a speech.

Shri Atal Bihari Vajpayee: The Hon. Minister did make a speech while moving the Bill for consideration. He could have said many things. I will wait for his speech.

Mr. Deputy-Speaker: Would you like these as amendments to the Bill?

Shri R.S. Pandey: I wanted to enlighten the House how the society is to be adjusted.

Shri K.S. Chavda (Patan): I rise to support the amending Bill before the House. The Elayaperumal Committee submitted its report in January, 1969. The Minister has come forward before the House today with this amending Bill. That shows that government is not serious in case of removal of untouchability. Otherwise government would have come much earlier because 4 years have passed. When the preaching of any reform fails, the law takes the place of preaching. In case of removal of untouchability, when the preachings of saints and great men like Mahatma Gandhi and Dr. Babasaheb Ambedkar did not remove untouchability to a considerable extent, then, Sir, Article 17 was provided in the Constitution and our Indian Parliament has passed the Untouchability Offences Act of 1955. But, Sir, I am sorry to say that there is wide gap between the legislation and the implementation.

Today the Scheduled Castes people in the villages are not allowed to fetch water from the same common well in the village. In the same way they are not allowed to worship God together with caste Hindus in the same village. Even the barbers and the washermen do not serve them in the villages. This is the position, Sir, even after 25 years of our independence.

Now the circumstances are more favourable than they were when Mahatma Gandhi and Dr. Ambedkar tried their level best to remove untouchability.

Still, Sir, the Government of India and the State Governments are not serious to remove untouchability lock stock and barrel. Otherwise it would have been removed by now.

The figure of murders of Schedule Castes people during the years 1967, 1968 and 1969 were 1112 for the whole country.

Out of them, nearly 556 murders were from Madhya Pradesh and U.P. A Harijan girl was burnt in 1970 in Madhya Pradesh. When the question was raised by me on the floor of the Rajya Sabha, the Prime Minister promised to make a statement regarding that case. But she never made a statement though she was and till now is the Minister of Home Affairs and if this is the position regarding the Prime Minister, naturally, Sir, the State Chief Ministers will follow the same thing and do nothing to improve the condition of the Scheduled Castes and Scheduled Tribes. This portfolio of the removal of untouchability and amelioration of the condition of the Scheduled Castes should be in the hands of the Chief Ministers in the States and in the case of the Centre it should be with the Prime Minister. Then only something can be done with regard to the removal of untouchability.

If she takes keen interest, then things can be improved. The Prime

Minister held about a month back a meeting for the development of her constituency, namely Rae Bareli, and all the Ministers were invited for that meeting, but only the Minister for Social Welfare was not invited. For the development of her own district, she has taken so much interest....

Mr. Deputy-Speaker: The Hon. Member has made a reference to it. That should be enough. Let him not divert his attention from the Bill.

Shri K.S. Chavda: I am not diverting my attention. The whole thing is only the Minister for Social Welfare....

Mr. Deputy-Speaker: Untouchables are being bypassed by many other matters. Let him now come to the main thing.

Shri K.S. Chavda: The main thing is that if the head of the whole nation takes the initiative, then something can be done.

Mr. Deputy-Speaker: Let him not go off the main subject to Rae Bareli.

Shri K.S. Chavda: At that meeting she said that she wanted to make Rae Bareli a model district. That is why I say that she should take this up first, namely the removal of untouchability.

Mr. Deputy-Speaker: That is relevant....

Shri K.S. Chavda: Here is the press report which mentions the names of all the Ministers who were present....

Mr. Deputy-Speaker: Let him not go into the details of all that. He is going away very far from the main subject. He has made a reference to that and that should be enough.

Shri K.S. Chavda: The main subject is the removal of untouchability, and I am coming to that also. If she takes the initiative, then something could be done. All the Ministers, Central and State were present there, but only the Minister for Social Welfare was not present....

The Deputy Minister in the Ministry of Irrigation and Power (Shri B.N. Kureel): No Minister was invited. The Ministers went on their own.

Shri K.S. Chavda: Shri Om Mehta, Shri H.N. Bahuguna....

Mr. Deputy-Speaker: Then Hon. Member has already made the suggestion that it will be most effective if the Prime Minister herself takes over this responsibility. That is very relevant and very pertinent and I have allowed it. But beyond that, if he goes off and goes into the details of what happened in Rae Bareli, then he will be going very far away from the subject, and the poor untouchables whom he is trying to defend would be the sufferers.

Shri K.S. Chavda: She wants to make Rae Bareli a model district. I was submitting that in the case of removal of untouchability also she should take up that responsibility. My point was that....

Mr. Deputy-Speaker: I have allowed that and that is quite relevant....

Shri K.S. Chavda: But the Deputy Minister says that no Minister was invited to that meeting. I should say something in reply to it and say that all the Ministers were invited....

Mr. Deputy-Speaker: I do not allow it.

Shri K.S. Chavda: That is quite relevant.

Mr. Deputy-Speaker: The Hon. Member has made the point. If he wants to go into the details and deflect the entire discussion into something else....

Shri K.S. Chavda: But the Deputy Minister says that I am wrong. Should I not say something in reply and save my position?

Mr. Deputy-Speaker: Rae Bareli is not untouchability. Now, the Hon. Member should conclude. I am calling the next Member.

Shri K.S. Chavda: This is unfair. She says that Rae Bareli should be made a model for the whole nation. Should I not refer to that and say that untouchability should be removed?...

Mr. Deputy-Speaker: He has made that point and I have allowed him.

Shri K.S. Chavda: The Deputy Minister said that no Minister had been invited. That is why I am quoting from the report....

Shri Shashi Bhushan (South Delhi)! The Hon. Member should be made a model Member of Parliament.

Shri K.S. Chavda: If I would have been in charge, there would not have been any untouchability at all.

Mr. Deputy-Speaker: I have a feeling, and I do not know how really concerned Members are for those whom some people consider untouchables....

Shri K.S. Chavda: If even you, Sir, fail to understand what I say, I do not know what to do.

Mr. Deputy-Speaker: The hon. Member has made his point and it is a pertinent point, and I think he should be satisfied with that.

Now, the Hon. Member should conclude, Shri B.R. Shukla.

Shri B.R. Shukla (Bahraich) : The real point of the controversy has been missed by many Members who have participated in the debate. The question is not whether untouchability is a course and whether it should be abolished or not. When we adopted the Constitution, we made a provision that untouchability in any shape or form shall not be tolerated or practised in this country. In pursuance of the constitutional directive, the Untouchability Offences Act, 1955 was passed. The question which this Bill raises for discussion is whether the punishment already provided for under the Parent Act should be enhanced so as to meet the situation.

The question is whether when we bring an amendment for enhancement of the punishment or for providing a minimum rigorous imprisonment for an act which amounts to an offence under the Act we have made out any case or not. Only if the existing penal provisions in the Act are inadequate amendment becomes necessary. The real point to consider is whether the punishment of fine or imprisonment upto six months has been inadequate to remove untouchability. For that we have to see how many cases have gone to courts and how many persons have been really prosecuted and convicted, and in spite of the conviction and light punishment under the Parent Act, those very persons have persisted in repetition of the offence. Only then it would be necessary to make a change. But if the implementation of the provisions of the Parent Act has been insufficient, there is no question of bringing an amendment Bill.

The principle of punishment is based on three grounds, retributive, reformative and deterrent. As for retributive punishment, if a person has beaten another person, instead of the person who has been beaten taking to private vengeance against the wrongdoer, he seeks the assistance of the court which awards the punishment. This should be settled through the agency of the court of law. Then there is reformative punishment and deterrent punishment. Deterrent punishment is punishment of such a nature as to strike terror in the hearts of potential wrongdoers and prevent them from committing the offence. I would submit that the punishment provided under the Untouchability (Offences) Act is neither the retributive type nor of the deterrent types but by its very nature it is of the reformative type. A very distinguished jurist, Mr. Salmonds in his famous book on Jurisprudence has said that law lags behind public opinion, as public opinion lags behind truth.

Mr. Deputy-Speaker: How does he define this Bill?

Shri B.R. Shukla: I am saying there is no case made out by government for bringing a bill of this type for making the punishment which should be minimum of one month imprisonment in the case of first offence, then adding another term for the second offence and adding a further term for the third offence. It means we are encroaching upon the discretion of judges because after a judge has come to the conclusion that a certain person has committed an offence for which he should be punished, what should be the quantum of punishment should be left to the discretion of the judge who decides it taking into account a variety of reason. Therefore, my submission is that Bill is uncalled for. The punishment is already there; to amend it is now uncalled for. The Bill says in the case of first offence under the Act, there should be a punishment of rigorous imprisonment of not less than one month. Such type of provisions do not improve the matter. I will give an illustration.

There are two other enactments in this country where the minimum imprisonment has been provided for. One is the Prevention of Food Adulteration Act where the compulsory punishment is not less than six months imprisonment and a fine of about Rs. 1,000. The very fact that the minimum punishment of six months has been provided has gone a long way for the wrong-doers to defeat the provisions of the law by adopting corrupt methods, because they know that once they are convicted, no mercy would be shown and therefore, they must go to the police officer and the food inspector and see that that is not allowed. Under the Gambling

Act also, the minimum punishment is six months rigorous imprisonment if a certain place or a certain house is used for gambling. That provision has not been very successful.

So, my submission is that this amendment should not be allowed to be passed, although being a Member of the party which is ruling, I shall only support it, but because it is a radical and social measure, I have ventured to put forth my point of view.

Shri B.S. Murthy (Amalapuram): I am unable to understand why this Bill has been brought forward in this way. Earlier, the provision was that punishment might extend upto six months. Now it says; one month onwards and the fine is Rs. 550. Is this an indication that untouchability is almost abolished in India? Is it true? It is not true. Why should we misguide ourselves and our people and the world? Every speaker here today was at pains to show how untouchability was on the increase. Just now Mr. Vajpayee said that in one of the central offices in Delhi the Scheduled Castes were not allowed to take water from the common pot. Scheduled Castes officers coming to Delhi are not given houses. I need not say how many persons have been murdered.

Mr. Deputy-Speaker: You were yourself in charge of this matter when you were a Minister.

Shri Shashi Bhushan (South Delhi): How many houses did you give them when you were in charge of that portfolio?

Shri B.S. Murthy: Generally speakers do not inconvenience other speakers. You have taken the liberty and I shall take the same liberty. When I was the Minister in charge of housing, I saw to it that at least five per cent of the houses were reserved for Scheduled Castes.

Mr. Deputy-Speaker: I wanted this to come from you.

Shri B.S. Murthy: I was able to manage to do that and the government accepted that suggestion. I am not speak-about what I did or did not.

It is not a fact that untouchability is on the decline; on the other hand it is on the ascendancy. In Andhra Pradesh a youngman was burnt alive in daylight. In Rajasthan....

Shri P.K. Deo (Kalahandi)...In your party's government, in Kanchikarla

Shri B.S. Murthy: Is the Swatantra Party better? Are you supporting it?

Shri P.K. Deo: I am not supporting it.

Shri B.S. Murthy: It is a serious matter. Nearly eighty per cent of the Members in this House are absent. I am requesting those who are present to look upon the Harijans as human beings. It is very bad. He quoted the Kanchikarla case. What difference does it make if it was under the Congress Government, or the Communist Government or the Swatantra Government? Crime is a crime. Even if he is a Maharaja, I do not bother.

Shri P.K. Deo: He should have resigned from the party.

Shri B.S. Murthy: He does not understand how it touches the chords of our hearts. After 25 years of independence, these are happening. He is talking of Kanchikarla happening under the Congress Government. What has he done? What have you done in the Swatantra Government in Orissa? Have you not been encouraging Scheduled Tribes girls to be sold? Shame on you.

Shri Atal Behari Vajpayee: What is happening?

Shri B.S. Murthy: Nothing is happening. We go to philosophy and say *karma.* I am glad Mr. Vajpayee is supporting urgent measures to remove untouchability lock, stock and barrel.

This is a Bill which will beguile the world. I do not know why Prof. Nurul Hasan has brought it. Untouchability is not on the decline. Has any trouble been taken to see how far the legislation so far available has benefited the Scheduled Castes? No. We have been requesting several times that a high level commission may be appointed to go into the whole matter as to what legislation is available at the Centre and what legislation is available at the States to improve the conditions of Scheduled Castes and Scheduled Tribes and find out what reforms are necessary to be made.

In the statement of objects and reasons, it is said that the Elayaperumal Committee made certain recommendations and based on that, this Bill has been brought. I am afraid there are a number of very important suggestions of the Elayaperumal Committee and all of them have been forgotten. I am not for any enhancement punishment but when you are bringing a legislation, do not beguile the people. We had said, six months; but today it is only one month. Originally we said, Rs. 500; but today it is only Rs. 50 to begin with. Whom are you deceiving? This is very bad. Sometimes State Governments come and tell the Centre, "We do not have money". When the Department of the Welfare of Scheduled Castes and Scheduled Tribes was under the Home Ministry and when Mr. Pant was there as Home Minister, he always appealed to the State Ministers that this is a very important thing. Is not removal of untouchability a nation-building process? Can all the other people have their own way without the willing consent and cooperation of 10 crores of Harijans? We have seen how $7^1/_2$ crores of people in Bangladesh have revolted and broken off the chains from their hands and formed an independent and sovereign State of Bangladesh. Do you think Scheduled Castes numbering 8 or 10 crores will always remain like this? Is it not because of this ill-treatment by caste Hindus that the movement of Bangladesh was originally started? Who were these Bangladesh people? Were they not 200 years ago Hindus? Was it not because of the ill-treatment and harassment by the Calcutta *babus* that they embraced Islam? Do you want the Scheduled Castes in India to follow the same thing? Beware ! I am giving you a warning. During the last 25 years, you had spent crores and crores on others. Did you not spend crores of money on Bangladesh? I want more money to be given to more Bangladesh, because they were originally my cousins.

But don't try to deceive the country by bringing in a legislation like this.

Mr. Deputy-Speaker: What shall we do with the Bill now?

Shri B.S. Murthy: You have asked me that. I will also give a reply.

If the government wants to pass it because it has brought in, I shall give my vote. But my heart will not be there; the heart of the millions of people will not be there. Because nothing adequate has been done. You come out and say that untouchability is on the decline and, therefore, not six months, you make it one month, and, not Rs. 500, you make it Rs. 50. Any person who violates the law can give Rs. 50 every time.

I am anxious to say that the question will not be ended with this legislation. The question is much more serious, much more difficult. I appeal to the Prime Minister to bring to bear her dynamism in solving this problem. She has solved many problems. She is going to solve many other problems. But of all these problems of the removal of untouchability lock, stock and barrel, is the one which will benefit India for ever and ever.

I am sorry I did not want to say anything against the Maharaja of Kalahandi. With these words, I commend this legislation to be accepted by the House. I would also request the Minister in-charge to bring forward another legislation which will be more beneficial to the sufferers, to the victims of religious oppression.

Shri B.V. Naik (Kanara): Mr. Deputy-Speaker, Sir, I welcome the Bill without any reservations unlike my esteemed previous speaker. But in the process, I would like to find out and take a sort of balance-sheet about what has been done regarding the existing provisions in the Removal of Untouchability Act.

There is a previous provision, trying to remove untouchability from access to shops, public restaurants, etc. I think, that has been a part success and a part failure. Coming to the use of utensils, it is a total failure. Then, about occupation, trade or business, legally, it may not come into question but still it is a failure. The use or access to rivers, streams, wells, tanks, water taps, etc.— it is a major failure. As regards the enjoyment of benefit under the charitable trusts. I have no information as to how far it has been successful. Coming to the use or access to public conveyance, I would not say it is a failure. The public conveyance is always permitted. Then about the use of dharamshalas, of course, the dharamshalas, in these days, are principally occupied by the under-privileged sections of society. Then I come to the question of access to religious premises. I myself feel that we are not trying to bring in anything in this section of our society which is God-fearing, by giving it such a high sort of pedestal, by making an access to the temples, as though it is the biggest thing in life. I do not think going to a temple or a church or a mosque is a very important thing at all. I think the less we have of this godliness or religious superstition, particularly among the weakers sections of the society and the under-privileged, the better for this section of society, if we want to improve them.

Then I come to the hierarchical nature of the Hindu society, even though it may hurt the sentiments of some of the people in the Hindu society. The first jolt that was given to the hierarchical system of Hindu society, or the negative system of society, was really given by the assault of Islam and the Mohammedans about a thousand years ago. After the recovery, because of the protected existence under the British, the Hindu system never had a challenge to its life. Unless we want to see that this system, this hierarchical system, this exploited system is going to be given another rude jolt we will have to take adequate steps. I hope it will not be a jolt by communism or a jolt by Mao. In spite of the effort of Mahatma Gandhi, we have not been able to do anything substantial about the removal of untouchability or the ill-treatment of Harijans. So, unless you want Mao's thoughts to come, you should better take adequate steps to see that the existing system is removed lock, stock and barrel, root and branch.

An Hon. Member: How is Mao relevent here?

Shri B.V. Naik: Mao will come if we do not take care of the society ourselves. At least, his thoughts will come. But there is time for us to change before that.

In regard to this emancipation, instead of letting these people to enter into conventional temples, I would urge upon the Minister of Education....

Mr. Deputy-Speaker: Say something about the Bill.

Shri B.V. Naik: I will do that at the very fag end.

Mr. Deputy-Speaker: There is not much time.

Shri B.V. Naik: We have a Harijan culture. We have a sort of super-imposed culture. In my constituency there is the cock fight and fowl sacrifice. In the course of years we have not found it possible to give stimulation to this sort of culture which is there. If we are in a position to make these people worship their own type of god, I think we will be able to make them understand.

I am not speaking in the DMK terms, but in regard to the emancipated Harijans I would like to put in a word of caution. The emancipation of our downtrodden or weaker section of society invariably leads to the limitation of those sections which does not really liberate them. In the circumstances, if we have to make a frontal attack on the Harijan problem, or for that sake take the entire two-thirds or half of the population, social emancipation will have to be there.

Mr. Deputy-Speaker: I always thought of you as one of thse new intellectually gifted Members of Parliament. Why not give some examples of relevance also?

Shri B.V. Naik: I was coming to that. Social emancipation depends on economic emancipation. As far as the details of this Bill are concerened, they are perfectly all right.

Mr. Deputy-Speaker: So, you support the Bill.

Shri B.V. Naik: Economic emancipation will mean for the next 5 to 10 years actual reduction, if not *status quo*, in regard to the real income of the organised section of society. I would, therefore, suggest that we have to do a certain amount of basic thinking in regard to the welfare of the weaker sections of our society, call them by any other name, and that will mean something deeper, much more radical than what has been given in this Bill, which I welcome for the time being.

Mr. Deputy-Speaker: We started this debate at 12.28 and four hours have been allotted. So, we should conclude by 4.28 p.m. and take up the discussion on the drought situation in West Bengal at 4.30 p.m. How much time would the Hon. Minister take?

Prof. S. Nurul Hasan: About 20 minutes.

Mr. Deputy-Speaker: So, I will call him at 4 o'clock. I have got with me some names from the Congress Party. I think I will be able to accommodate all of them if they try to be brief.

Shri R.D. Bhandare (Bombay Central) : I rise to support this measure on a single ground. I draw your attention and the attention of the House including my Hon. friend, Shri B.S. Murthy, to Explanation II. It says:

> "A person shall be deemed to incite or encourage another person to practise 'untouchability', if he justifies, whether on historical, philosophical or religious grounds, the practice, by such other person, of 'untouchability'. "

The measure which has been incorporated in Explanation II is a welcome measure. But. I don't know to what extent in India, either the

Police or the Magistracy or the Judges would interpret the meaning of this Explanation II.

Shri B.S. Murthy: And the past experience.

Shri R.D. Bhandare: Experience—we have gone through these processes. I need not repeat our experience.

I am, therefore, drawing the attention to the speech made by my great friend and my admirer, Shri Vajpayee....

Mr. Deputy Speaker: He is admiring you.

Shri R.D. Bhandare: Even if he does not, at least as a social hypocrisy I must say that he admires me as I do. He says, unwittingly perhaps, that the *Chaturvarna* had no origin either in the Shastras or in the Vedas. Forgetting that he is a Brahmin, as he is, there is *Purusha Sukta* in the Vedas which is the origin of *Chaturvarna* followed by *Panchavarna*. Now, if the word is uttered and justified on the ground whether of historical, philosophical or religious grounds then it is made an offence under this piece of legislation. I do not know what the meaning will be, what the connotation will be, what the interpretation will be, of this explanation.

Shri Atal Bihari Vajpayee: To justify untouchability on any historical ground—that is made an offence, but history cannot be made an offence.

Shri R.D. Bhandare: I hope you are not a lawyer....

Shri Atal Bihari Vajpayee: I have studied law.

Shri R.V. Bade (Khargone): It is not in *purushasuktha,* it is in *manusmruthi* only.

Mr. Deputy-Speaker: Let us leave it to the courts of law for interpretation.

Shri R.D. Bhandare: I wonder when my learned friends show their ignorance.

Shri R.V. Bade: It is not in *Purushasukta; panchama varna* is not there.

Shri R.D. Bhandare: I need not go to the extent of sasying more. You are a great pandit, but ignorant of these simple matters.

I hope Mr. Vajpayee agrees with me....

Shri Atal Bihari Vajpayee: I am not a great pandit.

Shri R.D. Bhandare: That much I know.

Therefore, Sir, reading of the explanation raises a number of questions. A number of questions arise in my mind.

Mr. Deputy Speaker: In support or in opposition?

Shri R.D. Bhandare: As I told you, this is a new innovation; I welcome it. I welcome it because this is a new innovation for the first time to be found in a piece of legislation.

My children are taking their education in the schools. I happened to read their books. The books to be taught to them say, Dr. Ambedkar is a chamar. They never mention that he was the Constitution-maker. Now, writing of these things does what? Does it encourage or discourage?

Prof. Madhu Dandavate (Rajapur): Burn the books.

Shri R.D. Bhandare: Professor Dandavate, it is not a new thing that you are suggesting; we have been saying so for ages together.

Prof. Madhu Dandavate: I also suggest, burn the scriptures which stand for inequality.

Shri R.D. Bhandare: I hope that courts of law, the political parties, the leaders, etc. will try to understand the meaning and the significance to carry on propaganda, to prepare for change of mind of the Indian people, so that they may change their attitude. I hope on the basis of this Explanation. Two, we shall recast our educational system so that the educational system will be the instrument of reconstruction of the Indian society. I hope this aspect of social changes will be emphasised duly and made a part and parcel of the programme of every party and every public man. We have to see whether power is shared by the classes for whose benefit this explanation is there. I do not know what interpretation will be given to this explanation.....

Mr. Deputy-Speaker: Let them interpret it. We are not here to interpret it.

Shri R.D. Bhandare: We are making a legislation, and I am quite aware of the consequences of the legislation. If an occasion arises to put an interpretation on the pieces of the legislation....

Mr. Deputy-Speaker: Let the occasion arise.

Shri R.D. Bhandare: When I am a legislator, why should I allow that occasion to arise? At the time of the legislation, I must foresee the danger which is lurking. . .

Mr. Deputy-Speaker: If he were opposing the Bill, I would have understood it. But when he is supporting it, why should he go into all those things?

Shri R.D. Bhandare: I wonder, when we are trying to understand the clause, the meaning and the connotation and when doubts are raised and questions and problems are raised, you interpret that either I must oppose the Bill *in toto* or I must accept it as it is and sit quite. We have to benefit from the experience cited by a number of friends. We suffer in experience and we become wiser by experience, and we never take any word at its own face value because we know that hypocrisy of the best form has been used in the choice of words for ages together in this country. Therefore, the question of interpretation arises. But, as I said, Shri Atal Behari Vajpayee will certainly carry on the propaganda in view of what I have said and instruct his own people to try to give the correct interpretation. . .

Mr. Deputy-Speaker: There are other Members also to speak. Now, the Hon. Member should conclude.

Shri R.D. Bhandare: What is your suggestion, Sir?

Mr. Deputy-Speaker: I think he has supported the Bill with eyes and mind open. Let the Hon. Member now conclude.

Shri R.D. Bhandare: I doubt whether a proper interpretation....

Shri Atal Behari Vajpayee: What about the Hon. Member's own party?

Shri R.D. Bhandare: I have joined the Congress Party and I shall try to emphasis and try to persuade....

Mr. Deputy-Speaker: I would request the Hon. Member that if he wants to enlighten Shri Atal Behari Vajpayee, he can do so outside. He can fix up some time and give him proper tuition.

Shri R.D. Bhandare: I can quite understand if you say that my time is up.

Mr. Deputy-Speaker: Yes.

Shri R.D. Bhandare: You should have said that first.

Mr. Deputy-Speaker: I have rung the bell so many times.

Shri R.D. Bhandare: No, you have always been telling me....

Mr. Deputy-Speaker: I have been ringing the bell so many times.

Shri R.D. Bhandare: I beg your pardon, if I appear to be rude to you. You have always been telling me to instruct these people, and, therefore, I wanted to give the interpretation. You should have told me earlier if my time was up.

Mr. Deputy-Speaker: His time is up. Now, let the Hon. Member sit down. Shri M. Ram Gopal Reddy.

Mr. Deputy-Speaker: Shri C.M. Stephen.

Shri C.M. Stephen (Muvattupuzha): Mr. Deputy-Speaker, Sir, I rise to support this Bill. But even while supporting that, there are certain questions occurring to my mind which I would like to spell out for the consideration of the House and of the Hon. Minister who is piloting this Bill. This amending Bill has got two novel features; one is that the imprisonment is made compulsory and the other is, Expianation 2 to Sub-section (2) of Section 7. This Explanation 2, I am afraid, may not cover the field which, probably, my friend Mr. Bhandare was having in view. Explanation 2 can apply only to a case in which a particular person is hauled up for an offence and it is shown that with respect to that particular person an abetment is proved, in the sense that he has justified the offence on historical or religious or whatever grounds. But there is an other clause which the Hon. Minister should have thought about bringing within the ambit of this legislation. That is what my friend from the DMK benches mentioned during his speech. Propaganda is going on unrelated to any particular offence from high places justifying untouchability on the grounds mentioned out in Explanation 2. No particular offence is committed, but campaign is going on, that untouchability is good for historical reasons, religious reasons and so many other reasons, whether that is not an offence and whether that could not be counted as an abetment deserves to be considered. Explanation 2 as framed, would not cover that case and I feel, Sir, in view of certain campaigns taking place in the name of Shankaracharya or some other high dignitaries, these amendments should have provided for bringing that too under punitive coverage. This is a lacuna which should have been filled up and unless that is filled up, Sir, in fighting a social malady like this, we will not be making any headway. Ban that campaign to create an impression that the nation treats untouchability as a great crime. Even as a treasonable speech is treated as something condemnable, so also the campaign in this direction should be treated as heinous and penal. That is the point I wanted to make.

With regard to enhancement of punishment, there are two-three questions arising.

The first question is, why has this enhancement become necessary? After all, the statistics spelt out by the report of the Commission show that in 1968, the total cases challaned was 203, convicted 35, acquitted 39 and compromised 52. If in a large country like India the aberrations amount to only 203 cases, is there a case for enhancement of punishment and bring in special legislation or is it that the cases have not been adequately dealt with? Certainly the latter, i.e., the reason. All cases have not been picked up and prosecutions have not been launched. Severe punishment has not been given. Therefore, society or administrative machinery has not been geared up to face the challenge with regard to this social malady. As an Indian, I feel like bowing my head in shame that in the 25th year of our independence, this Parliament has got to consider a legislation suggesting enhancement of punishment for untouchability, i.e., for treating a human being as untouchable.

When the Constitution was passed, it was contemplated that reservation will be necessary only for 10 years. But it was further extended. Now we say enhancement of punishment is necessary. That is to say, in this vital respect, we have not made any advance at all. The Schedule to the Parent Act contains a number of Acts which have been repealed under the repealing provision of that Act. This covers a long period, from 1946. Nevertheless, this malady remains. Are you going to fight it by enhancing punishment? I am all out to support enhancement of punishment, but what made this legislation necessary? Have you got statistics to show that although the cases were proved, the judiciary has not been awarding the punishment? That is the case here. That is the case with respect to labour legislation or any legislation seeking to protect the weak and unprotected. The judiciary gives a punishment which is only formal, although the law says imprisonment or fine or both. Whereas with respect to section 323 of the IPC although law says this or that and yet the magistracy does impose a punishment of imprisonment, when it comes to untouchability, the most heinous thing you can have which has been specifically spelt out as such by incorporation in the Constitution, the judiciary refuses to give the punishment of imprisonment. Is that not the statistics? If that is so, what is to be our concept about our judiciary? Are they keeping pace with the revolution we want to accomplish? I am pinpointing the source. The internal infrastructure of society has not been recast in such a manner as to face this malady. For that, a real change in the infrastructure is necessary.

During the period of Mahatma Gandhi, much more, work was done in terms of Harijan welfare than in all these 25 years after independence. He did not have any law or government to support him. He had the entire religion against him. But nevertheless, by a process of social revolution which he carried out like a hurricane from one end of the country to the other, this problems was tackled and the Harijan felt more secure during Mahatma Gandhi's time under his benign protection than now. But with this legislation, that revolutionary urge has gone. No political party is taking it up in that spirit. Nobody is approaching the problem in the spirit of explanation of the sins our forefathers committed against these masses of people. Unless that spirit comes in, this problem cannot be solved. Certainly, so far as this legislation is concerned; its value is that of a symbolic declaration that the whole country is behind anybody who attempts to carry it out.

This can be done, as has been suggested by the Commission, only by self-assertion and self-realisation on the part of the people of the Scheduled Castes themselves. I am saying this from my experience. Wherever the agricultural labourers; mostly of the Scheduled Castes, are organized and are coming forward to fight for their rights, nobody dreams of untouchability so far as they are concerned because they have got the strength and they go ahead. I say this from my experience in my State. Wherever agricultural labour is organized, it is not under any complex and nobody else is under any complex because he is aware of his rights. If these persons are to be rehabilitated, let there be enhancement of the punishment. I am not questioning that but unless you give him the place of power in the governmental machinery, in your secretariat, in your judiciary, in your first class cadre, unless you give him the place of power, he will not come to his own. Where you attempt to give him the place of power, so many obstacles are coming: Chapter 10 of the Commission's report is revealing enough about the gulf between your promises and what they are getting. Not that the Scheduled Castes people are not qualified to get, but so many things are coming up to keep them away. Scheduled Castes graduates float about without employment.

But it is said that qualified persons are not available. Let them organize themselves, and that will be the solution.

I view this legislation as a welcome measure only in one respect, that this is a re-avowal, re-pledging of the Indian nation on the 25th Anniversary of Indian Freedom, declaring to the whole world that we are pledged to the end that we are to achieve; nothing more than that. And it will have a salutary effect if the Scheduled Castes people themselves and the political parties who are behind them take up the challenge and go ahead in a revolutionary spirit in which Mahatma Gandhi addressed himself to the task. Otherwise, socialism will be a far cry; and we will be deluding ourselves and deluding the people.

With these words, I support this legislation.

Shrimati T. Lakshmikanthamma (Khammam): In this country from time immemorial, Harijans and women have been the worst sufferers at the hands of the society....

Mr. Deputy Speaker: There is no provision for women in this Bill.

Shrimati T. Lakshmikanthamma: We are also untouchables.

Puri Sankaracharya does not allow women to touch his feet.

There was a time when Harijans were not allowed to go with chappals in the streets where Brahmins lived and they were also not allowed to use umbrella. Also the woman, when the husband died, was to have her head shaven, and she was not allowed to eat more than once. Even now, so many things are happening. (*Interruptions*) The same conditions still exist. I am bringing this to the notice of the House because the House should be aware of the social conditions of Harijans, and along with Harijans also of women....

Shri Vasant Sathe (Akola): You want them also to be added in the Bill.

Shrimati T. Lakshmikanthamma: I am saying this, so that at a later date another Bill like this for women may also be brought forward.

Shri S.M. Banerjee: The country is headed by a woman.

Shrimati T. Lakshmikanthamma: Once she heads the country, she is not a woman, she is a man. In fact, she is the only man. That is what has been said. It has been said that in this country there has been only one man.

Shri S.M. Banerjee: If she calls herself a man, who is woman? (*Interruptions*)

Shrimati T. Lakshmikanthamma; All of us are women.

Some Hon. Members were reminding the House about what had happened in Kanchi Kacherla and other places. At Kanchi Kacherla, a Harijan boy was burnt, and the then Minister went to the length of supporting the incident.

I am glad to inform the House that the Minister is no more a Minister and he is no more in our party. I think such a person who has such views, does not deserve to be in our party. I am glad he is outside our party.

There was also an instance, which I know, where a Harijan boy went to a hotel because he was feeling hungry. It is not something which we see in some cinemas or read in some stories. But these things do happen in our society. The boy went to the hotel and ate something and since he was not able to pay the money, he was tied and his hands were burnt. There was also another instance where a child, just because she sat on a mat, in U.P., that child was taken and thrown into a well. These are not old stories; these are recent things, that had happened. I am glad that our government intend taking some stringent measures through this Bill.

So many people mentioned about socialism and more socialism. I am one with Mr. Shashi Bhushan and other Members that mere removal of economic disparities will not solve the problem. Socialism and more socialism is the only panacea for these economic ills. Yes, we go and touch the feet of Babu Jagjivan Ram. On the other day when Mr. Sanjivayya died....

Mr. Deputy-Speaker: Is touching the feet socialism?

Shrimati T. Lakshmikanthamma: It depends on the status you give to a woman or a Harijan or to the backward classes, whoever it is.

I am glad at least in our Andhra Cabinet, there are four Harijans in the Ministry and a number of backward class people also. There was a time when giving a Ministership to a Harijan was considered as though it was a favour being done to the community. But now, the country has started moving in a different direction. Now, we want to give them importance so that they will take their place in their own right. They are a force now. There is a story that the great Hanuman did not know his strength unless somebody reminded him that he was so powerful. So also, these sections. We know what a great force women are because of the equal vote they have along with men and they could now shape the destinies of a country. So also the Harijans and to her poorer sections. When we talk of backward classes, it is not that all are backward. There may be a few—one or two rich people among the backward classes. But, there are only two classes now, the rich and the poor.

There was a discussion about Vedas and Upanishads. According to the Shastras, a Brahmin is one who has the knowledge of Brahman. Brahman is the supreme origin. According to me, Avadutram who is a Harijan is Brahmin and Puri Sankaracharya is an Achut. A person is a Brahmin by attainment and not by birth. The great Viswamitra had to struggle to attain that Brahminhood.

I will give one more suggestion and I will conclude my speech. This is about the inter-caste marriages. There should be a provision wherein you give priority or preference to a person who marries a Harijan girl or Harijan boy.

Shri K.S. Chavda: In government jobs?

Shrimati T. Lakshmikanthamma: Government can do this much. (*Interruptions*) There are only a few classes of people who believe in this. The general upsurge among the masses is against all these social evils.

I will now give an example and I will conclude. In Tirupati, as an experiment, we gave a seat to a Harijan, who was a Christian student leader. All orthodox people came and said 'How did you give a seat?' Big people came and complained to the Prime Minister. But ultimately, that boy won by a 15,000 majority. That means the country is not thinking on these lines. The people also are not thinking on these lines. It is only a few classes, and among those few classes, only a few individuals who are thinking like this. They are getting extinct, I am sure. There is a peaceful revolution coming up and these forces that are coming in the way, will be wiped out.

[Shri K.N. Tiwari: *In the Chair*].

Prof. S. Nurul Hasan: I am extremely grateful to the hon. Members for having given their whole-hearted support to this Bill.

Shri S.M. Banerjee (Kanpur): The Speaker said that he is going to call the Minister at 4 p.m. I am not seeking to speak. I have only a suggestion. Because the second reading of the Bill may come up tomorrow at 4.30 we have another discussion, what I am suggesting is that many good amendments were suggested by Hon. Members but they could not send them because abruptly this Bill came. So...

Mr. Chairman: No please.

Shri S.M. Banerjee: Are you going to pass this Bill today?

Mr. Chairman: Yes, Sir.

Shri S.M. Banerjee: After all, there are so many Members who have spoken...

Dr. Kailas (Bombay South): It would be better if it is sent to the Select committee.

Shri S.M. Banerjee: We may have the second reading of the Bill tomorrow.

Shri K.S. Chavda: The Deputy-Speaker said that the Minister will reply at 4 p.m.

Shri K.S. Chavda: The time was fixed by the Deputy Speaker for his reply.

Mr. Chairman: I know what the Deputy-Speaker said and what he has told me and how I should conduct the House. Now, please take your seat.

The Minister of Education, Social Welfare and Culture (Prof. S. Nurul Hasan): So far as this particular measure is concerned, it is limited in character. It is not a measure which would by itself lead to eradication of untouchability. Hon. Members from all sections of the House have rightly pointed out that to eradicate the real malady something else is needed. We need a social revolution. We need a basic change in our outlook. It is necessary that social and political workers should mobilise the masses of our people to arouse their conscience against this canker of untouchability. I think there cannot be any difference of opinion on this. The way all sections of the House have expressed themselves on this issue of untouchability is a proof (if any proof is needed at this stage) that the people of India will not tolerate untouchability. Even though it may be practised to our utter shame and disgust, the people of the nation as a whole will not tolerate and if the people as a whole will not tolerate it, then, it becomes the duty of all of us, particularly of the government to take all such measures which are necessary for the eradication of untouchability.

Sir, various measures have been proposed; many measures have already been undertaken; many more are likely to be undertaken in the future the net effect of all of which would be to undermine the whole indeological, social and economic basis of the society which tolerates and engenders untouchability. I will not go into the details of all those measures.

I would only make one very brief reference to education. I am deeply conscious of my responsibility in the sphere of education, to ensure that the education system does not contribute in any way to the concept of untouchability, but on the other hand, to see that effective measures are taken to see that those who have had the benefit of education reject outright the concept of untouchability and the social and ideological basis of this particular attitude.

Shrimati Sahodra Bai Rai then left the House.

Prof. S. Nurul Hasan: I am only too painfully conscious also of the various incidents that have taken place against the Harijans. I am also conscious of the fact that as land legislation is going to be enacted in various States and changes of land relationships are in the offing, social tensions have increased and as a result of these social tensions attempts have been made to use violence against the Harijans. It is the duty of all political parties and all social organisations to ensure that Harijans are protected but the duty of the government is even more than that of the social workers and of the political leaders. It is with this aim in view that the government considered it necessary to bring forward this long-delayed measure before the House, a measure, which, as I said before, is based on the well-considered recommendations of the very high-powered committee, namely, the Elayaperumal Committee. It would have been easy for me to say that let us refer it to yet another committee. Then, the Fifth Lok Sabha's term would be over and again a measure would come, and again the society would undergo a change, and again there would be a Bill and again there would be a demand and yet another Select committee. I feel that even if we find that there are certain gaps or certain loopholes, we should point out those things; I heard with rapt attention all the agruments that were advanced in the House, and on the basis of the arguments, I am seeking your indulgence to move some amendments myself. But I would beg of Hon. Members not to postpone this further, because a postponement at this stage when these tensions are increasing is likely to create more complications than it would solve.

A reference was made quite rightly by almost all Hon. Members to the machinery for implementation. I am conscious again of the fact that our machinery is not what all of us would like it to be. But governments have been conscious—I am referring to the State Governments—of the need to enforce properly and adequately this Act. I myself addressed a letter in February to all the State Governments in which I made a special plea that the Collectors and District Superintendents of Police be held personally responsible to ensure adequate protection to Harijans against any kind of discrimination arising out of untouchability and that they should take prompt action *suo moto* in all instances where the practice of untouchability comes to their notice. The State Governments should take a note of the work done by the Collectors and the District Superintendents of Police in connection with the protection and welfare of Harijans, Adibasis and other backward classes and that special notice should be taken in connection with their annual confidential reports. A further request was made that the presidents of district panchayats be asked to take prompt action against taluk and village panchayats which were found to be discriminating against the Harijans in their jurisdiction.

Shri K.S. Chavda: What is the response from the State Governments?

Prof. S. Nurul Hasan: Some State Governments have started taking energetic action. The Government of the State from which the Hon. Members comes, has taken very important decisions in this respect, and I am happy to state that.

I would like to draw the attention of the House to another measure which the government of India have taken. We have requested the Chief Secretaries to the State Governments and drawn their attention to this particular Bill and we have also said that the State Governments may consider the need to make provisions similar to the provision that is sought to be made here in the Representation of the People Act, that is to say, debarring anyone from seeking election to zila parishad or village panchayat, who has been convicted of the offence of untouchability.

I am also extremely gratified that Hon. Members have made a special reference to this very significant Explanation No. 2 which has been inserted here, that is to say, any person who justifies whether on historical, philosophical or religious grounds the practice of untouchability will be deemed to have incited or encouraged another person to practise untouchability. This is a very important point added. After this, I would only submit that we should not go in for banning of books. As a teacher, I am a little worried when books are sought to be banned. I want ideology to be met with ideology. Books written in a given set of historical circumstances may have a totality of values which may be valid for the time, but parts of those books may not be valid today. Therefore, if every historical work is to be subjected to censorship by each subsequent generation, perhaps it would not be possible for us even to understand the proper development of society in any given age. Hence by evaluating a historical work, let us see what was the total contribution of that work in a given society at a given moment of time.

Shri B.S. Murthy: Are you prescribing them as textbooks?

Prof. S. Nurul Hasan: At the same time, it will be very difficult for us to ignore the feeling reflected in this House that in the matter of textbooks meant for schools, we have to be very careful about what sense of values we wish to inculcate. That was why I started my very speech by saying that in the educational system we will have to take measures to ensure that the values we inculcate in the new generation are not values which will tolerate this canker of untouchability.

Reference was made to the number of cases registered with the police and actual convictions obtained. I have with me the figures right from the beginning. I am particularly happy at the decline in the number of cases registered with the police. I am told these figures are incomplete, but even so, I think they do reflect a trend that the number of cases registered by the police, even though these are cognisable offences, is not on the increase, even though reports are that these offences are being committed on a fairly wide scale. In 1968, 214 cases were registered; 184 were challaned; 19 were convicted; 28 were acquitted; 53 were compounded, and 84 were pending.

Shri C.M. Stephen: Any information about the nature of convictions?

Prof. S. Nurul Hasan: If you just bear with me for a few seconds, I will be coming to it. In 1969, the cases registered with the police were 251; challaned 207; convicted 28; acquitted 13; compounded 46; pending 120. In 1970, cases registered 203; challaned 168; convicted 15; acquitted 14; compounded 83; pending 56. You will see from the percentage of cases compounded why it has been necessary for us to come forward with this Bill.

Another point which has been raised and quite correctly raised is that what has been the attitude of the presiding magistrates when convictions were done. Sir, the Elayaperumal Committee studied 70 cases, of which 23 ended in conviction; out of these 23 cases, 17 cases resulted in fine only. The amount of fine ranged up to Rs. 25 in 12 cases and between Rs. 25 and Rs. 100 in five cases, and of the two cases which ended in imprisonment, in one case the imprisonment was for only one week and in another case only up to the rising of the court. Therefore, it was necessary for the government to take due note of the very valuable recommendations of the Elayaperumal Committee and to bring forward this particular piece of legislation.

Sir, in my introductory speech, I had made a reference to the fact that the government had deviated in one respect from the recommendations of the Elayaperumal Committee, and that was that we should take the view that if for the first offence the minimum punishment is one month instead of three months, then perhaps there would not be so many acquittals, but as I had thought from the speeches that I heard here, I gathered that Hon. Members would prefer that the minimum punishment which has been prescribed should not be lowered. I am, therefore, going to crave your indulgence that the minimum punishment recommended by the Elayaperumal Committee, of three months plus Rs. 50 as fine should be incorporated in this Bill.

Shri S.M. Banerjee: Are you going to move an amendment?

Prof. S. Nurul Hasan: Yes.

Shri S.M. Banerjee: When are you going to move it? The Bill is going to be passed today. (*Interruptions*) If the government are moving an amendment, why not allow us also to move amendments?

Mr. Chairman: Let the Minister finish his speech.

Prof. S. Nurul Hasan: There have been many other suggestions which I am sure the government will benefit from by accepting them. For example, one suggestion was that the provisions of the Bill should be properly publicised and brought to the notice of the various authorities.

Prof. S. Nurul Hasan: Then the question about free legal aid to the Harijans was raised.

This is a cognizable offence and Harijans do not have to fight the case themselves; it is for the police to take up the case and fight it. My Hon. friend Shri Vajpayee made a specific reference to an incident about separate *surahi* being kept in the Central Secretariat. It is a serious matter and I would beg of him to let me know further details. We must take up this matter seriously and take strong action... (*Interruptions*). My Hon. friend was having some discussion and did not probably hear what I said; otherwise he would not have raised this matter. I have already said that it should be our special responsibility to fight against the concept of untouchability through educational institutions. I commend the Bill to the House.

Mr. Chairman: The question is:

"That the Bill to amend the Untouchability (Offences) Act, 1955 and further to amend the Representation of the People Act, 1951, be taken into consideration."

Shri Raj Bahadur: I move.

"That the debate on the Bill be adjourned".

***Shri Atal Behari Vajpayee:** Honourable Chairman, what is the motion? Is the motion to stop the debate? If so, why? Have not all the members participated in this debate? Is the Honourable Minister agreeing to referring this Amendment Bill to a Joint Committee? If yes, then there can be agreement on it. But why is the debate being adjourned at this point of time.

Shri Raj Bahadur: Even for the consideration of the motion to refer the Bill to a Joint Committee, time is needed... (*Interruptions*)

Mr. Chairman: First let me dispose of Mr. Vajpayee's point. According to rule 109 at any stage of a Bill under discussion in the House, a motion that the debate on the Bill be adjourned may be moved with the consent of the Speaker.

I am giving my consent.

Shri Raj Bahadur: I mentioned rule 109 myself and I have formally moved.

Shri Raj Bahadur: It is a matter which deeply affects the psychological

---

*As Originally delivered in Hindi.

satisfaction and actual satisfaction of our friends belonging to the Scheduled Castes and Scheduled Tribes. We must not do anything in a hurry which leaves a feeling in their mind that we are rushing with the Bill. I am not really happy with the adjournment, but I would rather like to take an uncomfortable step for us but I would not like that they should go with the impression that we are rushing with it without giving them the fullest opportunity to discuss it. You are quite right in saying that it was circulated on 13.4.72.

Mr. Chairman: As Mr. Vajpayee pertinently asked, what is the purpose for which the adjournment is being sought?

Shri Raj Bahadur: The purpose is to consider whether this Bill could not be referred to a Joint Select Committee.

Mr. Chairman: I think this is the opinion of the House also. The question is:

"That the debate on the Bill be adjourned".

The motion was adopted.

Shri S.M. Banerjee: I am extremely happy that it has been adjourned. I have given a motion which I sent to you saying that it should be referred to a Select Committee, the names of which are to be announced by the Minister of Parliamentary Affairs. It is already with you. As you know, Sir, amendments are moved upto 3 p.m. Now it is 4.20. I would request you to allow us as a special case to move amendments upto 5.30 or 6 p.m.

Mr. Chairman: You can give amendments till 5 p.m.

Shri Jyotirmoy Bosu: (Diamond Harbour): On a point of order, Sir, You have not only been misled the Table but you have been equally misled by the Minister of Parliamentary Affairs. His actions are unparliamentary. The rules are very clear on the subject. Rule 74 clearly says that when a Bill is introduced, the motion can be moved that it be referred to a Joint Committee. Now, has anybody under rule 74 formally moved a motion with the intention of sending the Bill to a Joint Committee?

Shri S.M. Banerjee: I have moved it.

Mr. Chairman: Before my friend Mr. Banerjee, my friend from this side, Shri Shambunath, also made that request.

Shri S.M. Banerjee: He mentioned it, but I moved.

Mr. Chairman: Your motion is not in order.

Shri Raj Bahadur: When a Bill is introduced, at any subsequent occasion the member in charge may make one of the following motions in regard to the Bill, and one of them is reference to the Select Committee of the House. I can move it even now.

Shri Atal Behari Vajpayee: But he is not in charge of the Bill.

Shri Raj Bahadur: I do not know whether Shri Jyotirmoy Bosu is more parliamentary or the chair is more parliamentary.

Shri Jyotirmoy Bosu: As far as the chair is concerned, the powers are quite well-defined. Rule 89 says that the Speaker may, if he thinks fit, postpone the consideration of the clause, not the Bill. As far as rule 74 is concerned....

Mr. Chairman: Kindly read rule 109.

Shri Jyotirmoy Bosu: I am referring to the rule relating to reference to Select Committee, and that is rule 74.

Mr. Chairman: Rule 75 (2) (b) says:

> "If the member in charge moves that the Bill be referred to a Select Committee of the House, or a Joint Committee of the Houses with the concurrence of the Council, any member may move as an amendment that the Bill be referred to a Joint Committee of the Houses with the concurrence of the Council or a Select Committee, as the case may be, or that the Bill be circulated for the purpose of eliciting opinion thereon by a date to be specified in the motion."

The Untouchability (Offences) Amendment and Miscellaneous Provisions Bill, 1976, discussed in the Rajya Sabha on September 3, 1976.

The Minister of State in the Ministry of Home Affairs, Department of Personnel and Administrative Reforms and Department of Parliamentary Affairs (Shri Om Mehta): Sir, I beg to move :

> "That the Bill to amend the Untouchability (Offences) Act, 1955 and further to amend the Representation of the People Act, 1951, as passed by the Lok Sabha, be taken into consideration."

Sir, the Untouchability (Offences) Act, 1955 was passed in pursuance of Article 17 of the Constitution which has abolished 'untouchability' and has made its practice in any form punishable by law. The Act has been in force for more than 20 years. A Committee was appointed under the Chairmanship of Shri Elayaperumal to go into the working of the Act and on the basis of the recommendations of that Committee, a Bill was introduced in the Lok Sabha in April, 1972.

The Bill was referred to a Joint Committee of the two Houses. The Joint Committee went thoroughly into the various aspects and made many far-reaching changes. The Bill as reported by the Joint Committee has been passed by the Lok Sabha with a few amendments.

The name of the principal Act is being changed to 'the Protection of Civil Rights Act'. So, in future, the name of the Act will be the Protection of Civil Rights Act instead of the Untouchability (Offences) Act.

The present amending Bill considerably tightens the provisions relating to the removal of untouchability. Privately owned places of worship along with lands and subsidiary shrines appurtenant to such privately owned places of worship which are allowed by the owner to be used as places of public worship are being brought within the purview of the Act. The direct or indirect preaching of untouchability or its justification on historical, philosophical or religious ground is being made an offence. The compelling of any person to do any scavenging, sweeping, removing of carcasses, flaying of animals or removing the umbilical cord is also being made punishable. The State Governments are being empowered to impose collective fines on the inhabitants of any area who are concerned in or abetting the commission of untouchability offences. All untouchability offences are cognizable. They will now become non-compoundable and in cases where the punishment does not exceed three months, they can be tried summarily. The punishment of untouchability offences is being considerably enhanced and now both fine and imprisonment will be awarded for untouchability offences. For the first offence the minimum punishment will be one months' imprisonment and a fine of Rs. 100 and the maximum six months' imprisonment and a fine of Rs. 500. For the second offence, the minimum punishment is six months' imprisonment and a fine of Rs. 200 and the maximum, one years' imprisonment and Rs. 500 fine. For the third and subsequent offences, the punishment can range from one years' imprisonment with Rs. 500 fine to two years' imprisonment with Rs. 1000 fine.

The significant characteristic of the present Bill is that public servants who wilfully neglect in the investigation of any offence punishable under this Act shall be deemed to have abetted an offence punishable under this Act. Persons convicted of untouchability offences shall be disqualified from contesting elections to Central and State Legislatures. The Probation of Offenders Act will not supply to untouchability offenders unless they are below the age of 14 years.

Thus the Bill will have a deterrent effect in curbing the commission of untouchability offences. The Bill also contemplates surveys and studies for determining the areas where untouchability is practised, the setting up of Committees for implementing the Act and the grant of adequate facilities to persons subjected to disabilities arising out of untouchability to enable them to avail of their rights.

Government is making every endeavour to uplift the Scheduled Castes and to ensure that the last vestiges of untouchability are completely eradicated from the country within the shortest possible time. Under the 20-point programme of the Prime Minister, various measures are being taken for the economic uplift of these downtrodden sections of the society. Most of them are agricultural labourers and petty artisans and for them, special measures for the grant of house-sites, agricultural lands, loans for settlement in trades, fixation of minimum wages and abolition of bonded labour are being undertaken so that their economic and social conditions improve and they are better able to assert their rights. The massive education programme for the Scheduled Castes both at the school stage as well as at the post-matric stage also helps them in improving their social and educational standards. The great strides achieved in filling posts in the country's public services at various levels have also contributed to raising the status of this community and also to giving them adequate strength to assert their rights. All these, together with the legal protection provided under the present Bill, will help in the complete eradication of this evil practice.

With these words, Sir, I commend the Bill for the consideration of the House.

The question was proposed.

The Vice-Chairman (Shri Lokanath Misra) : Now, there are 12 speakers in all. Therefore, under compulsion the Chair will have to restrict each speaker to 10 minutes and not a minute beyond ten. So, in all we will take two hours for the speakers and 15 minutes for the reply of the Hon. Minister so that by 5-15 punctually we finish this Bill and take up the other Bill. We must go according to the schedule. There will not be the slightest departure from the schedule. Mr. Bhola Prasad.

Shri Yogendra Makwana (Gujarat): Mr. Vice-Chairman, Sir . . .

The Vice-Chairman (Shri Lokanath Misra): Kindly be brief.

Shri Yogendra Makwana: Sir, I will confine myself only to the Bill, I will not go into all the other details.

Mr. Vice-Chairman, Sir, I rise to support and welcome this Bill introduced by the Home Minister. I congratulate the Home Minister for introducing such a revolutionary Bill. As I described it, it is really a revolutionary Bill in a way, because it has so many provisions which enable an untouchable to get those persons prosecuted who observe untouchability and it also enables him to protect himself against the possibilities arising out of untouchability.

Sir, first of all, I will like to refer to the title of the Bill. The title is changed and instead of "practising of untouchability", the words "preaching and practising of untouchability" have been used. Sir, those words look very simple, but they have a great effect. The word "preaching" is inserted before the word "practising".

The practice of untouchability was an offence in the principal Act. Now, preaching of untouchability also becomes an offence under this Bill. In the previous session and before that also, I have often remarked in this House against the religious heads of this country. Sometimes they make derogatory remarks against the Scheduled Castes. Sometimes they have preached untouchability. With the insertion of these words, Shankracharya of Puri and Doongri Maharaj or any other religious heads who were preaching untouchability will not be able to do it. They can be prosecuted under the present law. Sir, in sub-section (1) of section 1, the words "the Untouchability (Offences) Act" have been substituted by the words "the Protection of Civil Rights Act". This is also an important change in the principal Act because the civil rights of the so-called untouchables were not honoured by some of the people of this country. I do not mean all the people of this country. But some people who are orthodox and reactionary have been always attacking the untouchables.

Sir, another salient feature of the Bill is to be found in section 3 (iii) of the Bill. Whereas the minimum punishment was fixed for one month or fine under the principal Act, the word "or" has been substituted by the words "and also" in the new Bill. This is a very significant change because fine has also to be paid over and above the punishment of imprisonment. It will become a sort of deterrent to those who are observing untouchability. As I have said in the beginning, mostly the religious heads are responsible for untouchability. As the change in the title is an important thing, so also Explanation II after Explanation I in section 7 is a very important explanation. It reads like this:

"*Explanation II.*—For the purposes of clause (c), a person shall be deemed to incite or encourage the practice of "untouchability"—

(i) if he, directly or indirectly, preaches untouchability or its practice in any form; or

(ii) if he justifies, whether on historical, philosophical or religious grounds or on the ground of any tradition of the caste system or on any other ground, the practice of "untouchability" in any form."

Sir, these words are very important because all the religious heads have been describing untouchability as a part of religion as it is given in the religious books and sometimes they give some historical background to it. In the present day and in the present society, that background has been lost. Nowadays, the accepted principle is that every human being is equal. It has become an accepted universal principle. Therefore, such outdated discourses by the religious leaders should be banned.

Sir, there is also a provision under section 7(a) which gives an opportunity for untouchables to perform other occupations. In small villages, even the educated persons were asked to take the night soil on their head and to scavenge the streets, Sir, with this insertion of section 7(a), there is a ban on it. So, it will be a very good provision in the principal Act. Then, Sir, there is an insertion of an explanation at the end of Section 10. This is a most important explanation which is now inserted in the principal Act. It reads out like this: "A public servant who wilfully neglects the investigation of any offence punishable under this Act shall be deemed to have abetted an offence punishable under this Act."

Sir, in most of the cases of atrocities we have seen that the public servants have neglected their duty at the time of investigation. Even the FIRs are changed at many places, and the public servants, specially the police officers, instead of investigating and prosecuting the offender, help the criminals. And the history shows that even one person was not punished during these 25 years. Now, Sir, with the addition of this explanation to the principal Act, I hope, there will be a good check on the police officers who will try to play mischief and evade their responsibility. (*Time bell rings*) I will complete within a few minutes, Sir. Sir, I described this Bill as revolutionary and I must justify why I called it a revolutionary Bill, and I congratulate the Home Minister. He should also recommend to give me some more minutes.

The Vice-Chairman (Shri Lokanath Misra): All of us should be precise and concise also.

Shri Yogendra Makwana: Sir, this Bill is really a very good Bill. Sir, so many provisions are included here and I cannot go into details. As you say, Sir, the time is limited I will throw some light on some of the general aspects of the Bill. There was a very good provision suggested by the Joint Select Committee under Explanation 2, after Section 10, which is now deleted. I do not know why it is deleted. The Explanation reads like this : "Any appointing authority, in relation to any service or post in connection with the affairs of, (a) the Union or any State Government, (b) the corporation or undertaking, owned or controlled by the Central Government or the State Government or by both, (c) any authority or body established by any Central, State or provincial Act, (d) any local authority, who show any negligence in giving effect to the orders of the appropriate authority relating to the reservation of posts for the employment of the members of the

Scheduled Castes shall be deemed to have abetted an offence punishable under this Act." Sir, I would request the Hon. Minister to accept this Explanation even now at this stage. I would like to invite his attention and the attention of the House to the report of the Commissioner for Scheduled Castes and Scheduled Tribes. This is the latest report for the year 1973-74 in which he has mentioned about recruitment to the Central Government services and other services in different States. I will not read the figures because they are very negligible. But I will read the remarks of the Commissioner. He says: 'The figures in this Table reveal that the representation of Scheduled Castes in these services is still far from satisfactory. The position regarding Scheduled Tribes is much worse.' Sir, these are the remarks made by the Commissioner for Scheduled Castes and Scheduled Tribes. Why are these remarks there? It is only because the bureaucrats, the government officers, who are the recruiting officers who sit in the committees do not like and do not observe the provisions relating to reservations. Recently, Sir, we had an occasion to examine the Delhi authority where some rules are framed. But they have recruited their sons and daughters and their relatives only and the percentage of recruitment of the Scheduled Castes and the Scheduled Tribes is not maintained. It is not only negligible but in some cases it is not at all there. No Scheduled Castes man is taken in the Delhi Administration authority.

Sir, I appreciate this Bill very much because I have also had occasions, as a political leader of my district, to suffer so many attacks by high caste Hindus in the course of elections and at several other times too. In the course of elections the Harijans became the victims particularly because they favour the government or some party, especially the Congress Party which works for the upliftment of the Harijans and downtrodden people. That is why the Harijans who support the Congress Party in the interior parts are attacked. Several times in this House also. Sir, if you remember, the Prime Minister herself has given two examples of my own State and of my own district. In the course of the last elections, in a Christian locality in village in Kaira District the houses of workers of the Congress, were put on fire and several families were burnt.

In the case of election of my wife we were attacked at so many places and we were not allowed to enter five villages and we lost the election only because of these things. Therefore, I say that this Bill is a revolutionary

Bill and I heartily congratulate the Home Minister and the Prime Minister for introducing this Bill. It will be a red letter day in the history of India when it becomes an Act. With these words, Sir, I end my speech.

Shri S.K. Vaishampayen (Maharashtra): Mr. Vice-Chairman, Sir, I wish to extend my wholehearted support to this Bill. The Bill has been brought forward after a very careful consideration by the Joint Committee of the two Houses. At the same time, I consider that this Bill is a little belated. But it is a step in the right direction to end the scourge of untouchability. The Bill removes all the vagueness that was there in the earlier Act. The clauses have been so framed that there is some definiteness in regard to the action to be taken. It also lays a firm hand on those who would act against the spirit of the Constitution. I support the provision made in this Bill particularly for imposing collective fines. As I see it, untouchability has assumed a very acute form during the last three to four years. There are social boycotts, burning of huts of Harijans and even murders. So, this provision of collective fines is really a provision which will to a long way to see that this certainly very stringent but there should also be other measures which must be taken by the government as such. I should say that the Hon. Home Minister should issue directives to all the State Governments to have a special cell in their respective Home Departments.

Secondly, there should be vigilance committees at district level and they should have Member of Parliament as Chairman and the Collector as the Secretary of that committee. It is because I have the experience of such a vigilance committee. We have tried to see that offences of this nature which come under untouchability have become less.

Thirdly, I would like to say that this social evil is still much deep-rooted. According to whatever information I have, I would like to point out that the extent of atrocities committed during these years has increased. I would like to give figures of atrocities committed during the years 1972, 1973 and 1974 and this information has been given by the Home Ministry in a reply given in the Rajya Sabha on 27th February, 1975. I will only quote a few figures from two or three States. I will take my State first. In Maharashtra during 1972, 124 atrocities have been committed. In 1973 the number was 223 and in 1974 it was 277. This shows that the number has gone up year by year. Similarly, in Gujarat the number in 1972 was 246, in

1973 it was 248 and in 1974 it was 352. In Uttar Pradesh the figure is still rising high. The number in 1972 was 567, in 1973 it was 1179 and in 1974 it was 1178. So, this is still a deep-rooted malady and we will have to take other measures along with these stringent provisions to combat the menace. We shall have to undertake intensive promotional activity also. I will suggest that incentives must be given to those villages who have freed themselves of this particular malady of untouchability. There are a number of villages who have declared that there is no untouchability in their villages. All the communities have come together in gram sabhas and declared so. We should give some incentives to such workers, not of the Scheduled Castes and Scheduled Tribes, who are working in the field for the welfare of Harijans, for ending untouchability. They must also be given some special awards by the State Governments. Then, there are provisions made in our state. We have Zila Parishads. There are provisions for the welfare of the Scheduled Castes and Scheduled Tribes. But out experience is that these provisions are not spent. Not only they are not spent but the provisions are transferred to some other measures which do not help the Scheduled Castes and Scheduled Tribes. I have figures from Maharashtra which go to show that 10 Zila Parishads, despite the provision being there for the welfare of the Scheduled Castes and Scheduled Tribes, have spent zero per cent. Seven Zila Parishads have spent one per cent, four have spent one to five per cent and three have spent five to ten per cent of the provisions that were made in the Zila Parishad budgets. So, this aspect also should be gone into in each State and a directive should be issued by the Home Ministry that whatever provisions are made for the welfare of the Scheduled Castes and Scheduled Tribes should be spent on their welfare. Rather I would suggest, Sir, that these provisions should be earmarked and the allocations should not be transferred to any other department as such.

Then the question of untouchability has taken a new dimension and that dimension has an economic aspect also. Under the 20-point economic programme we are now helping the economically weaker sections, and amongst the economically weaker sections the percentage of the Scheduled Castes and Scheduled Tribes is as high as 50 per cent at some places and even 70 per cent at some other places because they are all landless labourers. Naturally because of the measures which are there under the 20-point economic programme, those who are going to benefit under them are coming into clash with the landed, vested interests in the rural areas. The question of untouchability has taken a new dimension and, therefore, it is necessary that the Scheduled Castes and Scheduled Tribes be organized into a movement by forming a united front with the other economically weaker sections so that all the economic injustices that are being done to these poorer sections in the rural areas are ended. And if all these measures succeed—the measures under this Bill, other promotional measures and also a movement by the Scheduled Castes and Scheduled Tribes and their leaders with a common united front with the other economically weaker sections in the rural areas—the day of deliverance is not far off. Thank you, Sir.

Shri K.K. Madhavan (Kerala) : Sir, it was long ago that the Constitution of India abolished untouchability. But even before that, there was a movement for the annihilation of untouchability, right from the days, when Dr. Ambedkar had to fight the social evil through his book, which was originally meant for a presidential speech at a meeting which did not take place. Later on it was published as a book. The meeting did not take place and he said many things in that which were very unpalatable to the would be audience. This book is well known under the title *Annihilation of Caste*. I for one say that abolition of untouchability alone cannot deliver the goods. We have to abolish the caste system also. Untouchability is a consequence of the caste system, and the caste system, in its turn, is a consequence of the "Chathur Varnjya" system. I do not want to deal with the theoretical aspect of this question. Whatever we have gained in India against untouchability is because of three factors: (i) by the resistance of the weaker sections of the society, the so-called untouchables; (ii) by governmental help; and (iii) the most important of all, by the efforts of an enlightened section of the society in India. Of the three factors, the third factor for which Mahatma Gandhi is largely responsible, is gradually going down, now I do not know what the reason is. I have my own explanation. In the present context, in free India, the erstwhile untouchables have a sense of right, an awareness of their rights, and they have begun to assert. It is only natural that when the weaker sections of the people become aware of their rights and they begin to strike back or when they begin to assert themselves, certainly, the exploiters will have with redoubled vigour, a new programme for suppressing the underdog. That is exactly what happens. In many States, the cases of atrocities on the Scheduled Castes and Scheduled Tribes are on the increase. It is admitted even by the official quarters. Why does this happen? This happens simply because the casteist monopolists who look down upon these weaker sections of people as their slaves, cannot to erate the later coming up. This is not untouchability, Sir. This is something worse than untouchability. This is an inhuman attitude which cannot be tolerated in any civilised society. This unsocial attitude is known under the nomenclature 'casteism'. Why does this casteism occur? This casteism occurs, I would say, because of untouchability, which has been declared, treated and punished as a crime. The basic law now being against it, it has now gone underground. It has gone underground into the minds of men and there it reigns raising its ugly head in the form of a war of nerves the Scheduled Castes and the Scheduled Tribes. I say, it is a perpetual war of nerves. This war of nerves cannot be defeated very easily. A war can be won only by a stronger force. In the case of a war of nerves also it can be won by a superior force combating the evil. That is what is happening in India. Some of our friends in this Hon. House were saying that certain social service organisations like the Ramakrishna Mission, the Arya Samaj and some other Samajams, that they should take up the work, that the Scheduled Castes leaders should themselves take up the work. We are prepared, Sir. We are actually doing that work. Nobody need advice us on that account. But I would ask, is it enough for Hon. Members to sit in their armchairs and exhort people to do the job for them? I would say, Sir, that it is the duty of these people, the leaders of this country, to take up the cause and fight it to extinction as the Father of Nation has done.

Now, Sir, though I admit that this is a progressive Bill and it provides for so many good things, still I have a feeling that there is a section which ought not to have found a place in this Bill. What is that section? That is clause 2 of section 17 of the Bill which seeks to amend section 15 of the principal Act. Now, clause (2) of section 17 of the Bill says : "Notwithstanding anything contained in the Code of Criminal Procedure, 1973, when any public servant is alleged to have committed the offence of abetment of an offence punishable under this Act, while acting or purporting to act in the discharge of his official duty, no court shall take cognisance of such offence of abetment except with the previous sanction (a) of the Central Government in the case of a person employed in connection with the affairs of the Union, and (b) of the State Government, in the case of a person employed in connection with the affairs of a State". Sir, why this exemption? Sir, this protection aggravates the caste mentality of the officers. My complaint is : "why do you provide this section?" I am getting hundreds of complaints against casteism being practised in government offices in the matter of appointments as well as administration at all stages in public sector undertakings are much worse.

Shri N.H. Kumbhare: This amendment is made at the instance of the government. This is a government amendment, otherwise there was no such provision.

Shri K.K. Madhavan: Casteism largely is the cause of our disability whereas untouchability is under control. The disease has assumed the new form of casteism in government offices and in farms and factories. In the farms where the workers refuse to be dictated by others, we find that by the substitution of the new provision in section 15 government servants will be protected and only the government will have the power to sanction prosecution against them. Sir, it is the right of a private citizen to complain if he is discriminated against. Why should the aggrieved Scheduled Castes citizen be denied of that right to take the matter to a court of law. If the wrongdoer is an officer of the Central Government it is only the Central Government which has the powers to take legal proceedings against him. If he happens to be a public servant of a State Government it is only the State Government which is competent to institute proceedings against him. Why should these public servants be given this exemption, this protection?

[The Vice-Chairman (Shri Ranbir Singh) *in the Chair*]

It is unwarranted, Sir, I should say that clause (2) of section 17 of the Bill should be taken away from the Bill for the simple reason that it places the victim of the wrong at a disadvantage when he files a complaint. This clause (2) of section 17 of the Bill is a black spot on this legislation. It is not consistent with the spirit of our democracy; it is not consistent with the spirit of the 20-point programme which has been hailed from all quarters. So, I would suggest that better wisdom should prevail against this clause.

Sir, I was referring to casteism entertained in government offices and at other public places. Such public places are not mentioned in this Bill or in the principal Act. That is the deficiency. This deficiency has to be made good. How should it be made good? I would suggest that the amplitude of this Act should be made wider so as to include anti-Harijan, anti-tribal, attitude and discriminatory actions of government officers punishable within the Act. Unless that is done, the administration would not improve, would not become free from casteism.

The Vice-Chairman (Shri Ranbir Singh): Try to wind up now.

Shri K.K. Madhavan: Sir, unless this is done our social system and our democracy will not progress. Thank you, Sir.

Shri Abu Abraham (Nominated): Mr. Vice-Chairman, Sir, every year, a few times we, in Parliament discuss the subject of untouchability of Harijans and we have done this for many years now. But since independence, it seems that the condition of Harijans has not changed very much. We still read in the newspapers everyday of open discrimination against Harijans, violence against them, their living conditions also remaining the same. We have cases of landlords attacking Harijan villages and the police doing nothing about it. The Harijans get arrested very often and the landlords get away with it. We have to consider why the situation is like this. Why, after so many years and after trying to do so much, have we made so little progress? I think it is because we have an attitude of doing charity to the Harijans like the salvation army used to do the poor in the old days. And this had got to change. What we have to do is to improve the political and economic power of the Harijans. Unless we do that, it will be very hard for any legislation to improve their condition.

Sir, this Bill is a progressive Bill, a radical Bill and its provisions, I am sure, will give to untouchables the legal right that they deserve and should have. But this is not enough. I think we have to attempt to make radical changes in the social structure, the basic structure of our society. Unless that is done, we cannot expect the conditions of the Harijans to improve very much.

The important point to be considered here is that Harijans themselves should have the means to defend themselves and to look after their interests. They will have to organise themselves. They will have to educate themselves. They will have to take a greater part in the democratic processes in this country. It is these things that matter and the government should try to help them, enable them to assert themselves and to organise themselves. But so long as the Harijans remain largely illiterate, they will neither be able to defend themselves nor make any economic progress. I know that the recent measures of land distribution to the landless has helped Harijan communities in many parts of the country but a great deal more needs be done. There has to be a massive attempt to educate the Harijans, to give them literacy, to give them the basic tools with which they can improve their conditions. Sir, for example, Kerala's work in this matter is worthnoting. A hundred years ago, when Swami Vivekananda visited Kerala, he said that this was the most reactionary State that he had ever been to: In those days, there was not only untouchability, but there was also unapproachability and unseeability. Today, if you go to Kerala, you can see the difference. This is not necessarily because of legislation, not even by propaganda or by charitable acts, but by organising the rural labour and the industrial labour and by giving them the tools and the means by which they could fight for their rights. This is what should have been done in other States also. This has been done in Kerala. Kerala has a very high level of education and this has made a tremendous impact in destroying the caste system. I do not say that it is completely destroyed. But it is very negligible now. Privately, people may have prejudices. But in most parts of Kerala, it is very difficult to see any open discrimination against the Harijans. The Kerala Government have built houses for the poor people. In these houses, the Harijans live side by side with the other people who belong to the higher castes. It is not so in other States. In the other States, separate housing schemes are there for the Harijans.

Shri K.K. Madhavan: For the information of the Hon. Member, I would like to state that in Kerala the Harijan population is not segregated generally.

Shri Abu Abraham: This is what I am saying. But in the old days, there were segregated areas where the Harijans lived. Therefore, our most important task should be the desegregation of the Harijan population. When we build hostels for students, they should be for every one. Why should there be Harijan hostels? If such is the case, why not we have buses and trains exclusively for the Harijans? It has been said that the

Railways have made a great contribution in changing the social pattern in this country because in our trains, the Harijans and other people travel together. In the same way, I think we should have common hostels, we should have hostels where the Harijan boys can stay along with the boys belonging to the higher castes. In any case, it has been proved to be a racket where these people have been exploited and people have been making money. This is a well known fact.

Sir, we say all the time that we are a secular State and we are getting more and more secular as years pass by. But the interesting thing is that while we say that we are becoming more secular, it seems to me that we are getting more and more religious. I do not see any attempt being made in this country to break the hold of religious orthodoxy on our society. Now, many distinguished people, political leaders, and high dignitaries seen to be encouraging orthodoxy. In this connection, I would like to give the example of the revival of the cow protection campaign. May I ask why the ban on cow slaughter has so suddenly been introduced in Tamil Nadu, Andhra Pradesh and Maharashtra? This has directly affected the poor people in this country. This has directly affected the Harijans in this country. I can only say this is a way of encouraging religious orthodoxy. The other day Shri Vinoba Bhave made an extraordinary remark that vegetarianism is the answer to the removal of untouchability. Now this is a direct insult to all people who eat meat. The implication of that remark is that people who eat meat automatically go down the social ladder. On the contrary, I say that people must all be encouraged to eat meat so that they can all achieve equality. This should be the aim of the government and they should not give in to Vinoba Bhave. Any agricultural scientist will say that we have too many cattle in this country and it is necessary to have a certain amount of slaughter and meat-eating.

Sir, the new duties of citizens include "the cultivation of a scientific temper" and is it too much to ask the government itself to show a scientific temper in this matter?

Shri Om Mehta: Sir, I am very grateful to the Honourable Members for the unanimous support that they have given to this Bill and I am grateful particularly to Shri Prakash Veer Shastri, Pandeje's arguments I heard at my residence as unfortunately, I was not present here. But it was a good speech, I must say—and then to Mr. Vaishampayen, Mr. Kumbhare—I think, Sir, Mr. Kumbhare has not spoken.

Shri N.H. Kumbhare: I had no opportunity to speak.

Shri Om Mehta: Sir, he has given an amendment and so, I thought that he must have spoken. I am grateful to Mr. Kalp Nath Rai, Rani Sahiban, Mr. Makhwana and many others. I am really thankful to all of them.

Sir, this is a very significant Bill. This was before the Lok Sabha for the last two years. Unfortunately, for one reason or the other, it could not be passed. It is good that it is being passed today and it is a very significant achievement so far as eradication of untouchability is concerned which, Sir, is a malady of our times. Sir, the word "untouchability" has been removed from our Constitution and this word is not there now. But untouchability is still practised in some parts of the country and it is a matter of shame for this country and for the people of this country who still practise it and I think it is high time that we took stringent action against those who still practised untouchability and to meet this need, Sir, we have brought forward this Bill.

Even before this Act came into being, we were not obvious of this fact. Our beloved Prime Minister wrote to the Chief Ministers of all the States to set up special cells under their personal supervision to look into the grievances of the Scheduled Castes and Scheduled Tribes people and other minorities. Such cells have been set up in a number of States. Not only this, Sir, the Home Minister has been issuing instructions from time to time to the States to look into the grievances of these down trodden people, these exploited people, and we have issued instructions to them to the effect that in each and every State, the district officers must be requested to obtain relevant information about all incidents involving the Harijans, irrespective of whether such incidents have arisen due to any caste consideration or not and send it to the State and Central Governments since communication of such information to the State and the Central Governments would help them in placing these matters in proper perspective.

Sir, we have said that investigation of all offences involving Harijans, where any caste considerations are suspected, should be promptly, efficiently and adequately supervised. Investigation of serious offences involving the Harijans, where caste considerations are suspected, should be treated as special report cases and entrusted to selected investigation officers. A suggestion made that such investigation should be conducted by an officer not below the rank of Deputy Superintendent of Police or Inspector of Police, was adopted wherever possible. Any failure to undertake prompt and efficient investigation or to exercise adequate supervision should be regarded as grave dereliction of duty on the part of the officers concerned.

Sir, it can now be confidently said that a new orientation has been imported into the official approach—A steady improvement has also been made in regard to the administrative response to the needs of the situation.

Sir, my friend, Mr. Vaishampayen has quoted some figures also to show that in Gujarat and Maharashtra the number of atrocities is increasing. He gave figures for 1972, 1973, 1974, 1975. Sir, there is no doubt that previously whenever atrocities were committed they were not being reported. The Harijans were thinking that there would be retaliation from the higher castes and they were reluctant to report these atrocities to the *thana* or to the government. Now, as the consciousness is growing, education is growing more and more such incidents are being reported. Sir, as politically, also they are becoming more and more conscious of their rights and privileges they are bringing more and more such incidents to the notice of the authorities.

Some points have been raised here that against these officers who are negligent or who do not register the cases whenever these poor people go to the police station, action should be taken. The present Bill is only to meet that situation. Where we find that there is a wilful negligence on the part of any officer to take any action against those who commit atrocities or to write the reports, action would be taken against that officer also.

Sir, not only that. We have said that in the case of those officers who do not go to the rescue of the Scheduled Castes and Scheduled Tribes, the offence will be a cognizable offence and there also action will be taken against him.

Shri Makwana raised a point about the services. Sir, as I said in the other House, in this Bill we could not bring a provision for the services. But the government is trying that whatever quota is fixed, it should be filled completely. Sir, I have been saying repeatedly in this House that full quota of Scheduled Castes and Scheduled Tribes has been filled in the all-India services, that is, IAS, IPS, IFS, in the past.

Wherever their representation is less, not only in Class IV services, but in Class I, Class II and Class III services also, in recent years we have tried to see to it that their number is increased. I should say that the number of Scheduled Castes officers is 35,061 in Class I, 54,129 in Class II, 16,32,397 in Class III and 12,38,818 in Class IV. In recent years, we have taken certain more steps. Reservation in promotion quota now applied to all the grades and classes where the element of direct recruitment does not exist. It is 66.33 per cent. Earlier this limit was 50 per cent. From 1974, recruitment to posts filled by selection has been extended to promotions from Class III to Class II, within Class II and from Class II to the lowest rung of Class I. Before 1974, such reservations were confined to Class III and Class IV posts. Carry forward provisions have been liberalised in favour of the Scheduled Castes and the Scheduled Tribes with effect from June 1975. Scientific and technical posts for research up to the lowest grade of Class I have been brought within the purview of reservation orders. Earlier, no reservation existed for such posts. The UPSC an other competent authorities have been authorised to lessen qualifications relating to experience if otherwise suitably qualified Scheduled Castes and Scheduled Tribes candidates are available. The position has also improved in the public sector undertaking where the representation of Scheduled Castes has risen by 26.5 per cent in Class IV and 14 per cent in Class III. In the case of Scheduled Tribes, the representation has risen to 12 per cent and 6 per cent respectively.

Sir, a High-Power Committee under the chairmanship of the Prime Minister meet regularly to review the progress relating to matters concerning Scheduled Castes and Scheduled Tribes including their representation in services. Instructions have also been issued that reservation orders will apply to staff recruited by voluntary agencies which receive subtantial grants-in-aid from the Government under certain conditions. We have seen to it that whatever orders are being issued by the Government of India, Department of Personnel, are implementd. It is not only the Commissioner for Scheduled Castes and Scheduled Tribes who keeps an eye on this. Also, a High-Power Committee of both the

Houses of Parliament, which is there, looks to it whether the orders issued by us are implemented or not. The report of the Commissioner for Scheduled Castes and Scheduled Tribes who keeps an eye on this. Also, High-Power Committee of both the Houses of Parliament, which is there, looks to it whether the orders issued by us are implemented or not. The report of the Commissioner for Scheduled Castes and Scheduled Tribes and, also the report of the High-Power Committee of both the Houses of Parliament are placed on the Table of the House.

A point has been raised here by Mr. Wajd. He said lakhs and lakhs of Harijans and other backward class people are still houseless.

Shri Sikander Ali Wajd: I said about nomads.

Shri Om Mehta: Nomads are those who have got no lands and no houses. When I talk of houseless people, that means nomads also. It does not mean that we are excluding them. We are proud of what we have done during the last two or three years under the leadership of our honourable Prime Miniser. There are lakhs and lakhs of houseless people. (*Interruptions*) No, I am not yielding. He has said whatever he wanted to say. Sir, apart from whatever Mr. Wajd has said, I have high regards for his ability, for his experience, for his poetry and also other things.

I think, Sir, he has seen the figures of what has been achieved after the launching of the 20-point programme. The first priority which we are giving in this is to giving houses to the houseless. That is agricultural labour and those who are without houses. Sir, up to this time. 70 lakh people have been provided with house sites. Not only that. We are seeing to it that actually their possession is given to those people who never had any house-sites up to this time and they should be able to build the houses there. When we talk of houses, I must say, in Delhi, when I was in the Housing Ministry, it was for the first time that we made a reservation of 20 per cent for the Scheduled Castes and Scheduled Tribes in all the flats which were being built by the DDA. We started separate reservations for the Harijans. Previously, a common list was being kept and, unfortunately, from the Janata houses and other houses, the Scheduled Castes and Scheduled Tribes were not getting any houses. So, we made it a special thing that 20 per cent of the houses built by the DDA would be reserved for the Scheduled Castes and Scheduled Tribes and they would get priority in that. Not only that, Sir, the money which was to be paid by them as first instalment or as registration fee was also reduced considerably. And there is no discrimination. For persons who are without houses, whatever possible is being done-to give them houses so that they can also live a happy and contented life.

Sir, some other points have been made by the Hon. Members, Shastriji made a point that there are separate schools for the Harijans. Sir, I should inform Shastriji that there are no separate schools. We allow other boys also to come to the Ashram school and schools which are opend for Harijans. But generally what happens is this. Mostly the schools which are opened for Harijans are in areas where their population is predominent. And as Mr. Makwana says in many of the schools, they have got 10 per cent reservation but many student do not come there. When we talk of untouchability, we do not want that. But still we should take certain steps by which this untouchability is not perpetuated. In schools and other places, we want that Harijan boys should be allowed to sit with other boys so that from the very beginning this idea that they are untouchables is not there in their minds.

Shri Abu Abraham: What about the reservation of 20 per cent? You were saying that 20 per cent of the housing is reserved for Harijans. Could you please tell us whether these houses will be separated for Harijans or will they be mixed houses?

Shri Om Metha: They will be mixed houses. This is only reservation. But it is not that we will fix certain blocks only for Harijans where the Harijans live. They will live with other communities in any colonies and wherever the houses are there.

The motion was adopted.

The Vice-Chairman (Shri Ranbir Singh): The question is :

"That the Bill to amend the Untouchability (Offences), Act, 1955 and further to amend the Representation of the People Act, 1951, as passed by the Lok Sabha, be taken into consideration".

The Vice-Chairman (Shri Ranbir Singh): We shall now take up clause by clause consideration of the Bill.

Clauses 2 to 16 were added to the Bill.

Clause 17—Substitution of section 15.

The Vice-Chairman (Shri Ranbir Singh): There is one amendment by Shri Kumbhare.

Shri N.H. Kumbhare: Sir, I did not any opportunity to speak on the Bill. I am in entire agreement with the Hon. Minister when he says that it is a really radical measure. The Bill is, no doubt, comprehensive and it is also more purposeful; I say the scope of the Bill is also enlarged.

The Vice-Chairman (Shri Ranbir Singh): Are you moving the amendment?

Shri N.H. Kumbhare: I am just coming to the amendment. I am just making the opening remarks.

The Vice-Chairman (Shri Ranbir Singh): May I know whether you are moving the amendment?

Would you like to speak on the clause?

Shri N.H. Kumbhare: Sir, I want to point out the relevant clauses.

"That at page 8, after line 7, the following be inserted namely :

> 'A survey of the district will be conducted by Assistant Director of Civil Rights for locating the area of social disability in such manner as prescribed and shall submit a report as to the nature of untouchability being practiced and the extent of social disability to which the Scheduled Caste people are subjected.
>
> *Explanations:* 'Area of social disability is a place or places where members of Scheduled Castes, on account of their subjection could not exercise their right, accrued to them, by reason of the abolition of untouchability under Article 17 of the Constitution.
>
> (1) On receipt of the report from the Assistant Director and after making an enquiry as may deem appropriate and on being satisfied as to the situation existing at the place, the Director of Civil Rights will make a declaration specifying the area of social disability and other particulars as may be prescribed.

(2) The area of social disability having been so declared the Assistant Director shall proceed to take such steps and in such manner as may be prescribed to deal with the situation, and shall endeavour to persuade the dominant class through conciliation and seek to create condition so that the members of the Scheduled Castes do not suffer from any social disability provided the said area will be kept under observation for such period as may deem necessary. Provided further the period of observation will not be for a period exceeding six months.

(3) The Assistant Director of Civil Rights after having succeeded in his efforts in creating favourable conditions submit a report to the Director who will make a declaration accordingly, in the manner as may be prescribed.

(4) The Assistant Director of Civil Rights having satisfied that he has failed in his efforts to create favourable conditions to facilitate enforcement of rights by members of the Scheduled Castes, submit a failure report to the Director of Civil Rights. This report shall contain the particulars as may be prescribed including the names of the persons who are likely to commit or attempt to commit or abets the commission of an offence.

(5) (A) The Sub-Divisional Magistrate having jurisdiction and specially empowered by the State Governmnt in this behalf may be given information of the names referred to in the failure report of the Assistant Director of Civil Rights and the S.D.M. may require such persons to show cause why they should not be ordered to execute bond with surety for their good behaviour for such period not exceeding 3 years as the Magistrate may direct.

(B) The Provision of the Code of Criminal Procedure, 1973, shall in so far as they are applicable apply to any proceedings under sub-section (1) as if the bond referred to therein were a bond required to be executed under section 110 of the said Code."

The question was proposed.

Shri N.H. Kumbhare: Sir, formerly only practice of untouchability was forbidden but now not only practice but preaching of untouchability is also forbidden. If anybody preaches or practises now he will be dealt with and will come under the clutches of the Law. Therefore, I say that the scope of the Bill has been enlarged. It has been made more deterrent because these offences have now been made cognizable. It is also non-bailable. If anybody is found guilty the magistrate has no discretion except to send him to jail because the minimum jail sentence is one month.

Sir, I would be failing in my duty if I do not say a word about the good work of the Joint Select Committee which was presided over by Mr. S.M. Siddiah, Mr. Mirdha was the Minister in charge of the Bill. But for their co-operation it would not have been possible to give such a good shape to it. I may however point out that it could have been made more comprehensive we could have been incorporated a scheme by which we could locate the areas of untouchability and deal with those areas. It is essentially a matter which comes within the purview of the Central Government and we desire that the Central Government should set up a machinery to enforce these provisions. As has been pointed out by my friends, laws are there. But laws become dead letters if we do not set up an administrative machinery to enforce those laws and therefore we want them to take the entire responsibility in this behalf and government should set up a machinery to enforce these provisions. Unfortunately that suggestion has not been accepted and the entire responsibility has been transferred to the State Governments. Of course, under the Act itself the Central Government will make the rules whereby a duty will be cast on the State Governments to set up a machinery. I have stated that government must make the entire provisions more explicit and, therefore, in regard to my amendment, I only want to cite an example. Even today if you go to a village there will be a well. If that well is located in a high caste locality, the Scheduled Castes people will not be allowed to fetch water from that well. So, according to me, it is an area of disability. Such areas have to be identified and located. Let the government play a more positive role. I have suggested that an officer should be appointed under the Act. A duty will be cast on the officer to have a survey made to find out how many places are there where the Scheduled Castes people, even though they have got a right given under the Constitution, are denied those rights. The reasons are obvious. They know that they have got a right but they cannot muster courage to assert that right because they are in a minority, because they have to depend upon them. In such a case the officer will go and find out himself how the position is. He will make an enquiry and if he comes to the conclusion that even though on the face of it there appears to be no discrimination, the caste Hindus are dominating and practising untouchability and preventing these people from taking water, suitable action should be taken.

So, in that case, under the survey, that area will be identified as an area of social disability. The Government will notify it and then there will be a stage of conciliation. As I said, the officer will go and try to bring about a conciliation and tell those elements that these are the provisions in the Act and that they must allow the Scheduled Castes otherwise they will have to suffer and go to jail. In that way, I think, people in the village will not be opposed to it. But, if there are certain elements still, the officer will make a note of those bad elements who are opposed to it and then he will make a report to the Director and the Director will file proceedings in the court. The court will then issue summons to them and tell them that they must create conditions whereby the Scheduled Castes people would have full freedom to go and fetch water. That is the scheme which is incorporated and I think it should be acceptable to government.

Unfortunately, Sir, one of the important recommendations has not been accepted by the Government. It reads like this:

> "A public servant who shows any negligence in the investigation of any offence punishable under the Act shall be deemed to have abetted the offence punishable under this Act."

I know the reasons and that way I am convinced that if the Government is going in for a separate legislation providing for reservations for the Scheduled Castes and the Scheduled Tribes, then such a provision could find a place. So, we would like to know from the Hon. Minister whether such a legislation is under contemplation. And if so, when are we going to have it?

Shri Om Mehta: Sir, I have already replied to points raised by the Hon. Member. Whatever he has said with regard to recruitments and other things, I have already given an assurance that we are trying to see whether orders issued by our Ministry are being implemented or not. Still, if he finds that they are not being implemented, we will have to codify these orders and find out how a suitable legislation can be brought in. We can consider it only after taking stock of the whole thing.

Sir, I must tell Mr. Kumbhare that by article 17 of the Constitution, untouchability has been abolished and disability arising out of untouchability has been declared to be an offence. Under article 35(a), sub-section (ii), Parliament has the exclusive legislative competence to provide for punishment for enforcement of the disability arising out of untouchability. The Act in question is, therefore, restricted to the above mentioned constitutional provision.

Sir, in this particular Bill, we also have got some provision for the machinery for the enforcement of this Act. Under that provision, some officers will certainly be appointed who will be going to find out if there are certain places where the Harijans who are very poor or in minority, are not able to take the shelter of the law or are not able to go to those whom they can go for protection. These officers will report about those areas and, as you know, Sir, we have got a provision of collective fines from those villages and that action will be enforced. That provision has also been kept.

Sir, with these words, I oppose this amendment.

The Vice-Chairman (Shri Ranbir Singh): Mr. Kumbhare, do you want to withdraw the amendment?

Shri N.H. Kumbhare: Yes, Sir.

The Vice-Chairman (Shri Ranbir Singh): The question is :

"That leave be granted to the mover to withdraw the amendment."

The motion was adopted.

The amendment was, by leave, withdrawn.

Does he mean to say that the Scheduled Castes and the Scheduled Tribes should not have some share in the industry? Does he mean to say that there should not be proper roads where there are concentrations of people belonging to the Scheduled Castes and Scheduled Tribes? I do not know what he means. But all that he says is that there is only one need and that is giving scholarships and providing schools and colleges near their homes. I think this is a stupid scheme. With all respect to the learned friend, I should say that it is a stupid proposal, because he does not see reality.

Shri U.K. Lakshmana Gowda (Karnataka): It is very harsh.

Shri K.K. Madhavan: When harsh things are said, hard replies are needed. He does not see what the problems of the Scheduled Castes and the Scheduled Tribes are. I do not deny the necessity of education. Due emphasis should be laid on education. At the same time, one cannot close one's eyes to the other problems that face them. My Hon. friend himself was admitting that one of the main problems is economic backwardness. I say he had not understood the problem. It is not economic backwardness only. If economic backwardness is the only problem, then certainly there are other people also who are backward. But, fortunately, the framers of our Constitution and the moulders of our administrative system, however, imperfect they may be now, have rightly analysed the problem. The problem of the Scheduled Castes and Scheduled Tribes has different facets. That is why they have earmarked funds for housing, for industry, for co-operative institutions, for education, for drinking water facilities and for so many other things. My learned friend thinks that only by giving education to a few students and by establishing a few new schools and colleges in the vicinity of their homes all these problems will be solved. As a matter which needs a multi-faceted programme. In India both the Central Government and the State Governments are alive to the situation and they have evolved a working programme, a comprehensive working programme for ameliorating the conditions of these backward people. I do not know what prompted out my friend to bring forward a Resolution like this. My only inference is that he has not seen the Scheduled Castes and the Scheduled Tribes in the right perspective. He has not lived among them. He does not know the sentiments of these people. He does not know the emotions of these people. He does not know the aspirations of these people. His is not the perspective of a social reformer. Evidently he is not a social reformer, as is patent from the words and tone of his speech. Had he been social reformer he would certainly have come to the proper solution to this problem. I am not interested in his pedigree. I am not interested in his background of education. I am not interested in his birth and other things. This is a personal matter and I do not want to go into that. By whatever standards I measure him, seeing the contents of the Resolution which he has placed befors us. I have reason to think that he has not cared to see the conditions and such surroundings of these unfortunate people, the Scheduled Castes and the Scheduled Tribes. I can understand his saying that the administration is top-heavy. In that case it was his duty to give proper suggestions, healthy suggestions, positive suggestions as to how the administration could be streamlined instead of recommending outright the abolition of all the institutions, departments and organisations. It is equally surprising, Sir, that from the other side also a sympathetic response has come in favour of the Resolution. Strangely, Sir, this is a matter where the reactionaries and the revolutionaries agree as against the Scheduled Castes and the Scheduled Tribes. If there is any inadequacy in an administration, it ought to be improved. My learned friends here do not say that certain other departments which are notorious for their imperfections and malpractices should be abolished. But they are very happy at that. But there is extra unanimity when there is a proposal to abolish all these institutions, departments and organisations which are positively meant for the welfare of the Scheduled Castes and the Scheduled Tribes. I do not understand this humanity in spite of their political differences. All that I can infer is that the cultural background of these people is the same old one. In spite of the political differences, that they profess, they have the same feelings and they have the same psychological response to the problems of the Scheduled Castes and Scheduled Tribes. Sir, it is time that this type of defective approach to the problem is put an end to. What is required is a positive programme the basis for which has been laid by the Father of the Nation, by Pandit Jawaharlal Nehru and by all our great leaders who knew the problem and who organized this welfare programme—both official as well as non-official. Sir, I am not very happy; I am not satisfied that we have done all the things for them. I am not satisfied. I am dissatisfied because these are, as I said the other day, problems which have been created during centuries and ages and they cannot be wiped off in a day or two. It requires patience; it requires determination; it requires self-sacrifice. It was for this that Mahatma Gandhi said that everybody, every enlightened citizen in this country should be prepared to do something for these unfortunate people. He ended the fast only on the promise by leaders of this country that they would take up the responsibility of removing the unfortunate condition of these people. The leaders gave an undertaking and it was only after that Mahatma Gandhi gave up his epic fast.

My learned friends I wish to stress the importance, the human emotions behind, this huge problem. There may be differences between the leaders. But fortunately, with the exception of a few handful of people, the large majority of the thinking people in this country are agreed on the problem and the approach, that the problems of the Scheduled Castes and Scheduled Tribes are very big, multitudinous and complicated and that they ought to be solved by effective means. Unfortunately this attitude is wanting among some of our latest political leaders. They profess revolution, but their course is that of reaction. That is the paradox. The main requirement for approaching this problem is to have enlightened type of people organised in such a way that we can show to the world that we are dedicated to the cause of these people. The Resolution, I think, reminds me of Judas. A poor woman, Mary of Magdalene came to see Jesus. She brought ointment which she applied to his feet. But Judas came forward and said: "What a foolish woman! If she had instead of purchasing this ointment distributed this money to the poor people, hundreds of poor people could have been served and saved." From the Resolution, and from the tone of the mover of the Resolution and of the persons who supported the Resolution, I feel that 'Judas-ism' has not totally disappeared from this country. Sir, I oppose this Resolution.

The Act has now come into force from November 19, 1976.[2] The intention of the legislation is to protect the civil rights of the untouchables. The title of the Act has been changed to Protection of Civil Rights Act.[3] This Act aimed at abolishing untouchability completely.

Under the new Act, punishment has been considerably increased and there is a provision for both, fine and imprisonment. For the first offence, the minimum punishment is one month imprisonment and a fine of Rs. 100/- and maximum six months imprisonment and a fine of Rs. 500/-. If the offence is committed a second time, the punishment will be six months imprisonment and a fine of Rs. 200/- the maximum being six months imprisonment and a fine of Rs. 500/. For the third and subsequent offence, the punishment may range from one year imprisonment and a fine of Rs. 500/- to two year imprisonment and a fine of Rs.1000/-.

Until now, untouchability offences though congnizable, could be compounded but they become non-compoundable under the new Act. It also provides that persons convicted of untouchability offences shall be disqualified from contesting elections to the Central or State legislatures.

The new Act also gives greater powers to the State Governments to deal with the offenders. The State Governments have been empowered to impose collective fines on the inhabitants of any area if they commit or abet the commission of an untouchability offence. They are further required to provide adequate facilities including legal aid to persons subjected to any disability on account of untouchability. The Act also requires the State Governments to appoint officers for initiating supervision over prosecutions to set up special courts, to constitute committees at appropriate levels, to undertake periodic surveys and identify areas where untouchability is practised and take suitable remedial measures for enforcement of the provisions of this Act. This Act has brought the law in favour of the Scheduled Castes.

The Protection of Civil Rights Act, 1976

1. This Act may be called the Protection of Civil Rights Act, 1955.
2. It extends to the whole of India.
3. It shall come into force on such date the Central Government may, by notification in the Official Gazette, appoint.

Definitions

In this Act, unless the context otherwise requires,

(a) "Civil Right" means any right accruing to a person by reason of the abolition of "Untouchability" by Article 17 of the Constitution.

(aa) "Hotel" includes a refreshment room, a boarding house, a lodging house, a coffee house and cafe;

(b) "Place" includes a house, building and other structure and premises, and also includes a tent, vehicle and vessel;

(c) "Place of Public entertainment" includes any place to which the public are admitted and in which an entertainment is provided or held.

"Entertainment" includes exhibition, performance, game, sport and any other forms of amusement;

(d) "Place of public worship" means a place, by whatever name known, which is used as a place of public religious worship or which is dedicated generally to, or is used generally by persons professing any religion or, belonging to any religious denomination or any section thereof, for the performance of any religious service, or for offering prayers therein and includes,

(i) all lands and subsidiary shrines appurtenant or attached to any such place;

(ii) a privately owned place of worship which is, in fact, allowed by the owner thereof to be used as a place of public worship, and

(iii) land or subsidiary shrine pertaining to such privately owned place of worship as is allowed by the owner thereof to be used as a place of public religious worship.

da. "Prescribed" means prescribed by rules made under this Act;

db. "Scheduled Castes" has the meaning assigned to it in clause (24) of Article 366 of the Constitution.

(e) "Shop" means any premises where goods are sold either wholesale or by retail or both wholesale and by retail (and includes),

(i) any place from where goods are sold by a hawker or vendor or from a mobile van or cart;

(ii) a laundry and a hair cutting saloon;

(iii) any other place where services are rendered to customers.

Punishment for Enforcing Religious Disabilities

Whoever on the ground of "untouchability" prevents any person:

(a) from entering any place of public worship which is open to other person professing the same religion[4] or any section thereof, as such person, or,

(b) From worshipping or offering prayers or performing any religious service in any place of public worship, or bathing in, or using the waters of, any sacred tank, well, spring or water course (river or lake or bathing at any ghat of such tank, water course, river or lake) in the same manner and to the same extent as is permissible to the other persons professing the same religion[5] or any section thereof, as such person, (shall be punishable with imprisonment for a term of not less than one month and not more than six months and also with fine which shall be not less than one hundred rupees and not more than five hundred rupees).

For the purposes of this Section and Section 4, persons professing the Buddhist, Sikh or Jain religion or persons professing the Hindu religion in any of its forms or development including Virashaivas, Lingayats, Adivasis, followers of Brahma Samaj, Prarthana Samaj, Arya Smaj and the Swaminarayan Sampraday shall be deemed to be Hindus.

Punishment for Enforcing Social Disabilities

Whoever on the ground of "Untouchability" enforces against any person any disability with regard to:

(i) access to any shop, public restaurant, hotel or place of public entertainment, or

(ii) the use of any utensils, and other articles kept in any public restaurant, hotel, dharmashala, *sarai* or *musafirkhana* for the use of the general public or of (any section thereof); or

(iii) the practice of any profession or the carrying on of any occupation, trade or business (or employment in any job); or

(iv) the use of, or access to, any river, stream, spring, well, tank, cistern, water tap or other watering place, or any bathing ghat, burial or cremation ground, any sanitary convenience, any road or passage, or any other place of public resort which other members of the public (or any section thereof) have a right to use or have access to; or,

(v) the use of, or access to, any place used for a charitable or a public purpose maintained wholly or partly out of State funds or dedicated to the use of the general public (or any section thereof) or,

(vi) the enjoyment of any benefit under a charitable trust created for the benefit of the general public (or of any section thereof) or,

(vii) the use of, or access to, any public conveyance; or

(viii) the construction, acquisition, or occupation of any residential premises in any locality, whatsoever; or

(ix) the use of any dharmashala, *sarai* or *musafirkhana* which is open to the general public, (or to any section thereof); or

(x) the observance of any social or religious custom, usage or ceremony (or taking part in or taking out, any religious, social or cultural procession).

Punishment for Refusing to Admit Person to Hospitals, etc.

Whoever on the ground of "untouchability"

(a) refuses admission to any person to any hospital, dispensary, educational institution or any hostel, if such hospital, dispensary, educational institution or hostel[6] is established or maintained for the benefit of the general public or any section thereof; or

(b) does any act which discriminates against any such person after admission to any of the aforesaid institutions, (shall be punishable with imprisonment for a term of not less than one month and not more than six months and also with fine which shall be not less than one hundred rupees and more than five hundred rupees).

Punishment for Refusing to Sell Goods or Render Services

Whoever on the ground of "untouchability" refuses to sell any goods or refuses to render any service to any person at the same time and place and on the same terms and conditions at or which such goods are sold or services are rendered to other persons in the ordinary course of business (shall be punishable with imprisonment for a term of not less than one month and not more than six months and also with fine which shall be not less than one hundred rupees and not more than five hundred rupees).

Punishment for Other Offences Arising Out of "Untouchability"

1. Whoever

(a) prevents any person from exercising any right accruing to him by reason of the abolition of "untouchability" under Article 17 of the Constitution; or

(b) Molests, injures, annoys, obstructs or causes or attempts to cause to lose one's right, or molests, injures, annoys or boycotts any person by reason of his having exercised any right; or

(c) by words either spoken or written or by signs or by visible representations or otherwise incites or encourages any person or class of persons or the public generally to practice "untouchability" in any form whatsoever; or

(d) insults or attempts to insult, on the ground of "untouchability" a member of a Scheduled Caste,

(shall be punishable with imprisonment for a term of not less than one month and more than six months and also with fine which shall be less than one hundred rupees and not more than five hundred rupees).

I . A person shall be not deemed to boycott another person who

(a) refuses to let to such other person or refuses to permit such other person, to use or occupy any house or land or refuses to deal with, work for hire for, or do business with, such other person or to render to him or receive from him any customary service, or refuses to do any of the said things on the terms on which such things would be commonly done in the ordinary course of business; or

(b) abstains from such social, professional or business relations as he would ordinarily maintain with such other person.

II. For the purpose of clause (c) a person shall be deemed to incite or encourage the practice of "untouchability",

(i) if he, directly or indirectly, preaches "untouchability" or its practice in any form; or

(ii) if he justifies, whether on historical, philosophical or religious grounds or on the ground of any tradition of the caste system or on any other ground, the practice of untouchability in any form.

[(1A) Whoever commits any offence against the person or property of any individual as a reprisal or revenge for his having exercised any right accruing to him by reason of the abolition, of "untouchability" under Article 17 of the Constitution, shall, where the offence is punishable with imprisonment for a term which shall not be less than two years and also with fine.]

2. Whoever

(i) denies to any person belonging to his community or any section thereof right or privilege to which such person would be entitled as a member of such community or sections;

(ii) takes any part in the ex-communication of such person on the ground that such person has refused to, practice "untouchability" that such person has done any act in furtherance of the objects of this Act, [(shall be punishable with imprisonment for a term of not less than one month and not more than six months, and also with fine which shall be not less than one hundred rupees and not more than five hundred rupees)].

[7A Unlawful Compulsory Labour When to be Deemed to be a Practice of "Untouchability"

1.Whoever is deemed under such-section-(1) to have enforced a disability arising out of "untouchability" shall be punishable with imprisonment for a term which shall not be less than three months and also with fine which shall not be less than one hundred rupees and not more than five hundred rupees.

For the purposes of this section, "compulsion" includes a threat of social or economic boycott.]

Cancellation or Suspension of Licences in Certain Cases

When a person who is convicted of an offence under Section 6 holds any licence under any law for the time being in force in respect of any profession, trade, calling or employment in relation to which the offence is committed, the Court trying the offence may, without prejudice to any other penalty to which such person may be liable under that section, direct that the licence shall stand cancelled or be suspended for such period as the Court may deem fit and every order of the Court so cancelling or suspending a licence shall have effect as if it had been passed by the authority competent to cancel or suspend the licence under any such law.

In this section, "licence" includes a permit or a permission.

Resumption or Suspension of Grants made by Government

Where the manager or trustee of a place of public worship (or any educational institution or hostel) which is in receipt of a grant of land or money from the Government is convicted of an offence under this Act and such conviction is not reversed or quashed in any appeal or revision, the Government may, if in its opinion the circumstances of the case warrant such a course, direct the suspension or resumption of the whole or any part of such grant.

Abetment of Offence

Whoever abets any offence under this Act shall be punishable with the punishment provided for the offence. A public servant who wilfully neglects the investigation of any offence punishable under this Act shall be deemed to have abetted as offence punishable under this Act.

Power of State Government to Impose Collective Fine

1. If after an inquiry in the prescribed manner, the State Government is satisfied that the inhabitants of an area are concerned in, or abetting the commission or, any offence punishable under this Act, or harbouring persons concerned in the commission of such offence or failing to render all the assistance in their power to discover or apprehend the offender or offenders or suppressing material evidence of the commission of such offence, the State Government may, by notification in the official Gazette, impose a collective fine on such inhabitants and apportion such fine amongst the inhabitants who are liable collectively to pay it and such apportionment shall be made according to the State Government's judgement of the respective means of such inhabitants and in making any such apportionment, the State Government may assign a portion of such fine to a Hindu undivided family to be payable by it provided that the fine apportioned to an inhabitant shall not be realized until the petition, if any, denied by him under sub-section (3) is disposed of.

2. The notification made under sub-section (7) shall be proclaimed in the area by beat of drum or in such other manner as the State Government may think best in the circumstances to bring to imposition of the collective fine to the notice of the inhabitants of the said area.

3. (a) Any person aggrieved by the imposition of the collective fine under sub-section (1) or by the order of apportionment may, within the prescribed period, file a petition before the State Government or such other authority as that Government may specify in this behalf for being exempted from such fine or for modification of the order or apportionment; provided that no fee shall be charged for filing such petition.

(b) The State Government or the authority specified by it shall, after giving to the petitioner a reasonable opportunity of being heard, pass such order as it may think fit; provided that the amount of the fine exempted or reduced under this section shall not be realizable from any person, and the total fine imposed on the inhabitants of an area under sub-section (1) shall be deemed to have been reduced to that extent.

4. Notwithstanding anything contained in sub-section (3) the State Government may exempt the victims of any offence punishable under this Act or any person who does not, in its opinion, fall within the category of persons specified in sub-section (1) from the liability to pay the collective fine imposed under sub-section (1) or any portion thereof.

5. The portion of collective fine payable by any person (including a Hindu undivided family) may be recovered in the manner provided by the code of Criminal procedure, 1973 (2 of 1974), for the recovery of fines imposed by a Court as if such portion were a fine imposed by a Magistrate.

Enhanced Penalty on Subsequent Conviction

Where any act constituting an offence under this Act is committed in relation to a member of a Scheduled Caste, the Court shall presume, unless the contrary is proved, that such act was committed on the ground of "untouchability".

Limitation of Jurisdiction of Civil Courts

1. No Civil Court shall entertain or continue any suit or proceeding or shall pass any decree or order if the claim involved in such suit or proceeding or if the passing of such decree or order or if such execution would in any way be contrary to the provision of this Act.

2. No Court shall, in adjudicating any matter or executing any decree or order, recognize any custom or usage imposing any disability on any person on the ground of "Untouchability"

Offences by Companies

If the person committing an offence under this Act is in a company, every person who at the time the offence was committed, was in charge of, and was responsible to the company for the conduct of the business of the company, shall be deemed to be guilty of the offence and shall be liable to be proceeded against and punished accordingly;

Provided that nothing contained in this sub-section shall render any such person liable to any punishment, if he proves that the offence was committed without knowledge or that he exercised all due diligence to prevent the commission of such offence.

Notwithstanding anything contained in sub-section (1) where an offence under this Act has been committed with the consent of any director or manager, secretary or other officer of the company, such director, manager, secretary or other officer shall also be deemed to be guilty of that offence and shall be liable to be proceeded against and punished accordingly.

For the purposes of this section:

(a) "Company" means the body that corporate and includes a firm or other association of individuals; and

(b) "director" in relation to a firm means a partner in the firm.

Protection of Action Taken in Good Faith

1. No suit, prosecution or other legal proceeding shall lie against the Central Government or a State Government for anything which is in good faith done or intended to be done under this Act.

2. No suit or other legal proceeding shall lie against the Central Government or a State Govenment for any damage caused or likely to be caused by anything which is in good faith done or intended to be done under this Act.

Offences to be Cognizable and Triable Summarily

1. Notwithstanding anything contained in the Code of Criminal Procedure, 1973 (2 of 1974), every offence punishable under this Act shall be cognizable and every such offence, except where it is punishable with imprisonment for a minimum term exceeding three months, may be tried summarily by a Judicial Magistrate of the first class or in a metropolitan area by a Metropolitan Magistrate in accordance with the procedure specified in the said code.

2. Notwithstanding anything contained in the Code of Criminal Procedure, 1973 (2 of 1974), when any public servant is alleged to have committed the offence of abetment of an offence punishable under this Act while acting or purporting to act in the discharge of his offical duty, no Court shall take congnizance of such offence of abetment except with the previous sanction

(a) of the Central Government in the case of a person employed in connection with the affairs of the union; and

(b) of the State Government in the case of a person employed in connection with the affairs of a State.

Duty of State Government to Ensure that the Rights Accruing from the Abolition of "Untouchability" May be Availed of by the Concerned Person

1. Subject to such rules as the Central Government may take in this behalf, the State Government shall take such measures as may be necessary

for ensuring that the rights arising from the abolition of "untouchability" are made available to, and are availed of by the persons subjected to any disability arising out of "untouchability".

2. In particular, and without prejudice to the generality of the provisions of sub-section (1) such measures may include:

(i) the provision of adequate facilities, including legal aid, to the persons subjected to any disability arising out of "untouchability" to enable them to avail themselves of such rights;

(ii) the appointment of officers for initiating or exercising supervision over prosecutions for the contravention of the provisions of this Act;

(iii) the setting up of special courts for the trial of offence as under this Act;

(iv) the setting up of committees at such appropriate levels as the State Government may think fit to assist the State Government in formulating or implementing such measures;

(v) provision for a periodic survey of the working of the provisions of this Act with a view to suggesting measures for the better implementation of the provisions of this Act;

(vi) the identification of the areas where persons are under any disability arising out of "untouchability" and adoption of such measures as would ensure the removal of such disability from such areas.

3. The Central Government shall take such steps as may be necessary to co-ordinate the measures taken by the State Government under sub-section (1).

4. The Central Government shall, every year place on the table of each House of Parliament a report on the measures taken by itself and by the State Government in pursuance of the provision of this section.

Act to Overside Other Laws

Save as otherwise expressly provided in this Act, the provision of this Act shall have, effect notwithstanding anything inconsistent therewith contained in any other law for the time being in force, or any custom or usage or any instrument having effect by virtue of any such law or any decree or order of any court or other authority.

16 A. Probation of Offenders Act, 1958 Not to Apply to Persons above the Age of Fourteen Years

The provisions of the Probation of Offenders Act, 1958 (20 of 1958) shall not apply to any person above the age of fourteen years who is found guilty of having committed any offence punishable under this Act.

Power to Make Rules

1. The Central Government may, by notification in the official gazette, make rules to carry out the provisions of this Act.

2. Every rule made by the Central Government under this Act shall be laid, as soon as may be after it is made, before each House of Parliament while it is in session for a total period of thirty days which may be comprised in one session or in two or more successive sessions, and if before the expiry of the session immediately following the session or the successive sessions aforesaid, both Houses agree in keying any modification in the rule or both Houses agree that the rule should be made, or shall thereafter have effect only in such modified form or be of no effect, as the case may be; so however, that any such modification or annulment shall be without prejudice to the validity of anything previously done under that rule.

Repeal

The enactments specified in the schedule are hereby repealed to the extent to which they or any of the provisions contained therein correspond or are repugnant to this Act or to any of the provisions contained therein.

(IX) Provisions and Plans for the Welfare of the Scheduled Castes by the Central Government

Representation in legislature under Articles 330 and 332 of the Constitution, concession of reserved seats was initially for a period of 10 years from the commencement of the Constitution, but has been extended, through amendments, up to 1995. There is no reservation of seats in the Rajya Sabha and State Vidhan Parishad.[7]

Following introduction of Panchayati Raj, safeguards have been provided for proper representation of members of the Scheduled Castes by reserving seats for them in the Gram Panchayat and other local bodies.[8]

(XI) Reservation in the Services

Fifteen per cent of the vacancies are reserved for Schedule Castes in which recruitment is made on all India basis and 16 $^2/_3$ per cent of the vacancies to which recruitment is made on all India basis otherwise by open competition. For Scheduled Tribes reservation is 7.5 per cent in both the cases. Reservation in direct recruitment to Group C and D posts, which normally attract candidates from one locality or religion is fixed in proportion to the population of Scheduled Castes and Scheduled Tribes in respective States/Union Territories. In promotions, reservations of vacancies is allowed and 15 per cent of the vacancies for Scheduled Castes and 7.5 per cent for Scheduled Tribes on the result of competitive examinations limited to departmental candidates in Groups B, C and D and in promotion by selection in Groups B, C and D and to the lowest rung of Group A in grades or services to which element of direct recruitment if any does not exceed 75 per cent. Reservation has also been provided for Scheduled Castes and Scheduled Tribes for promotions on the basis of seniority; subject to fitness in Groups A,B,C, and D posts in grades or services to which element of direct recruitment if any does not exceed 75 per cent.[9]

The only field where some concrete achievements have been made amongst the Scheduled Castes is in education. This is clear from the fact that while in 1948-49 only 647 scholarships for post-matric studies had been granted, in 1990 this figure rose to 14 lakh. This means that much has been done in this sector.[10] As a result, a wave of rising expectations is found among the educated Scheduled Caste youth. They are becoming more and more conscious, still social justice is denied to them.

The main reason for unsatisfactory progress of the Scheduled Castes is lack of proper implementation of the various welfare schemes undertaken for their development from time to time. The basic reasons that appear to be responsible for this area, are: firstly, general lack of a sense of urgency on the part of those responsible for the implementation of the schemes; secondly, insufficient financial provisions for the welfare schemes, due to a low priority accorded to them in the various five year plans; and thirdly, lack of people's participation in the implementation of the schemes, particularly due to a lukewarm attitude in that respect on the part of political parties and want of revolutionary urge and zeal on the part of social workers.

While analysing the shortcomings in the administrative system, a social welfare officer, who prefers to remain anonymous, said that the elected leaders at Zilla Parishad and Panchayat Samiti level are the main hindrances in implementing the schemes for the Scheduled Castes. The elected leaders belong to the upper castes and they have absolutely no interest in implementing any scheme for the Scheduled Castes. Whatever they do is just symbolic and for show.

The Commissioner for Scheduled Castes and Scheduled Tribes observed in the report of 1970-71,[11] that the efforts made by the Government since independence to help these communities to better their standards, for their proper integration with the mainstream of society, have not met with due success. The welfare measures undertaken during the various five years plans have also not had the desired impact on them and they continue to suffer from poverty and social degradation.

This Act based on the experience gained in the implemention of the Untouchability (Offences) Act, 1955 and the recommendations of the Elayaperumal Committee, was exhausitively amended and also renamed in 1976 as the Protection of Civil Rights Act. This amended Act prescribes punishments for the preaching and practice of "untouchability" for the enforcement of any disability arising therefrom and for matter connected therewith. The scope of the Act was enlarged in 1976, by including the offences of practising and preaching untouchability which include:

1. insulting a member of a Scheduled Caste on the ground of untouchability.
2. preaching untouchability directly or indirectly.
3. justifying untouchability on historical, philosophical or religious grounds or on the ground of tradition of the caste system.

The penal sanction was also enhanced in 1976 by prescribing that (a) in the case of subsequent convictions, the punishment may range from one to two years imprisonment and (b) a person convicted by the offence of "untouchability" shall be disqualified for election to the Union or a State legislature.

(XII) Objective of Protection of Civil Rights Act

For rebuilding the social structure and to weld the various elements of society into a common nation, the Government has taken vigorous action to abolish untouchability. All kinds of other social disabilities have also been abolished by law. No person can be prevented on the ground of untouchability from entering a place of public worship, offering prayer therein or taking water from a secured tank or spring.

Nothing can prevent a person from exercising his rights. A Harijan cannot be excommunicated or subjected to boycott, molestation or injury. The Protection of Civil Rights Act provides penalties for offences committed on all these grounds. The offences committed under this Act are cognizible. Free legal aid is also offered to the Harijans in dealing with cases arising out of denial of rights conferred on them by the Constitution.

While the equality of rights and opportunity is guaranteed to all citizens, specific measures are provided for safeguarding the interests of the weaker sections of the population that include the Scheduled Castes, the Scheduled Tribes and other backward classes.

No discrimination is allowed against any on grounds of religion, race, caste, class or place of birth. Every citizen is free to enjoy his civil rights regardless of his caste, creed and profession. No restriction or condition can be imposed with regard to access to shops, use of wells, tanks, bathing ghats, roads and places of public resorts maintained wholly or partly out of State funds or dedicated to the use of general public.

In order to bring the backward classes up to the level of other citizens, special and positive steps have been taken to remove the causes responsible for the backwardness of these people. The law of the land now gives them protection from social injustice and all forms of exploitation, special programmes of financial aid have been formulated by the Central and State Governments to help these communities to overcome their special handicaps and enable them to come up quickly to the level of the hitherto privileged section of the population. They can now participate equally in all spheres of national life.

(XIII) The Mandal Commission Report

The Central Government has been implementing the proposal suggested by the Mandal Commission.[12] Its report was submitted to the Government of India on December 31, 1980. It recommended increase in the reservation of seats for other backward classes also. The Scheduled Castes and Scheduled Tribes already have 22.5 per cent reservation of seats. This leaves only 27 per cent seats to the other backward classes.

This has resulted in strong opposition from those sections of society which are affected by this promotion. Resentment is aggravated by the fact that there is severe competition in the educational field and in the field of employment. It is a fact that some enjoy the privilege of having reserved seats when others are being rejected. The frustration has resulted in intense hatred towards these new "privileged" classes.

The Scheduled Castes and the backward classes have prepared themselves to fight for their due share inspite of the oppression from the non-backward classes. They see it as an attempt by the upper classes to maintain the status quo. With this impression and with a newly emerging leadership, awareness of their rights, and realization of their collective power as a political unit, they are keen on getting the opportunities which were denied to them for centuries.

The Central Government accepted the Mandal Commission Report on August 13, 1990 (No. 360/2/90 ESH (SCT).

In this chapter an attempt has been made to highlight the philosophy of the Indian Constitution and the legal provisions to eradicate the caste system. The focus has been on the post-Independence era. There is a special mention of the Kaka Kalelkar Commission and the Untouchability (Offences) Act 1955. The report of the Elayaperumal Committee 1965 and the weakness of the Untouchability Act are discussed thoroughly.

References

1. June 1, 1955, vide notificaton No. SRO 1109 dated May 23, 1995, Gazette of India 1955, New Delhi, Extraordinary Part II Section (iii) 1971, p. 1.
2. 19/11/1976 vide SRO 734 (E) dated November 16, 1976, published in the Gazette of India Extraordinary, New Delhi, Part II Section (ii), 1976, p. 401.
3. *Ibid.*, by Act 106 of 1976 S 4 (w. e. f. November 19, 1976).
4. *Ibid.* The words "for belonging to the same religious denomination" omitted by S 5 (w. e. f. November 19, 1976).
5. *Ibid.*, by S 5 (w. e. f. November 19, 1976).
6. *Ibid.* The words "attached there to" omitted by S 7 (w. e. f. November 19, 1976).
7. *India* by Research and References Division published by Ministry of Information and Broadcasting, Government of India, 1976, p. 105.
8. *Ibid.* India, p. 105.
9. *Ibid.* India, 1992, p. 227.
10. *Ibid.* India, 1992, p. 226.
11. RCSCST. Reports of the Commissioner of Scheduled Castes and Scheduled Tribes Manager of Publication, Government of India, New Delhi, 1970, p. 3.
12. Reservation for backward classes. Mandal Commission Report of the Backward Classes Commission. Central Government Publication, New Delhi, 1980.

5

The Scheduled Caste and the Scheduled Tribes (Prevention of Atrocities) Act, 1989

In the year 1989 an Act called the Scheduled Castes and the Scheduled Tribes (Prevention of Atrocities) Act, 1989[1] was enacted to prevent the commission of offences of atrocities against the members of the Scheduled Castes and Scheduled Tribes, to provide for special courts for the trial of such offences and for the relief and rehabilitation of the victims of such offences and for matters connected therewith or incidental thereto.

The Scheduled Castes and Scheduled Tribes (Prevention of Atrocities) Bill: Debates in the Parliament

Mr Deputy-Speaker: We go to the next item.

The Minister of State of the Ministry of Welfare (Dr. Rajendra Kumari Bajpai): I beg to move:

"That the Bill to prevent the commission of offences of atrocities against the members of the Scheduled Castes and the Scheduled Tribes, to provide for Special Courts for the trial of such offences and for the relief and rehabilitation of the victims of such offences and for matters connected therewith or incidental thereto be taken into consideration."

Mr. Deputy-Speaker, Sir, this House is aware of the deep concern our government has for the welfare of the Scheduled Castes and Scheduled Tribes. A separate Welfare Ministry was created in 1985, specially for the welfare of weaker section of the society. Many new initiatives have been taken, particularly in the last few years to improve the lots of Scheduled Castes and Scheduled Tribes in trying to discharge a mandate of the

Constitution. Poverty alleviation programmes which provide a special attention to the Scheduled Castes and Scheduled Tribes have been expanded and intensified.

(Shri Somnath Rath *in the Chair*)

First the IRDP and other programmes were improved considerably and now these have been replaced by a bigger scheme of the Jawahar Rozgar Yojana. It is because we think that if we have to improve the economic conditions of the weaker sections of the society, specially Scheduled Castes and Scheduled Tribes and those who are below the poverty line, they should be given employment. For that, Jawahar Rozgar Yojana has come in a big way.

Drinking water wells and irrigation wells have been provided for this group. The need of housing has been met by the Indira Awas Yojana. The programme for liberation of scavengers has been given a greater impetus. I want to tell the House that though in the Constitution, we have abolished untouchability it also true that unless and until we remove this sort of work i.e., scavenging, there will not be much impact. So, the liberation of scavenging programme is very important for removing untouchability from our society. The education of Scheduled Castes and Scheduled Tribes which is of crucial importance to their growth and development has received much greater attention. Education is very important to fight not only poverty but it gives them strength to fight social injustice as well. We want Scheduled Castes and Scheduled Tribes people to stand against social injustice and for that awareness should be created through education. So, education programme is very important and under the new education policy and under the 20-point programme, we have laid emphasis to this aspect. The number of students studying beyond the matriculation stage has gone up to 13 lakhs. This is an open-ended scheme where we are providing scholarships to our Scheduled Castes and Scheduled Tribes boys so that they can go for higher studies. Coaching centre are provided to them so that they can take the advantage or avail the opportunity of competing with other sections of the soceity.

A special drive is currently on for filling up the backlog which had arisen as a result of non-fulfilment of reserved seats for SC/ST. Efforts are also being made to free them from bonded labour and to find land for cultivation.

As well all know, about 45 per cent of the Scheduled Castes population are landless labourers and they are mostly living below poverty line. So, they have to be given these facilities and we have to give them opportunity and some of them are bonded labour too. We will free them through this Bonded Labour Act and they will be rehabilitated by giving them land and money as well.

We are witnessing today the signs of fruits of development reaching the Scheduled Castes and Scheduled Tribes. But it is not all. With greater spread of education and with the socio-economic condition improving, the relations in society sometimes come under tension as a result of this change. As the situation is changing and the change is coming into the society, we see that in the countryside, in rural India specially, there is some kind of tension also and that is because of atrocities on Scheduled Castes and Scheduled Tribes in some parts of the country or the other. Higher caste groups sometimes do not like change in the socio-economic structure and tension develop. These are the causes of atrocities and the Bill is intended to prevent these atrocities and so I am dealing with that. The demand for justice, for equality, for a human living standard, for knowledge, for education and freedom leads in some cases to a realisation by groups who are not enlightened enough to recognise the healthy signs of growth.

People are still not going to tolerate the growth of the development of Scheduled Castes or of those people who were till now working under them. They can come up and demand their rights. Sometimes tension erupts in the locality. In such situations, atrocities or a variety of offences are committed on members of Scheduled Castes and Scheduled Tribes. These are the causes.

I have had occasion to tell this House regarding the recent trend in the increase of such offence against members of the Scheduled Castes and Scheduled Tribes. The other day while we were discussing this matter in the House, a question was put and I have answered such questions many times in the last four years about atrocities on Scheduled Castes and Scheduled Tribes. Last week I was saying that I will be coming with some Bill on atrocities. Sometimes there was heated discussion on this point.

This question is constantly raised in this House that there is increase of such offences against members of Scheduled Castes and Scheduled Tribes. Sometimes Hon. Members are also agitated on this. During 1988, there were a little over 15,000 offences against Scheduled Castes and 3,300 cases in respect of Scheduled Tribes. Of these, heinous offences such as murder, arson, rape and grievous hurt accounted for about 3300 cases in respect of Scheduled Castes and 783 in respect of Scheduled Tribes. There are other minor offences also. This shows the tendency, trend and thinking of the upper caste people. They do not want that Scheduled Castes and Scheduled Tribes people should be respected in the society like others. The nature of these offences in many States indicated that these were not isolated instances but represented a trend in the country. In cities and towns and areas where the society was generally aware of the need to bring about such changes, the upward socio-economic mobility of the Scheduled Castes and Scheduled Tribes was accepted and tensions did not arise. But in certain rural areas things are very bad. In rural areas, traditions seem to be difficult to dislodge. It is difficult to dislodge the prejudices and traditions there. Hence, the Government thought that certain special measures would be necessary at this point of time. So, we are bringing in the Scheduled Castes and the Scheduled Tribes (Prevention of Atrocities) Bill. In this Bill, we have also defined as to what are the atrocities and we will specifically deal with those things.

Sir, the causes of such incidences were related generally to land or to continued exploitation or enforcement of traditional demeaning practices. It is regrettable that such instances have been reported such as in Kerala where a member of Scheduled Castes was forced to eat human excreta. There are reports of a bridal party being chased and houses of this community razed to the ground merely because the bridegroom had the temerity to ride on a horse through the village streets. That bridegroom was riding on a horse. He was going through the village streets. So, the upper-caste people felt as to how he could ride on a horse and to the houses of those poor Scheduled Castes people were razed to the ground. The efforts of the government to provide land have been frustrated in many cases. This is another example of atrocities on such people. In some States where the land is allotted to Scheduled Castes people, forcible dispossession or illegal occupation. Caste people forcible dispossession or illegal occupation of such land is reported to government. This is because of the fact that the upper-caste people are strong people. They think that these poor Scheduled Castes people should have no right on such lands. They forcibly occupy the land. So, land is also a cause of such atrocities. In Madhya Pradesh, recently the government launched a special programme to see that possession or effectively restoring land to members of Scheduled Castes and Scheduled Tribes who had been given pattas for the land, is implemented. Such programmes are taking place as a special drive. That is our policy. That is the guideline from the Central Government. So, they are trying to implement the programmes. But still there are cases where things are not properly implemented or if pattas are given to Scheduled Castes or Scheduled Tribes people, the upper-caste people in the village or those who are in possession of such land still try to hold the possession of the land or they grab the land meant for weaker sections. They will not part with that land. So the Scheduled Caste is not able to occupy that though he has got pattas. It is the one point of under cause or the pattern of atrocity that is committed on womenfolk. In unfortunate incidents the women folk of Scheduled Castes and Scheduled Tribes sought to be dishonoured and assaulted with the object of teaching a lesson to that community. This is a very ugly sort of thing and a very cruel mode of thing which is resorted to by certain people. And this is the worst type of atrocities committed on Scheduled Castes people in dishonouring women. In tribal areas sexual exploitation is now to occur and the willingness of the innocent tribal women is secured by exercise of authority or influence. The community is sometimes sought to be pressurised by denying them access to public places for easing themselves or for cremation or a water source, etc. Such type of things are still going on in some parts of India. Now in the 20th century, this is very shameful for the society. We have to not only create awareness but we have also to stop it with strong hand. We are going to take this strong measure.

Instances have occurred of fouling of water source or dumping carcass in the vicinity of their houses. It is to humiliate and tease the Scheduled Caste people. All these when taken together form a pattern which calls for more stringent legislative measures.

The Bill which is before this House seeks to classify most of such instances as Atrocities on Scheduled Castes and Scheduled Tribes. We have defined these atrocities and included all these atrocities in this Bill. Although many of these offences could probably be covered under the normal law of the land, we are witnessing today a difference in degree which calls for a differentiation in kind in respect of these offences. It was necessary to bring this Bill. The Bill hence proposes to specify higher punishments as also laying down some minimum punishment for such offences. We have elaborately mentioned the various kinds of atrocities which we have included in this Bill.

I will only mention two or three points though there are so many other points which are the salient features of the new legislation. For the first time, we have defined this term in this Bill, that is, what will constitute atrocity. It says:

"Forcing a member of Scheduled Caste or Scheduled Tribe to drink or eat any inedible or obnoxious substance as the human excreta or acting with as intention to cause injury, insulting or annoying by dumping excreta, carcasses and other similar items in the locality, taking off their clothes forcibly particularly of the women folk, forcibly dispossessing them of their land and keeping them as bonded labour and forcing them to do beggar, interfering in the rights guaranteed to them for representation in public bodies, through elections, utilising legal process for causing harassment and injury by instituting false, malicious or vexatious suits or legal proceedings against them and subjecting their women folk to assault and sexual exploitation by persons in a position to dominate their will".

Property is often the basis of atrocities on Scheduled Castes and Scheduled Tribes. Hence, wrongful dispossession of the property is made an atrocity under the Bill. The Bill also provides that upon conviction, in addition to a sentence to be passed, the movable and immovable property belonging to the convicted persons and used in the offences would be liable for forfeiture. This is very important and that is why it is made very stringent.

The Bill includes offences relating to property of persons and carrying punishments of ten years and above under the Indian Penal Code and committed by non-Scheduled Castes and non-Scheduled Tribes on the ground that the victims happen to be members of Scheduled Castes or Scheduled Tribes, as atrocities.

The Scheduled Tribes living in Scheduled Areas or Tribal Areas are harmed in many ways by vested elements. Article 19(1) provides for the protection of the interests of the Scheduled Tribes. The Bill, therefore, provides for externment of a person who is likely to commit an atrocity as defined in the Act against a member of a Scheduled Tribe in a Scheduled or Tribal Area, from that area for a period extending to two years.

The Bill provides for minimum punishment of six months imprisonment and fine for the offences.

Some of the other features of the Bill are appointment of Special Courts and Special public prosecutors, conferment of powers exercisable by a police officer or any officer of the State Government and protective and preventive measures that are to be taken by the law and order machinery to check the atrocities. The Bill further contemplates arrangements for effective implementation of the Act, and among other things, provides for economic and social rehabilitation of the victims of atrocities. These are the salient features of the Bill.

We say that prevention is better than cure and the Bill also looks after the preventive measures. If an area is declared prone to atrocities it will become the bonded duty of the law and order machinery to take all possible measures for instilling a sense of safety and security. Schemes would be formulated under the general guidance of the Government of India to provide for such measures as also for providing prompt and adequate relief and rehabilitation in the unfortunate event of atrocities taking place. We have kept all these provisions not only on the preventive side, but at the same time to see the rehabilitation part also.

The Bill places a special responsibility on the public servants who are not members of Scheduled Castes or Scheduled Tribes to take action to protect the interests of Scheduled Castes and Scheduled Tribes against atrocities being committed or taking of protective and rehabilitative measures.

The Bill overall aims at ensuring this when the fruits of development and spread of education is now reaching the Scheduled Castes and Scheduled Tribes the benefits therefrom are not taken away or denied by vested interests. I am sure these measures will be welcomed by all and enlightened sections of society and that we shall in our country succeed in removing the stain of such inhuman treatment towards a section of our people by vested interests. The dream of Mahatma Gandhi for the uplift of these groups is being brought to reality by our government and I seek your cooperation in passing this Bill and taking message to that far corners of our country. I hope that after giving your comments, this Bill will help in creating a proper atmosphere in the whole of the country and this Bill is going to have effect all over.

With these few words, Sir, I beg to move the motion for consideration.

Mr. Chairman: Motion moved.

"That the Bill to prevent the commission of offences of atrocities against the members of the Scheduled Castes and the Scheduled Tribes to provide to special courts for the trial of such offences and for the relief and rehabilitation of the victims of such offences and for matters connected therewith of incidental there to, be taken into consideration"

Shri Ram Ratan Ram (Hajipur): Mr. Chairman, Sir, first of all, I would like to congratulate the Prime Minister and also the Welfare Minister, Dr. Rajendra Kumari Bajpai, of going ahead with this very progressive Bill, after the lapse of forty years of our independence.

Just now, our respected Welfare Minister has mentioned about the dream of Mahatma Gandhi. No doubt, the dream of Mahatma Gandhi is going to be fulfilled after the lapse of forty years of independence.

So far as the question of atrocities, tortures, land grabbing, rape and whatsoever is incorporated in this Bill, is concerned, it has been going on for centuries after centuries. It is not that it is just coming up today. It has been there for the last so many centuries.

I would like to congratulate the Prime Minister and also the Welfare Minister—who has got the motherly affection for the members of the Scheduled Castes and the Scheduled Tribes—for bringing forward this unique Bill. With this unique Bill, no doubt, the members of the Scheduled Castes and the Scheduled Tribes will have some relief. I would like to thank Dr. Rajendra Kumari Bajpai for this. Before I go ahead—as the Hon. Minister has said just now—I would like to read the Statement of Objects and Reasons, which says:

"Despite various measures to improve the socio-economic conditions of the Scheduled Castes and the Scheduled Tribes, they remain vulnerable. They are denied number of civil rights. They are subjected to various offences, indignities, humiliations and harassment. They have, in several brutal incidents, been deprived of their life and property. Serious crimes are committed against them for various historical, social and economic reasons.

Because of the awareness created amongst the Scheduled Castes and the Scheduled Tribes through spread of education, etc. they are trying to assert their rights and this is not being taken very kindly by the others. When they assert their rights and resist practices of untouchability against them or demand statutory minimum wages or refuse to do any bonded and forced labour, the vested interests try to cow them down and terrorise them. When the Scheduled Castes and the Scheduled Tribes try to preserve their self-respect or honour of their women, they become irritants for the dominant and the mighty. Occupation and cultivation of even the government allotted land by the Scheduled Castes and the Scheduled Tribes is resented and more often these people become victims of attacks by the vested interests".

So, all these details are here. No doubt, this Bill is very unique. There is nothing left out in this Bill. Even a slightest point is not left out, so far as the question of prevention of the atrocities and the crime is concerned.

But what is it that was not there is the Indian Penal Code by which action could not be taken but the main things is one the civil side—the executive and the police are not really very sincere to implement these measures and go ahead with the very object and vision of the government. That is the whole question. We have already enacted so many Acts but the whole question is till today the judiciary is silent on this matter. It takes years and years for a case to get settled. Do you think these poor people can afford to pursue the cases for years and years? They cannot afford to do so with the result the offenders get scot free and thereby our people are put to a lot of harassment. No doubt, this Act will give some benefit and relief to our members but I want to touch the basic point. Whenever a crime, atrocity, torture, etc. is committed against the members of the Scheduled Castes and Scheduled Tribes first of all they have to go to the police station to lodge an FIR. Here in this Act nothing has been mentioned about the police officers. Crimes, atrocities, tortures, etc. are there but when they go to the police station the police officers there refuse to record the FIR. What is the way out for this? What action do we propose to take against those police officers who are still silent on the matter? In that respect I would have been grateful to the Hon. Minister if some way had been found out to curb such police officers as well. Now no case can stand unless an FIR is there and the police report is there. Our people go to the police station. The police officers there refuse to register the FIR. On the other hand our people are put to difficulty by being accused that they are making a false statement. So our people are afraid of going to the police station. They rather prefer to tolerate the inhuman treatment.

Mr. Chairman: May I draw the Hon. Member's attention to Clause 4 of the Bill?

Shri Ram Ratan Ram: Mr Chairman, my point is, will my people go to the police to lodge the FIR and also will the police officers there be sincere enough to take note of that? There are provisions even in the IPC. My point is what action you propose to take against such police officers who refuse to record the FIR and on the other hand put our people to harassment and torture. They go to the police station. They are asked to sit there for one or two days. No action is taken. So, what action has been proposed to be taken against such police officers? There should be a remedy to tackle such a situation. A special court will no doubt be there. Our prosecutor will be there. A separate advocate will also be there. Everything has been provided in this Bill. But there is no mention about action against such police officers. That is what I wanted to bring to the notice of the hon. Minister.

Everything is mentioned in detail in this Bill. But so far as the question of externment is concerned, the option has been given to the offender. On page 6, it has been said:

"Where the Special Court is satisfied, upon a complaint or a police report that a person is likely to commit an offence under Chapter II of this Act in any area included in 'Scheduled Areas' or 'tribal areas', as referred to in Article 244 of the Constitution, it may, by order in writing, direct such person to remove himself beyond the limits of such area, by such route and within such time as may be specified in the order, and not to return to that area from which he was directed to remove himself for such period, not exceeding two years, as may be specified in the order."

My point is that option has been given to the man who is going to commit a crime of who has already committed a crime. Will the man, who has been asked by the court to remove himself, carry out the order or not? That question has to be considered. Why should an option be left to the criminal. Suppose such person does go from the areas as defined, what is the guarantee that he will not come again and commit the offences? Such lacunae are there.

I am very thankful to the Hon. Minister for having brought forward such a progressive Bill after 40 years of our independence for the welfare and protection of people belonging to the Scheduled Castes and Scheduled Tribes. Our people are getting education. It is a marvellous and unique. We are happy and satisfied. But still there are some lacunae. Some options have been given which should not be there.

So far as the question of casting of vote concerned, what is the remedy? Booth-capturing is still there. Our people are not allowed to cast their votes in favour of the candidates whom they like. Separate booths are there. Booths are also set up in the localities of the Scheduled Castes and Scheduled Tribes. Since I come from the tribal area. I know that the tribal population is concentrated much more than the Scheduled Castes. The Scheduled Castes are not that much concentrated as the tribals. And that is why, government was kind enough to create booths for the Scheduled Castes in every locality so that people can exercise their franchise. In spite of the fact that there are booths in every locality and village, there are goondas persons who bribe and do not allow people to caste their votes. There is no doubt that remedy is there in this Bill. But I would like to point out to the Minister that remedy is also possible by appointing a police officer when the question of adult franchise comes. I would like to say that some police arrangement must be made. But at the same time, I have got an apprehension about the police officers. The police officers are there to create offences themselves. They train the criminals. They ask the criminals to commit crimes. So, more Scheduled Castes and Scheduled Tribes officers should be appointed and posted at the police stations and unless our people are posted at the police stations itself and made the officer-in-charge. I do not think that the objective of the government will be fulfilled by the Act since the power is in their hands. At the very initial stage, people will have to go to the police station to report the crime. Unless this is done, nobody can go to the court, whether it is a special court or whatever court it may be. The question of going to court comes later on. First of all, one has to go to the police station to report. Somehow our people have gone to the police station to have FIRs lodged after the offences like murder, rape, etc. were committed, as mentioned in this Act. But whole question is about the witnesses. The court will have to proceed according to the witnesses. The court cannot hang anybody simply on my saying, as a member of a Scheduled Castes or a Scheduled Tribes, that my daughter has been raped or my son has been murdered by this man or that man. The court of law cannot convict a person like that. So, witness is necessary. Wherefrom will be witness come? That is my point. Some torture is going on by some persons who still cannot be influenced. They still terrorise the people by saying that if they go to the court as witnesses, none will be allowed to remain in the village, all of them will be burnt or murdered. No doubt, there is action taken. Even if there is any apprehension, our people will go to the court or the police station and report by saying that an apprehension is there. And action will be definitely taken by this Act. But a sort of fear is there in the minds of people. People are afraid. When my whole village gets burnt and when we will not survive, what will the court do? This sort of feeling is there among the people. We have to look into this aspect also. The government cannot go into all these details. They cannot post a magistrate for every door or every village. We have to find some ways so that the minds of our people are free from such weaknesses and fear. All those people who come and frighten and threaten people will have to be set right. This aspect will have to be looked into. We cannot depend on the government all the time that they would do everything for us. We have to do something ourselves also. Of course, the Bill as brought forward by the Hon. Minister is very unique and marvellous and I would like to express my thanks for the same.

I would like to make one more point regarding the grabbing of land. The government was very kind to allot land to our landless people. Most of our people are landless, and bonded labourers in the villages. Though the land had been allotted to these poor people, in many cases it has been grabbed from them and it is a very big problem to restore the possession to them. Though the Bill deals and takes care of the various problems relating to the bonded and landless labourers and grabbing of land by unauthorised people, yet it would require a lot of effort to put these provisions into practice. By this Central Act, we are going to give protection to these poor people throughout the country, but at the same time, in many matters we have to depend on the State administration. This legislation will be applicable throughout the country, and the State Government should be very sincere and honest in implementing it and particularly, they must take care of the Scheduled Castes and Scheduled Tribes so far as the land problem is concerned. We have given land to the landless people and most of these people have been dispossessed from the land, and the possession has not been restored to them. They have to go to the court of law. How many of our people have got enough money to go to the court of law? Of course, the provision is there that you will finance our people for this. In fact, these innocent people are afraid of going to the court. Thought, this problem has been definitely dealt with very nicely and adequately in this Bill, it is very difficult to restore the possession of the land, allotted to these people, once they are dispossessed of it. The law is there, the magistracy is there, the officers are there, yet we are not getting the required protection. I do not think the special courts will ever go to the spot to restore possession of the land to these people.

In this context, I would like to suggest that the cases relating to the land problem as also atrocities on these people should not take more than thirty days; these should be disposed of within that period. Only then, we can have faith and confidence that something is going to be done for us.

With these words, I conclude and would like to convey my heartiest thanks to the Prime Minister as also the Welfare Minister for bringing forwards this Bill, which would definitely provide relief to the poor people.

[*Translation*]

Shri Ganga Ram (Firozabad): Mr. Chairman, Sir, the Scheduled Castes and Scheduled Tribes (Prevention of Atrocities) Bill, 1989 moved by the

Hon. Minister of Social Welfare is the culmination of deep studies made on the problem process of which was started 4 to 5 years ago. During this period, the hon. Minister had several rounds of discussion with the Hon. Members of Parliament and organised seminars and conventions of the representatives of the Scheduled Castes and the Scheduled Tribes to interact with them about the difficulties being faced by them. This is not only an exhaustive Bill but an improved one also as it contains all the good provisions of the earlier laws and the subject. Therefore, she deserves all praise for introducing this Bill.

After 40 years of independence, a concrete step has been taken to prevent the atrocities on the people belonging to Scheduled Castes and Scheduled Tribes and constitute 25 crore of the total population of the country. It was Mahatma Gandhi who in 1932 had staked his life to make these castes as an integral part of the Indian society and he also did a lot for their betterment. Words fall short to describe the efforts of Pt. Jawaharlal Nehru and Dr. Baba Saheb Ambedkar in ameliorating the lot of these poor sections of our society and infusing the feeling of self-respect among them. I would like to quote what Pt. Jawaharlal Nehru said about Dr. Ambedkar.

"I imagine that the way he will be remembered most will be as a symbol of revolt against all the oppressive forces and features of Hindu society. He rebelled against something against which all should and ought to rebel and we have in face rebelled in various degrees."

[*Translation*]

After going through this Bill, it appears the Hon. Minister and for that matter the Government of India brought this Bill with a view to giving a warning to the oppressors, and who exploit the poor in order to remove social inequality.

The Hon. Minister has explained in detail the objects of moving this Bill in the House. The Acts and laws made till date on the subject, mainly the Removal of Untouchability Act, 1955 and the Protection of Civil Rights Act, 1987 could not be proved effective. All of us agree that the implementation of these Acts have been very poor.

A number of schemes have been launched for upliftment and

development of the people belonging to Scheduled Castes and Scheduled Tribes and weaker section of society which constitute 25 per cent of the total population of the country. The credit for the schemes such as 20-point programme, IRDP, NREP, Jawahar Rozgar Yojana, Special Component Plan and the Scheduled Castes and the Scheduled Tribes Financial Corporation goes to none other than the Congress Party. During the stewardship of the hon. Minister, Central Government has set up a separate Financial Development Corporation for these sections, whose jurisdiction runs throughout the country. Indira Awas Yojana and many other schemes were also launched, but unfortunately they could not be effectively implemented by the present machinery of the government. This reminds me of a few lines of a couplet of a poet:-

Kitne Badal Baras Rahe Hain, Phi Bhi Paudhe Taras Rahe Hain,

Yahi Chaman Ko Acharaj Bhai, Pani Kahan Chala Jata Hai?

It is a pity that despite several measures taken by the government, all these facilities have not reached the rural areas at the grassroot level. We must find out the reasons for this. Besides enacting this legislation we must also consider the effective implemention of measures taken for their upliftment because atrocities are closely inter-related to their upliftment.

I do remember that during the Janata Party rule, when I was in Lucknow, a decision was taken to withdraw reservation facility for SC/ST. However the Government of Janata Party was dismissed that very evening thereby saving the helpless poor. On coming to power, the Congress Party not only continued the policy of reservation, but also implemented it effectively. Recently, the young Hon. Prime Minister has tried his best to clear the backlog of reserved vacancies very earnestly. For this the Hon. Prime Minister and the Hon. Minister of Social Welfare both deserve to be congratulated. This created great fervour and enthusiasm among the poor all over the country, especially the constitutional amendment Bills of Panchayati Raj and the Nagarpalika have infused great confidence in the people. Under Panchayati Raj system, reservation for them has been given upto the grassroot level only.

Many people do not understand the meaning of reservation. I would like to explain its meaning before the House. We keep on demanding reservation in appointment and promotion in services and in allotment of gas agencies etc. Explaining the meaning of reservation, Dr. Ambedkar had stated that the reservation had been made for social upliftment of the people who had been subjected to social discrimination for thousand of years and in order to achieve the goal, some sort of discrimination against some people would have to be done. That discrimination can be termed as reservation for which down from Mahatma Gandhi to all the leaders of the present generation trying to achieve in right earnest.

The opposition has done nothing in this direction except making hue and cry. The House is the witness to their behaviour and sincerity shown during the last four years when they raised the issue of Bofors only and nothing else. Opposition never discussed the issues pertaining to the poor and on the other hand wasted time of the House. They do not know against whom they are levelling charges. They are levelling charges against the person who is trying to anchor the ship of the country from the turbulent sea. To them I can-say, *"Tum sahil wale kya jano, yeh tufan kaun uthata hai, yek kishti kaun dubota hai."* It is the opposition which is raising storms to drown the ship which is being anchored by our leader. Therefore, under the present conditions, neither we nor the people have any expectations from the opposition parties. The poor people are looking towards the Congress Party headed by the Hon. young Prime Minister only and the Hon. Minister of Social Welfare, who have political will and the determination to act upon. The present Bill to stop atrocities is bold and praiseworthy, though many programmes are already in progress.

A little time ago, Shri Ram Ratan Ram, who is a veteran Member of the House pointed out some shortcomings in the Bill. But before I go into them, I would like to refer to the last report of the Scheduled Castes and Scheduled Tribes Commission regarding atrocities. Commission has stated, which I quote.

[*English*]

"A review of the available atrocity data for the years 1982 to 1984 presents a somewhat disturbing trend. The overall number of cases of atrocity against the Scheduled Castes that had declined from 15,051 in 1981 to 14,847 in 1983, recorded an increase to 16,586 in 1984. In 1987, the highest number of atrocity cases was reported from Madhya Pradesh (6128) followed by Uttar Pradesh (4200), Bihar (1845) and Rajasthan (1648).

These States together with Tamil Nadu (489), Gujarat (690) and Maharashtra (579) among themselves accounted for about 95 per cent of the cases of atrocities reported during the year under review."

[*Translation*]

This has been stated by the Commission. The report of the Commissioner for Scheduled Castes and Scheduled Tribes for the year 1986 is also available now. At present Shri B.G. Sharma is the Commissioner. He has made an indepth studies of the problem throughout the country and his report is before us. As regards atrocities, total number of serious crimes committed in 1986 has been given in the report. Earlier, only serious crimes were treated as atrocities. Under the G.O. of the Ministry of Home Affairs, serious crime includes murder under section 302 of IPC, grievously hurt under sections 324 and 376 IPC, rape under section 376 IPC, arson under section 436 IPC and some other serious crimes but in the present Bill, the Hon. Minister has made the definition of the serious crime more exhaustive. The Commissioner for the Scheduled Castes and the Scheduled Tribes in his report has stated that in 1986 alone, as many as 15416 serious crimes, earlier used to be known as atrocities, were committed. Out of them, as many as 3945 crimes were committed against the people belonging to the Scheduled Tribes. In our country, there are 1085 Scheduled Castes and 639 Scheduled Tribes. As regards their population in the country, population of Scheduled Castes and Scheduled Tribes are about 15 crore and 10 crore respectively. Atrocities have also been committed in the same proportion against them. The causes of atrocities as pointed out by the Commissioner and the Hon. Minister are cent per cent correct. In the Objects and Reasons of the Bill, it has been correctly stated that the atrocities are committed on them because feudal elements in the society do not tolerate that the poor people should live with honour and peace in the society. The poor the Scheduled Castes and Scheduled Tribes wish to lead a peaceful and happy life in this independent India, without being forced to bear insults. In the objects of Bill, it has been accepted that they are subjected to atrocities. This Bill has been brought forward with a view to stop atrocities on them so that they may lead a respectable life. This is the need of the hour. Even on moral ground, nobody has got any right to insult one. It can be observed from the statement of objects and reasons attached to the Bill that maximum atrocities are committed in Madhya

Pradesh followed by Uttar Pradesh, Bihar and Rajasthan. After a deep study of the matter as to why Madhya Pradesh is on the top of the list, I came to conclusion that feudalism was the sole reason for it. This area has been under the control of feudal big zamindars and nawabs for a pretty long time. There were several small princely states who used to force the people to work. Their outlook was so feudal that in order to satisfy their false ego, these people did not allow common men to sit down on the cots before them. Mostly incidents of atrocities have occured minly in North India, e.g., Jahangirabad, Deoli, Sadupur, etc. I would like to tell about Deoli incident which occurred in 1982 in which as many as 23 persons were massacred. Two main accused named Santosha and Radhe were not allowed to be arrested on behest of the then Chief Minister of Uttar Pradesh who is the leader of opposition today and is leading them. He helped those accused and made them surrender in the courts only. This ghastly crime was committed in 1980-81 and the case is still pending in the court. The case is being get delayed by big zamindars and feudal lords who have been helping them. Not only this, Santosha filed even nomination for the post of Pradhan from the jail itself. They are providing protection to those criminals. People of Janata Dal are providing protection to persons having criminal record. I think that if such people come in power what benefit they will provide to Scheduled Castes and Scheduled Tribes. The future of the Harijans will become bleak if they come in power.

Hon. Minister has rightly said that bonded labour is one of causes of atrocities on them. An act to abolish bonded labour system was passed in 1976 on the initiative of our leader late Shrimati Indira Gandhi but bonded labour still exists in our country in one form or the other. In a conference, a high police official had expressed his views that political awareness among weaker sections, Scheduled Castes and Scheduled Tribes, for which credit goes to our Party, was one of the reasons for atrocities on them. The Congress Party has infused a sense of self-respect among them. Now when their self-respect is hurt, conflicts arise and atrocities are committed. Their women are raped and entire village is burnt. I have seen in Uttar Pradesh that atrocities are committed merely for such reasons. Bihar Government faced a lot of difficulties in implementing provisions of Minimum Wages Act. People who commit atrocities do not give minimum wages to these poor people. The Commissioner for Scheduled Castes and

Scheduled Tribes has mentioned in his report that farm labourers are given 5 kilograms of flour and some quantity of rice as daily wages or Rs. 8.50 in cash and it is also not known if it is actually paid or not, whereas an amount not less than Rs. 18.50 a day has been prescribed as the Minimum Wage under the Minimum Wages Act. Demand of minimum wages is one of the major causes of atrocities and harassment to Harijans.

Many aspects of the problem have been covered in this Bill. However, I would like to draw the attention of Hon. Minister towards some of points about which he has just made a mention. It is good that a provision has been made to set up special courts which was a long standing demand. In this regard, I would like to submit that cases of atrocities should be disposed of in summary trials, particularly in view of the fact that a number of years are wasted in investigation of the case and justice is not provided to them, as has been said by Shri Ram Ratan Ram. More the delay, more the injustice is done to them. While drawing attention towards section 4 of the Bill, the hon. Minister has stated that if public servant is found involved in it, he will also be punished. I would like to say in this connection that police officers also commit atrocities on Scheduled Castes and Scheduled Tribes. The Hon. Minister should think as to how he will tackle this problem of involvement of police officials in commissioning atrocities on these classes.

[Mr. Deputy-Speaker *in the Chair*]

Their FIRs will be written by the police officers. What provision has been made for this? The government should make special arrangements for the areas from where a large number of cases of atrocities are reported. It is true that different State Governments have appointed special IGs and DIGs for this purpose. But it would have been better if a provision is made specifically in this Bill itself. Of course, a provision has been made in section 4 with regard to atrocities to be committed by the public servants, still there is a need to look into this matter.

I would like to say one thing about the onus of proving the crime. You should think about it. Under section 5 of Prevention of Corruption Act and section 161 of IPC onus of proving innocence lies on the accused. Similarly, onus of proving innocence should be laid on the accused under this Bill. In that case, he will have to prove that he has not committed atrocities or he has not abused or insulted the complainant, then it will be a great thing. People will get justice. I welcome and support this Bill provisions of which are well considered.

I would like to conclude my speech with recital of a few lines of a poem of Shri Rangji:-

Ab na sahan hogi bebasi ki yatna,
Ant swayam kar raha srijan ki sadhana,
Aadmi ka kal aaj aadmi bana,
Ek-dusare se aaj ho rahi ghrina,
Aadmi ko aadmi ka pyar chahiye
Aaj desh ko naye vichar chahiye

and

Vartman ki ore dekhta
Aaj bhavishya mahan,
Kya jane kis khyan ho jaye
Navyug ka Nirman

By moving this Bill, government has done a very good work. I hope that 25 per cent people of this country will get relief from this Bill, their problems will be solved and their difficulties and troubles will be reduced.

With these words, I support the Bill.

Shri Harish Rawat (Almora): Hon. Deputy-Speaker, Sir, I would like to thank the Minister for Welfare for moving this Bill. This Bill is a warning to the people who kept on committing atrocities on the people belonging in Scheduled Castes and Scheduled Tribes by taking undue advantage of some lacunae in the law. I feel that the Hon. Minister has consolidated the various offences so as to include them in this Bill. This Bill has been drafted after indepth studies and careful consideration. I would like to extend my thanks to all those people who have assisted in drafting this Bill and consolidating the list of atrocities, etc.

Mr Deputy-speaker, Sir, laws were already there for giving protection to the people belonging to Scheduled Castes and Scheduled Tribes but the people who were entrusted responsibility to implement the law, belonged to the class who were aversed to it. That is why the law was not implemented properly. This is the reason why we have been raising this issue from time to time in this House.

I am in complete agreement with Shri Ganga Ram that with the awareness among Harijans, atrocities on Harijans have also increased. I would even like to add that whenever a government comes into power which thinks about the welfare of the Harijans and wants to give protection to them either at the Centre or in the States, incidents of atrocities increase as Harijans and Tribals resist atrocities in the hope that the present Government is benefactor and protector of their rights.

A debate was held in 1982 in this House on atrocities on Harijans. At that time Members belonging to Janata Party expressed view that incidents of atrocities on Harijans had gone down during the period from 1977 to 1980 when they were in power at the Centre, whereas the fact was otherwise atrocities were committed in greater degree but they were not reported because the victims did not want to go to police stations to lodge reports. If at all some of them went to police stations to lodge reports, their reports were not lodged by the police. When Congress Government as formed in 1980, a new awareness was created among Harijans and Tribals who began to feel secure. They again began to resist atrocities perpetrated on them in the villages.

I feel that the drawbacks and loopholes in IPC and criminal Procedure code will be plugged to a great extent after enactment of this Bill. Now accused will not take undue advantage of the loopholes to escape punishment for the crime. These drawbacks have been removed.

Hon. Deputy Speaker, Sir, it has all along been the policy of our government and the Congress Party that the weaker section should be protected. Even during the days of freedom struggle, Congress Party was the champion of the cause of weaker sections. Removal of untouchability was a part of our national struggle. When Gandhiji talked about freedom from the British rule, he also talked about removal of untouchability and religious discrimination. The Congress Party has inherited these ideals as its legacy. Voice has always been raised against those who commit atrocities. It is the reason why our government always thinks in this direction. So far as necessity of enactment of laws are concerned, necessary laws have been enacted to check atrocities on Harijans and weaker sections, even then atrocities on them have not stopped because of economic base of the people belonging to weaker sections, Harijans and Tribals is very weak. No atrocity is committed on the person who is economically sound. He can go to the court and seek protection. He can even resist but the Harijans and Tribals who are landless and unable to go to the court for remedy are subjected to atrocities. Even police does not heed to their complaints. He has no time to register their complaints.

Government has taken several steps in this direction. Very recently, Jawahar Rozgar Yojana has been introduced and representation of Harijans and weaker sections has been provided in panchayats. This been done because the government wants to make these sections economically self-reliant and to provide representation to them at the grass-root level. In this way, they will be able to express their views and raise their voice freely without any fear. Unless the weaker sections will be given ownership right of land, they will not be able to resist the atrocities being committed on them. Therefore, I would like to request the government through you that there is need to allot land to every Harijan under Land Reforms Act so that he is able to build his house on the land of his own and cultivate it for agricultural purposes. This is the primary duty of the government. Those who do not own agricultural land should be provided other means of livelihood. The government and the whole society should think in this direction so that the Harijans and the Tribals can become self-reliant. I think this will enable us to control the atrocities to a large extent and to solve the problem. With these words, I support this Bill and thank the Hon. Minister of State of the Ministry of Welfare, the Hon. Prime Minister and the government in this regard.

Shri Bapulal Malviya (Shajapur): Mr. Deputy Speaker, Sir, I support the Scheduled Castes and Scheduled Tribes (Prevention of Atrocities) Bill. Today, the Hon. Prime Minister has assured that all the reserved vacancies shall be filled up within a maximum period of three months and ceaseless efforts are being made to fulfil this pledge. This is a very significant step. It is for the first time since independence that the Hon. Prime Minister has taken the initiative of clearing the backlog of reserved vacancies. The Hon. Prime Minister has made a major contribution to the upliftment of the Scheduled Castes and Scheduled Tribes through the

Jawahar Rozgar Yojana. The Bill under consideration will also go a long way in solving the problems of the Scheduled Castes and Scheduled Tribes as is evident from its provisions.

Two of the provisions of this Bill are very appropriate. I would like to submit the social problems of the Scheduled Castes and Scheduled Tribes in the rural areas and expect that the Hon. Prime Minister will provide assistance in solving them. Apart from these problems, the primary problem is that of land. The 20-Point Programme Coordination Committee was constituted during the tenure of Shrimati Indira Gandhi. Lease deeds of land were given through these committees but they were not given actual possession of their land. What is the reason behind it. In this connection, the work of the Madhya Pradesh Government is laudable. The former Chief Minister of the State, Shri Arjun Singh and the present Chief Minister Shri Motilal Vora have done praiseworthy work. A committee by the name of 'Adhikar Abhiyan Samittee' has been constituted there and I am also a member of this committee. This committee has been doing commendable work. Those persons who were given lease deeds for land 15 to 20 years ago have been given actual possession of their land. The Collectors and Tehsildars in the State have been told that if the lease deed holders are not given possession of land, action will be taken against them. They were also told that if the Department of Revenue is incapable of carrying out this task, the assistance of Police should be taken. The results have been very encouraging 75 per cent of the lease deed holders have got possession of their land and only 25 per cent have still to get it. I think they will also get their possession shortly. Similar committees should be constituted all over the country. If a piece of land belonging to a Harijan happens to be located in between two plots of land belonging to an affluent person, his piece of land is forcibly occupied and he is evicted with the result that he is compelled to sell it off. As per my experience, if a Harijan has a piece of land in the village and it is also fertile, the caste Hindus would entrap him by turning him into an alcohol addict and would provide money for puchasing the same and in this way, they would eventually rob his piece of land. As in the case of Adivasis, there should be restrictions on the sale of land belonging to the Harijans as well. There should be a law to the effect that the land cannot be occupied forcibly. The land belonging to the Harijans are not registered with the result that they are often evicted by those to whom they owe money. The Hon. Minister has stated that 3000 cases of atrocities have come to their notice. Besides these cases, there are several cases which are not reported because the poor Harijans are prevented by the village musclemen from filing their complaints to the police in this regard. In this way many atrocities are committed on them, but the rich and influential people in the village do not allow them to report the matter to the police and even harm them physically. Some Harijans came to me with their complaints and they informed me that they had to take a separate and a longer route because they feared that the musclemen in their villages would prevent them from going to lodge the complaint. FIRs in this regard should be filed in the local police stations but they are unable to do so and they have to approach the SP for this purpose. These days the political leaders and even the police officers have little say with the result that cases are not registered. Only these influential people hold away and everybody is at their mercy. This is a very big problem. Presently, police stations have been set up exclusively for the Harijans. But in these police stations also, the situation is same. The policemen who register their complaints demand bribes and in this way atrocities are committed on the Harijans. It has also been observed that the Prevention of Untouchability Act has also not proved effective. It is necessary to make this law effective. During the Janata wave in 1977, a Harijan Congress worker was much harassed by the BJP workers. He was made to wear the clothes of a woman and made to dance on the streets. Such atrocities should be checked by framing necessary legislation. So far as I think, social programmes are based on social perspectives....

Shri Virdhi Chander Jain (Barmer): Provisions have been made in this Bill.

Shri Bapulal Malviya: I am putting forward one suggestion. You will observe that Harijans are discriminated against on social occasions and at public places. They are not allowed to sit at the same place with the caste Hindus. If the caste Hindus sit on the mats, the Harijans are told to sit somewhere else. If the Harijans sit on the mats, the caste Hindus sit on raised platform. This kind of discrimination which is practised everywhere should be removed. Atrocities are committed on women but they are prevented from reporting them. Much discrimination is practised in the rural areas. The Harijan children are not allowed to sit along with the children of other castes. In the tea-clubs of the teachers, the Harijan teachers are not included. The messengers also do not fetch tea for them nor do they wash their clothes. Consequently, the Harijan members of the staff refuse to become members of the staff tea-club. These are minor problems which should be removed. I think, the government should look into this aspect of practising discrimination even in places which are open to all. There are private temples in rural areas and the Harijans are not allowed to worship in these temples. The newly wed Harijan couples cannot enter into any temple and offer their prayers to the deity. Therefore, I would like to suggest that measures should be taken to build separate temples for Harijans in the Harijans colonies in order to avoid any confrontation. With these words, I thank the Hon. Minister for moving such a magnificant Bill and I would like to offer my support to it.

[*English*]

Shri Syed Shahabuddin (Kishanganj): Mr. Deputy Speaker, Sir, man's inhumanity to man has no limits. Indeed no species of life on this earth is as cruel to itself as the Homo-sapiens. This morning we woke up to the horrifying news of Gohpur, which is the latest case of atrocities. But my mind goes back to a few years ago when I visited a Harijan village in Andhra Pradesh, where everybody had been terrorised out of the village, except a lone woman, an old woman who had lost her mind and was loitering through the streets with a blank face and there was a dog following her. I could see the charred remains of rice in the granaries of various houses which had been turned into carbon. Madam, these atrocities are not only directed against a community, they are directed against the nation, they are directed against humanity, and it is with this sense and purpose that we have got to fight them out.... (*Interruptions*).

Shri Bipin Pal Das (Tezpur): When did that incident take place in Andhra Pradesh?

Shri Syed Shahabuddin: Around 1981 or 1982. I had a meeting of the National Executive of the Janata Party there at that time and then I visited that place.

Shri Bipin Pal Das: What is the name of that village?

Shri Syed Shahabuddin: I have forgotten the name. I will give it to the

Madam Minister some time.

Sir, man does not live by bread alone. He essentially needs dignity, he essentially needs a social existence, social recognition, social respect as a human being. Therefore, I congratulate the Hon. Minister for bringing this Bill before us. It has been overdue. We have long contended ourselves with an illusion that by passing the Protection of Civil Rights Act, we have done all that was needed, that by putting in beautiful phrases in the Constitution we have done all that was needed. I am happy that the government has realised that atrocities need to be dealt with a firm hand, with all the power this is at the command of a civilised State, with all the feelings and emotions that we can bring to bear on this despicable situation as human beings and as citizens of a country which swears by Mahatma Gandhi.

These atrocities cut across the political complexion of the State Governments and, therefore, one should not look at it as party question. It is a shame for the country. It is a national problem and we have got to look at it and deal with it as a national problem.

The other day a case was referred to here in the House of a Harijan being forced to eat human waste. I came across the other day a case in which a citizen of free India.... (*Interruptions*)

An Hon. Member: It was a place in Karnataka where Janata regime was there.

Shri Syed Shahabuddin: I also came across a similar case of a Harijan only recently, who had been forced to drink urine, in Uttar Pradesh in the very constituency of the Prime Minister and I have brought that case to the notice of the Prime Minister. Not that I am holding the Prime Minister responsible for that case of atrocity. Far from it. But what I am trying to say is that this is a social and a national malaise which cuts across political barriers and, therefore, we have got to unite here in this House to fight against this evil.

Here is a list of atrocities committed in 1987 and 1988. The figures are here. I do not know how far the figures represent the truth because many of these figures are only partial truth. It is only where a person finally gets across the many administrative, social and legal barriers to record his anguish and his pain and his shame that they appear here in the reply. But even as it is, they are rather revealing. I have got the figures for Bihar, Gujarat, Kerala, Madhya Pradesh, Rajasthan and Uttar Pradesh. I have chosen all those which have recorded more than 500 cases in a given year. There, six States alone account for 85% of the cases of atrocities recorded. I think some special effort has to be made by the Central Government and I would request the Hon. Minister to draw the attention of the Chief Ministers of these States to make a special study as to why is it that these State are responsible for so many atrocities. Therefore some very special methods are necessary to fight this evil in those States.

Mr. Deputy-Speaker, Sir, I would like to place a few suggestions before the Hon. Minister. It is absolutely necessary that the weaker sections like the 'Harijans' and the 'Adivasis' have due representation not only in the Police Force, but in the Intelligence machinery and in the Magistracy because the police does not act by itself. It is all these three agencies which together by their sins of omission and commission make such atrocities possible. Therefore, I would plead with the Hon. Minister to ensure that there is due representation in all these three branches and that not a single seat which is in the reserved/quota remains unfilled. What is more important is to have a composite pattern of deployment in the particular districts which are atrocities prone. For example, in every 'thana', in such areas, in every scheme of deployment of the magistrates in these areas, in these districts, you must ensure due representation of the weaker sections, I would suggest to the Hon. Minister for her consideration that in every district let there be one *thana* specially for recording the cases of atrocities and it should be manned from top to bottom by the weaker sections only. Just have one *thana*, call it by whatever name you like because the poor illiterate Harijans and Adivasis and weaker sections are not permitted access to the normal *thana*. They are shoved away. They are treated as sub-humans and they are not permitted to record their anguish. Whereas in such a separate *thana* their pain and sufferings shall be shared by the people in power and they shall be humanely impelled to record these cases of atrocities and it is these *thanas* which should then be responsible for investigating these cases of atrocities. The *thana* alone will not do. The political parties casting aside all the differences, and other social organisations, all those who speak in the name Gandhiji and Nehru must organise themselves into committees for the protection of civil rights at district level, at the town level so that any Harijan, any Adivasi, any member of the weaker section who feels aggrieved can go to them and seek their learned assistance and seek their expert help. Let these voluntary institutions be given full support by the government

Sir, I would like to suggest one thing which is not there in the Bill. Any person who is convicted of an act of atrocity as has been defined in this Act, should be disenfranchised from voting, from standing as a candidate in any elections in this country. He has no right to commit an atrocity and then come up and demand a share in running the society. Total disenfranchisement of any person who has been convicted of any offence under this Act including public service should be applied. I would like to draw the attention of the Hon. Minister to historic judgement recently by the Madras High Court, by the Justice Khadar. Of course, it was given in a different context. But the basic situation remains the same. His argument was that the State's primary duty is to protect the life and property of the citizen and if for some reason the police system of the State fails, the State is morally bound to compensate the citizen for the loss that he has suffered. Here in this Bill you talk about some compensation, some relief and rehabilitation as a gesture of generosity. No. It should be taken as a matter of right, as a matter of State obligation for the failure of its machinery for the failure to perform the duty that it is supposed to exist for. Therefore, there must be full compensation for all losses suffered, and for loss of lives and injury you must have a prescribed scale as there is in the case of Industrial Accident Act. Depending upon the age of the person, the earning period ahead of him, his earning capacity, you work out a definite reasonable sum that he would have earned had he lived. Similarly in the case of loss of property, there should be a compensation on the basis of full substitution, not that you give a Harijan a paltry sum of Rs 100/- to buy a few bamboos to re-erect his shelter. Whatever he has lost due to the negligence of the State, due to the failure of the machinery, must be fully compensated on the basis of substitution. Substitution cost should be the criterion for all losses of property. Of course, punitive line is mentioned there. But I would like to emphasize that the entire society is responsible for these atrocities, those who commit them and also those who remain silent spectators. Therefore, take the mohalla as a unit, take the panchayat as a unit or take the revenues village as a unit and let everybody contribute towards the punitive fine so that out of the punitive fine, you can pay the compensation that I have just demanded.

Sir, as far as the public servants are concerned, there is a lovely clause which I welcome fully. They are subject to prosecution, but they must be punished even administratively because sometimes it may not be possible to bring home the charge, to prove it in a court of law. Therefore, there must be administrative punishment for anybody who is negligent, who is found not to have acted in time, who is found to have looked the other way while the atrocities have been committed and atleast there should be a black mark in his record. He should at least be subjected to suspension.

Sir, I fully support the view of Mr. Ganga Ram that there should be a summary trial. Merely a special court would not do. A special court must have a summary procedure and a time-bound activity in order that these atrocities can be controlled.

I am fully conscious of the fact that violence and atrocities will continue to mount in our society because we are passing through a state of transition. People are standing up and demanding their rights. People are asking for the minimum that are due to them under the law of the land. They do not want anything more and yet for that cry, they are punished. Even today, I have seen a report from Bihar where some Harijans merely for the sin of asking for minimum wages were fired upon one person was killed and 30 others injured. Therefore, you have to steel your nerves, if the State, is to exist as a civilised State, you have got to gird up your loins, you have to stand up to this challenge and you have got to take a full measure of the situation of whatever power has been vested in you by the people of India and bring it to bear upon those mischievous elements who are bringing disgrace to the country until Gandhi's dream is realised, until justice dawns in our society, until we learn to treat each other as human beings and no as 'them' not as another group, but as human beings and as common citizens of a free India.

[*Translation*]

***Shri Harihar Soren** (Keonjhar): Mr. Deputy Speaker, Sir, I rise to

*Translation of the speech originally delivered in Oriya.

support the Scheduled Castes and Scheduled Tribes (Prevention of Atrocities) Bill. Sir, 40 years have passed since we achieved independence. The Government of India have taken a number of steps for the welfare of Scheduled Castes and Scheduled Tribes. But, it is a matter of great regret that these people are still neglected. They are still suppressed and oppressed by the upper caste people. So, this Bill will go a long way in protecting the Scheduled Castes and Scheduled Tribes from the atrocities. So, I welcome this Bill. The Honourable Minister, Smt. Bajpaiji is looking after this Ministry. She has studied the problems of the Scheduled Castes and Scheduled Tribes. Therefore, she has brought this Bill before the House. There are some good provisions in this Bill. But, mere passing of the Bill and making Act will not be able to stop atrocities on Scheduled Castes and Scheduled Tribes. We have to find out the root cause for the atrocities which are being perpetuated on them. If we make a proper analysis of it we will see that social, economical and educational backwardness are the main reasons as to why atrocities are being perpetuated on them. The entire Scheduled Caste and Scheduled Tribc population in the country is not educated. Due to their illiteracy, they are not able to know many things which are going on in the country. Since the economic condition of these people is not sound, they are not able to get respectable status in the society. Of course, our government have launched several schemes for the upliftment of the Scheduled Castes and Scheduled Tribes. The government want to enhance their status in the society by conferring many economic benefits on them through various schemes. But the duty of the government will not be over by launching those schemes and by allocating funds under those schemes. The government is to see as to whether the schemes launched for the welfare of Scheduled Castes and Scheduled Tribes are effectively implemented or not, the government is to see as to whether funds earmarked under those schemes are properly utilised or not. So far as my information is concerned, the officials who are put incharge of implementing various schemes for the socio-economic development of Scheduled Castes and Scheduled Tribes are not doing their duties honestly and sincerely. They are not able to provide benefits to all the beneficiaries.

Similarly the officials who are supposed to maintain law and order and to protect the lives and property of the Scheduled Castes and Scheduled Tribes are not able to give them due protection at the appropriate time.

They are not able to check atrocities perpetrated on them (Scheduled Castes and Scheduled Tribes).

If we will not be able to give due protection to the SCs and STs, the situation will further aggravate in future and it will be beyond control. Sir, I would like to say a word about the Reservation policy of the government. I thank the government for making reservation of posts of SCs and STs. In the past the posts reserved for SCs and STS were not being filled by SCs and STs, on the plea of the non-availability of suitable candidates from among them. I am grateful to the government that special drives have been launched to clear the backlog of employment of SC and ST candidates. This will protect the interest of the candidates. In this context I would like to say onething. Sir, at some places we find that the SC and ST candidates are able to secure the marks supposed to be secured by general candidates. That means they are qualified to get the posts reserved for general candidates. But it is seen that whatever best may be their performance they are appointed only against the posts reserved for them. If we take this attitude then the upliftment of SCs and STs will not become possible.

[Shri Sharad Dighe *in the Chair*]

Sir, you know the present situation in the country. At one place it is Uttarakhand, at another place it is Jharkhand, at some other place it is Bahujan Samaj Vadi and at some other place it is Bodo in the name of the movements are rising their ugly head. I do not support these movements. But we can not reject the issue simply by saying that the movements are unlawful. What are the root causes of their movements? Is it a fact that the people involved in those movements are being neglected since long, is it a fact that they are being suppressed by the upper caste people, if so, how will the government protect them? How will the government take action against the people who are exploiting them? All these factors should be studied very carefully. If we will be able to stop atrocities, if we will improve their economic conditions and if we will give them proper status in the society, they will never be involved in any kind of movement. Atleast I know that the tribals are simple and innocent and they are peace loving people. So, we must provide them protection and we must give them social justice. The Honourable Minister an experienced Minister. I request her to study the burning problems of SCs and STs. Then she should take immediate steps to tackle those problems. Otherwise you cannot cow down them. Because 40 years after independence now a kind of awareness is being created among them. They know that due justice has not been given to them in all these years. Therefore, please find out someways to remove their problems and restore peace in the society. Sir, our government have drawn up various schemes for the upliftment of SCs and STs. Most of those schemes are being implemented in the country. But it is regrettable that the state governments are not very sincere in the effective implementation of those schemes. Therefore, I would like to urge upon the central government to send necessary instructions to the state governments to implement those schemes with right earnestness and sincerity. Because it involves the upliftment of SCs and STs.

Sir, my second request is with regard to the better administration in the tribal areas. Some provisions have been made in this regard in the 5th and 6th Schedules of our Constitution. These provisions have been made to tackle the problems of tribals. Separate administrative systems have been provided in some tribal populated areas under the provisions made by the 6th Schedule of the Constitution. It is seen that the people are living peacefully in those areas. They are not being exploited by the upper caste people. The development process is taking place in full swing in those areas. The people living in those areas are very much satisfied with the existing administration. But the situation in other tribal areas which are under 5th schedule is different. The people have many grievances. In order to help them getting the full benefit of the various schemes which are being implemented by the government and in order to give them due justice it is very necessary to bring all the tribal areas under the 6th Schedule and necessary administrative system should be introduced in those areas. With these suggestions I thank you very much and conclude my speech.

[*English*]

Shri Digvijay Singh (Rajgarh): Sir, I rise to support the Bill and congratulate our Prime Minister Shri Rajivji and our Welfare Minister Shrimati Bajpaiji for bringing this Bill which, I hope, shall go a long way to curb the atrocities on Scheduled Castes and Scheduled Tribes.

Sir, it is unfortunate that in spite of giving Scheduled Castes and Scheduled Tribes the constitutional protection and protecting them under the Civil Rights Act 1955 and various provisions of Cr. P.C. and IPC, we have been unable to curb the atrocities on SC and ST. We must realise that it is the structure which is coming in the way. We find that the system is not responding to the needs of today and it is not solving the problem at the ground level and, that is why, whenever we find a situation like this, we again come back to bring in some kind of different law to make the penal provisions more stringent. What is needed is a political will at the state and district level so that the enforcing authority and the political masters take stringent action against those persons who are committing these atrocities on Scheduled Castes and Scheduled Tribes.

I welcome the penal provisions made against those officers who are negligent in their duty regarding the provisions made in this Bill. But I do not understand why the officers belonging to Scheduled Castes and Scheduled Tribes have been exempted from these penal provisions. I feel that officers and the public servants belonging to this section of Scheduled Castes and the Scheduled Tribes have a greater responsibility to see that these penal provisions of this Bill and the provisions of this Bill are faithfully implemented because ultimately it is their kith and kin who are to be helped. I request the Hon. Minister to consider and delete this provision.

I do not understand why, although after making the penal provisions, we are not monitoring the percentage of conviction in such cases. Simply booking them under the law and bringing them before the court is not the answer. We have to ensure, through a close monitoring of such cases, that conviction is to a higther level and then only, we shall be able to curb this. We have cut across by setting up special courts in this Bill. But that is not all. After all, he still has a right to appeal to the High Court and the Supreme Court. This itself will take years before the accused can be punished. The judicial structure today in this country, I am sorry to state—is heavily loaded against the poor. Although, we have provided for payment of travelling allowances and miscellaneous expenses for witnesses and the victims, still it is the duration of the actual crime committed and the punishment given which is detrimental to such happenings occurring again and again. This is why, I feel that it is time when the government itself thought about the restructuring of the whole judicial process whereby the right to appeal is restricted.

It is a very welcome sign that the provisions have been made to rehabilitate the victims of such atrocities to an extent possible. What is needed is that, as rightly pointed out by Shahabuddinji, we have to fix the quantum of the rehabilitation and the compensation paid. Otherwise, it may differ from state to state and according to the whims and fancies of different persons.

As I pointed out earlier, untouchability is an offence under the present law. But is it being enforced? Have we eradicated untouchability from our country? I am sorry to state that we have not. Still in the villages we have separate wells for Harijans, separate temples of Harijans. Why have we not been able to take action against those persons who are practising untouchability in the rural areas? I am sorry to say, a person of the stature of Sankaracharya of Puri openly advocated untouchability through the Press and he did not contradict that report. We have not taken action against him. We want more Jayendra Saraswathis in this country—the Sankaracharya of Kanchi—who are working for the uplift of the Harijans and working against untouchability.

It is the responsibility of the caste Hindus to see that atrocities are not committed against SC and ST people. We have to change our frame of mind and accept them as brothers. Then only will we be able to make progress on this issue.

I feel that some of the provisions made are a little harsh. Simply throwing of waste in front of the house of a Harijan has been made a cognizable offence. Those people who know the village closely would realise that this would be a daily occurrence. How many cases will you register? This would give way for the police officers at *thana* level to harass people. So we have to reconsider this. Throwing of agriculture waste is not such an offence as could be made cognizable; this could be deleted from the Act.

I strongly support the stringent penal provisions made regarding the usurping and the wrongful occupation of the land allotted to the SC and ST. There is ample scope for this provision because we find that the land allotted in the rural areas has been by and large taken away by the powerful people. It is there even in Madhya Pradesh. I should be ashamed of myself to come from a state where the highest atrocities take place in this country. We have take a very positive step in the state of Madhya Pradesh whereby through a special programme of Adhikar Abhiyan, we have taken up restoration of land to the title holders. You would be happy to know that 62000 people who were not in possession of their land and were only holding Pattas has been given land under this programme.

The problem is more socio-economic than prohibitive or regulatory. We realise that 66 per cent of the rural landless in this country are from SC. What is needed is mass oriented agrarian reform, faithfully implemented and monitored by specially constituted land tribunals and manned by people belonging to the SC and ST or by persons who have a definitely known leanings for the SC and ST. Then only will we be able to implement faithfully these land reforms.

Today, although we have fixed the minimum wages, they are not being given. Although we have fixed minimum wages. I know from any experience, they are not being given. Until and unless such things are monitored closely by some special committees or by the land tribunals, we will not be able to justify our intentions.

Land absorbing and land augmenting technical innovations have to be made. You would agree with me that most of the disputes which arise in the rural areas are through non-payment of wages or poor payment of wages. The government has to step in where we provide adequate work for at leas about hundred days in a year. We are very happy, the Hon. Prime Minister Shri Rajiv Gandhi has come out with special programmes under the Jawahar Rozgar Yojana. The other point is politically decenation until we politically decentralise power and give power directly to the elected representatives of the people, we will not be able to enforce these laws and all these programmes.

Another thing is the grass-root mobilisation of the Scheduled Castes and the Scheduled Tribes and bringing about an awareness amongst them that they enjoy fundamental rights under the Constitution, and that they enjoy civil rights under the Civil Rights Act. Until and unless they know the provisions of the Act, we will not be able to bring them up to the mainstream.

Administrative restructuring and planning from below is another feature which is important. Shri Rajivji has rightly taken the initiative to decentralise the power to Panchayati Raj and also provide work for the landless. Now that we have taken the initiative, the ball is in the court of the state leaders—the politicians in the state capitals to implement these laws and regulations.

I would like to say a word about the tribals. We have a large tribal population and especially in my state of Madhya Pradesh, they are about 22.5 per cent. The Jharkhand movement has been going on for a very long time. We have to give a serious thought to it. I congratulate the Hon. Home Minister for starting a dialogue with the Jharkhand leaders. What are they asking for? They want to be the masters of their own destiny. What are they asking for? They are only asking for self-rule. If we can give it to the Gorkhas of the Darjeeling, why cannot we give it to the tribals of the Central India? It is a serious thing which we have to consider with an open mind. Let us not reject it outright. After all, you cannot deliver the goods at the lowest level until and unless you have the people's involvement in the system, people's involvement in the delivery of the schemes, policies and the programmes. Therefore, I faithfully urge upon the Minister to convey my feelings to the Hon. Prime Minister and to the Home Minister to consider this very seriously.

Prof. N.G. Ranga (Guntur): Your Chief Minister also. That is the real trouble.

Shri Digvijaya Singh: Certainly, Sir, I have said it earlier. The ball is in the court of the Chief Ministrs because ultimately they are the people who are to implement the laws at the grass-root level.

In the end, I once again congratulate the Hon. Prime Minister. He has shown by his actions—whether by filling the vacancies in the Scheduled Castes and the Scheduled Tribes quota or by giving reservations in the Panchayati Raj System and now with the present Bill he has brought forward—that he is cast in the same mould of the Congress giants like Pandit Jawaharlal Nehru, Mahatma Gandhi who have brought in a revolution in this country. Here, of course, what remains will be eradicated by this Bill.

Shri P.M. Sayeed (Lakshadweep): Mr. Chairman, Sir, I congratulate the Hon. Minister for having brought this Bill before this House. It is a well-thought-out Bill. It deals with almost every aspect regarding the atrocities committed against the Harijans and Adivasis in our country.

As you know, we have passed many laws in this very House on eradication of untouchability, civil rights and many other laws. But, why is it that the atrocities are on the increase? My humble view is that, of late, on account of the increase in the percentage of literacy and also of the improvement in the economic field, the Harijans and Adivasis are trying to assert their rights. Naturally, they will assert their rights. Some old feudal, affluent, powerful, high-caste sections of our society will naturally resist with more vigour to see that the rights these communities want to assert get defeated. When these atrocities are going on in this country what are we do to do? The point I want to make is that this Bill after having been passed should not meet the same fate as the earlier Acts like eradication of untouchability and civil rights had met with.

There are many salient features in the present Bill which is proposed to be passed. For example, for the first time we are fixing the responsibility on the officers who are going to implement this piece of legislation at the grassroot level. Supposing this piece of legislation also meets the same fate as the earlier ones then what do we propose to do. My suggestion for that would be that at least, in the first instance, you will be in a position to know such atrocity prone areas in the country where atrocities are committed on the Scheduled Castes and Scheduled Tribes. Now such are as will get identified. Secondly the officers who have got sympathy towards these communities must also be identified and some awards should be given to them whenever they implement the provisions of this Bill in letter and spirit.

Mr. Chairman, Sir, I would also like to congratulate the Hon. Prime Minister for this. He has toured the length and breadth of this country and seen the plight of the Harijans and the Adivasis. Even the Hon. Minister herself has arranged so many seminars, conventions, meetings of the Scheduled Castes and Scheduled Tribes MPs and MLAs and other experts. After having studied the problem in depth she has brought this measure. We only hope that this will meet the requirements of the country. It is really very sad even after forty years of independence the Scheduled Castes and Scheduled Tribes population of our country — which is about 25 per cent — are not able to assert their rights and we are not in a position to give them their due share. The intention of the government is very well spelt out in this measure. I would have been happy if the opposition had been here and participated in the debate and given their suggestions. Instead of that they have chosen to remain outside and accuse the government of bringing in all these measures with an eye on the coming general elections. The other day when the Panchayati Raj Bill was being discussed many Hon. Members had touched this point. For four long years that aspect had been deliberated upon and fifteen thousand experts had cooperated and discussions were held at length. After that, it was brought before the House. The Harijans and Adivasis are now goint to be given reservation in each village panchayat according to their population. Why should we not ask the State Governments to make such laws to see that these measures are implemented through them? There will be an inbuilt mechanism through which they themselves can spot out where exactly the troubles are taking place.

I feel that it is good measure and has to be endorsed by one and all in this House. I think, if it is implemented with the same intention with which this has been brought before the House, the age-old atrocities and other inhuman things which are being inflicted by various high-castes, powerful and affluent sections of the rural society, will definitely be checked. Therefore, I wholeheartedly support this measure and congratulate the Prime Minister once again. Thank you very much.

Shrimati Basavarajeswari (Bellary): Mr. Chairman, Sir, I am happy to thank the Hon. Minister for having brought forward this historic and revolutionary Bill. We have already passed the historic Panchayati Raj and Nagarpalika Bills.

Most of us refuse to become the Minister of Social Welfare—myself and Dr. Rajendra Kumari Bajpai being exceptions. When ministerships are offered, most of them would like to become Industry Minister, Finance Minister or Minister for some other department. But nobody is willing to become Minister for Social Welfare unless he or she is very much sympathetic and can involve in the welfare of the poorer sections of the society. In that way, I congratulate Madam Bajpai for having taken charge as minister for Welfare and having 'brought this historic Bill. I too was Minister for Social Welfare in Karnataka State. I know something about the atrocities on and welfare of the people belonging to the Scheduled Castes and Scheduled Tribes.

Prof. N.G. Ranga: So, we congratulate you both.

Shrimati Basavarajeswari: We have already taken several measures to uplift the socially and economically backward people. But still we could not overcome this problem. We have taken up a lot of antipoverty programmes like IRDP, NREP, RLEGP. But what benefits have reached them? I am very sorry to say that the benefits have not reached them fully. There are various reasons which I am going to explain shortly.

As stated by the Hon. Minister, we have given scholarships for their education. We have distributed the surplus land for their socio-economic gains. We ask them to cultivate the wasteland wherever it is available. We have asked them to cultivate forest land wherever it exists. We have worked out so many schemes for the welfare and economic upliftment of these sections. But what is going on? The real fact is that the schemes through which we are doing our best to help them, are not reaching them. The reason behind this. Unless and until we bring total prohibition in this country, I don't think we would be in a position to bring them on par with others. Whatever amount we give and whatever wages they earn and whatever economic benefits we give for them are being misused by this section of the society. The first and foremost thing which we have to think is of total prohibition in this country. We may lose some revenue by this. But we should not mind. We are the followers of Gandhiji and so, we should be proud to say that we are going in for total prohibition in this country. If we want the poor ladies to be protected from all these evils, this is the only measure. By this measure, we can make them economically and morally well-off.

The next point is about education. We are trying our best to give education to everybody. We have been implementing the ICDC project for the welfare of children and also nutrition programme. I would like to know as to many centres have been started in the colonies. So many 'anganwadis' have been started under the ICDC project but I find that very few of them have been started in Harijan colonies. When we start more and more 'anganwadis', we should try to see that children who are brought in one environment are shifted to another environment. Only then, the whole scheme will be successful. We have to change their environment first. How best to change their environment will depend on starting more and more 'anganwadis' in the colonies instead of doing the same in the towns where there are more facilities to enjoy. We should try to see that more 'anganwadis' and health centres are started in the tribal areas and Harijan localities and so also the schools. We have started more schools under the new education policy. We are going to strengthen secondary education under this new education policy. There are a number of single-room schools in the Colonies. There are hundreds of children studying in such schools. We should try to strengthen education in these colonies by providing more and more schools and more and more teachers. We should make it compulsory for children to attend their schools. I would like to know from the Hon. Minister as to how many drop-outs are there. You try to make a survey of the whele subject and try to find the number of drop-outs. Children attend schools at the most upto fourth or fifth standard or SSLC. After that, very few go to college due to poverty.

And for the same, parents are not in a position to send their children to college. We have to provide them with some alternatives so that they need not depend upon the wages of their children. They take their children to the fields just to supplement their income. How can we create a feeling among people that they can live without the wages of their children?

These things should be taken care of. Moreover, they have their own differences, such as, they belong to this group or that group. I do not understand as to why there are disparities. Whenever I visit them, I have been telling them not to try to establish such kinds of disparities and we all belong to the same nation and they all belong to the same weaker sections of the society. And if they fight among themselves, what will be the outcome? We must remember Madam Gandhi on the floor of this House. She had brought the political awareness among the minorities, backward classes and Harijans. She had taught us about our rights. But till now, we are not utilising those rights properly. Minister stated, while defining atrocity, that when we ask for our rights, atrocities are committed on us. What has happened in Karnataka? We are pained to see that such things still continue in this country. In Karnataka there was a reformer in the 12th century, Lord Basava. Prof. Ranga knows that. He wanted to eradicate social evils in our society. He made revolutionary reformation in Karnataka. He was a great reformer. He made one Harijan girl marry a Brahmin boy. But he was so much harassed and tortured that he had to leave the kingdom and he committed suicide. He did his best in those days in the 12th century. And today, in the 20th century, we are shameful to see that such things are being practised. As Shri Shahabuddin said, this is not to be viewed politically. It is a national issue. Everybody should take it that we are all one in these matters. We should try to love each other.

As survey was undertaken and it revealed that persons who belonged to the same community, Scheduled Castes or Scheduled Tribes, once they achieved something, they were not very much in favour of developing their own brothers and sisters. Why is it so? Why do they forget their own brothers and sisters? The survey also revealed that they were ashamed to go to their own colonies. Why should it be so? In fact, they should be involved more in these kinds of things. We must put an end to this sort of attitude.

Then, under the Land Reforms Act, surplus land has been given to these poor people. Wherever we have given land, there should be some checks and balances to find out whether the land given to these people is being cultivated by them. Legally, their name may be there in the record, but who is the person actually cultivating it? The fact is that it is being cultivated by somebody else. Who takes the amount of fertilizers given to them? The moment they get the fertilizer, they sell it. What about the implements and seeds being given to them? That is not going into their hands. What is the reason for that? You should find out and set these things right. You should not think only one line, you should think the other way also.

What about the facilities being extended to them under the various schemes like IRDP? We give them buffaloes, cows, bulls and so many other things. If you go and see next day, you will not find them there. That is why we are not achieving the development that was anticipated by us. The real benefits are not reaching the beneficiaries. You should try to find out the reason. You must have a check on the persons who are not utilizing the aid being given to them. Unless we do this, I do not think, the benefits will reach the proper persons. We should be very careful in these things.

Dr. Ambedkar, during the days when the Constitution was being drafted was awake at 2 o'clock in the night one day. I read that in one of the books. When one of his friends asked him why he was awake at that time, he said: "How can I sleep unless my poor people can sleep during the night?" There is still a lot to be done. Poverty is still there; so many social evils are still prevalent in our society. Even today the devdasi system is very much prevalent. Girls are being offered in the name of God freely. Such social evils need to be eradicated. Devdasi system, nude processions etc. in the name of God are very much prevalent in States like Maharashtra and Karnataka. Unless we put an end to these systems, I do not know how we can call ourselves as civilized persons. We are ashamed to see that our sisters are being offered in the name of God freely, which ultimately leads to prostitution. These things should be immediately curbed, Some of the States, I think, enacted laws to rehabilitate these unfortunate devdasis and their children, but that has not proved effective. Those devdasis and children are very much there. Some serious though has to be given, so that these ladies and children are rehabilitated and kept in proper and good environment, so that the children can be given proper education. Unless these evils are checked, I don't think by bringing this legislation we are going to improve the entire social and economic structure of this community. The word 'atrocities' has been defined very nicely but the only thing is that it has to be implemented also by way of morally as well as legally enforcing the law. At the same time people should be given proper education and teachings. All the 'swamijis', 'gurus', Lords and 'dharmagurus' should come forward to teach the people that we are all one. Unless our leaders come forward and give a call to the nation, we don't think that we can enact it firmly and the condition of these people will improve. With these words, I thank you very much.

[*Translation*]

Shri Manikrao Hodlya Gavit (Nandurbar): Mr. Chairman, Sir, I am grateful to you for providing me an opportunity to express my views on Scheduled Castes and Scheduled Tribes (Prevention of Atrocities) Bill. The Hon. Minister has taken a good step by moving this Bill. I would like to thank her for this step. In view of the provisions made in this Bill and the views expressed by the Hon. Members of the Parliament, I can say that if the provisions of this Bill are implemented properly by the Centre and the State Governments, the Scheduled Castes and the Scheduled Tribes will get justice.

Mr. Chairman, Sir, as you also belong to Maharashtra, you are well aware of the atrocities being committed on the people belonging to Scheduled Castes and Scheduled Tribes in almost all States of the country. It is known to all the Hon. Members of the House including myself being a Scheduled Tribes, besides other people, police personnel also commit atrocities on them. Despite enactment of laws, atrocities are still being committed by the public as well as the police. Whenever a victim of atrocities goes to police station to lodge a complaint he is confined in police lock up where he is threatened to the extent that he loses his confidence in lodging a complaint. Such types of atrocities are not reported. In the tribal society in my district, exorcism is practised. The exorcist is called 'Bhagat' in local dialect. These *Bhagats* often have long hairs on their heads and treat the people of their diseases. A complaint was lodged against a *Bhagat* of my area that he had stolen a thing from the field. Despite the fact that *Bhagat* owns 27-28 acres of land, the police dragged him by the hair, and lodged him in the police lock-up. He was not only beaten but he was also made baldpated by the police. When he made a complaint, it was not lodged. When I came to know about it and enquired from the Superintendent of Police, he did not deny the fact that the complaint had not been registered. Whenever a poor man or a tribal goes to the police to lodge a complaint, his complaint is registered but later on it is said that no atrocities has been committed. It is said that when the Department of Welfare was a part of the Ministry of Home Affairs, it had more say in the States. But now it has been made an independent department. So I would request the Hon. Minister to do the needful so that the Department could exercise more authority over the States.

The Minimum Wages Act has been made for the poor and the Scheduled Castes and Scheduled Tribes. But it has not been implemented properly in many states. Attention should be paid to this also.

Recently, our Hon. Prime Minister Shri Rajiv Gandhi has made an extensive tours of the areas inhabited by the people belonging to Scheduled Tribes. We visited the huts of these poor people. He saw there the magnitude of poverty and felt their needs. For this reason, this Bill has been brought here.

The Hon. Prime Minister has instructed that the backlog of reserved vacancies for the persons belonging to Scheduled Castes and Scheduled Tribes under the Government of India and the State Governments should be cleared. Their quota of reservation as provided in the constitution should be fulfilled. Recently, I have received a complaint that the postal department in Maharashtra has advertised some posts under special drive in a newspaper named *Lok Satta*. Applications were to be sent within seven days. I would like to submit to the Hon. Minister that how a candidate can send his application within seven days. No candidate belonging to these categories would apply to the post. As a result thereof, backlog will not be cleared and the officer concerned will write to his superior that "candidate not available". When a super class I officers in Maharashtra circle have this type of attitude towards us, what can we expect from the lower level officers? Our Hon. Prime Minister wants that the backlog should be cleared. But how it can be cleared when they are given 7 days' time to send applications. Attention should be paid in this regard. The time schedule as directed by the Hon. Prime Minister for clearance of the backlog should be extended further. The last date by which backlog is to be cleared is 31st October, 1989. It should be extended further.

I have heard that special courts have been set-up for trial of cases of atrocities committed on the people belonging to Scheduled Castes and Scheduled Tribes. When their complaints are not registered in the police stations, who will heed to their complaints in the court?

A big irrigation project by the name of Sardar Sarovar Project is being set up on Narmada river at a place where borders of Madhya Pradesh, Maharashtra and Gujarat meet. Land of 33 villages of Maharashtra and some tribal villages of Gujarat is being acquired for this project. Nothing has been done so far for their rehabilitation. Neither any alternative land nor adequate compensation for their land is being given to them. They are given land by the government, on town planning rate, whereas the land of poor is acquired at throwaway prices at Rs. 4 to 5 thousand an acre only. The government is in favour of doing something in this regard. Unless government takes some steps justice cannot be done to the people belonging to the Scheduled Castes and Scheduled Tribes.

District Rural Development Agencies have been formed to implement all these programmes. This agency is also responsible for implementing the schemes under the Jawahar Rozgar Yojana. The funds provided to the Gram Panchayats under Jawahar Rozgar Yojana will be spent through this agency. I would like to submit that officers of clean record only should be posted in these agencies, all the money will be pocketed by them and the tribals and the poor will get nothing. That is why I am giving stress time and again on the fact that the government should take steps to provide justice to the poor with much alacrity.

I would also like to submit that a large number of persons belonging to communities other than the SC/ST have availed of facilities by producing bogus caste certificate. On the basis of bogus certificates, they got admission in various educational institutions such as ITIs, medical colleges and engineering colleges, etc. These bogus tribals living in cities are enjoying facilities meant for the tribals living in hill areas. They obtain caste certificates on the basis of affidavit. Thus the genuine tribals are deprived of their facilities. I urge upon the government to weed out bogus tribals. In 1977, the Government of India removed the area restriction. Due to this decision, a number of non-eligible persons could get caste certificates showing themselves as tribals. Those certificates as still valid.

Recently a Central Minister paid a visit to a Department of Central

Government. He said there that the caste certificates should be issued on permanent basis. I told him that I am a tribal myself and I never heard such thing. Such authority helps the bogus people.

In the end, I would like to submit that if the Hon. Minister is really sincere to check the atrocities on Harijans and Tribals, then he should give a serious thought to my suggestions.

Shri Janak Raj Gupta (Jammu): Mr. Chairman, Sir, the disease got aggrated with every dose of medicine. It is not for the first time that we are confronted with the fact that a lot of atrocities are committed on the Harijans. There is hardly a State where this malady is not present. Of course, somewhere it is in lesser degree and somewhere it is in acute form. A number of laws have been enacted from time to time by the government to check atrocities on the Scheduled Castes and Scheduled Tribes. There is no doubt that it has been checked to some extent. The Bill moved by Shrimati Bajpai is the need of the hour. It was a long felt demand of the people. Provisions of this Bill needs to be implemented strictly.

Before I could say something about the provisions of the Bill, I would like to draw the attention of the Hon. Minister towards section 3 of the Bill. In this connection I would like to suggest an amendment. In section 3 (A), for "whoever, not being a member of a Scheduled Castes or a Scheduled Tribes, ...". The word "whoever" is sufficient and words "not being a member of a Scheduled Caste and Scheduled Tribe" should be deleted. Only then the purpose of this Bill will be served. Suppose, an officer belonging to Scheduled Castes or Scheduled Tribes commits atrocities on Scheduled Castes and Scheduled Tribes and tries to deprive them of their rights he will not be punished under the provision of this Bill as many of our learned Members have stated that as soon as economic conditions of a person belonging to the Scheduled Castes and Scheduled Tribes improves, he does not want to live in the colony or locality in which he used to live earlier with his other brethren

(*English*)

Mr. Chairman: It is already 4 p.m. The House shall take up discussion under Rule 193. So, you can continue next time. You, please resume your seat.

The Minister of State of the Ministry of Welfare (Dr. Rajendra Kumari Bajpai): Madam, I beg to move:

"That the Bill to prevent the commission of offences of atrocities against the members of the Scheduled Castes and the Scheduled Tribes, to provide for Special Courts for the trial of such offences and for the relief and rehabilitation of the victims of such offences and for matters connected therewith or incidental thereto, as passed by the Lok Sabha, be taken into consideration."

This House is aware of the deep concern that our Prime Minister and our government have for the welfare of the Scheduled Castes and the Scheduled Tribes. Many new initiatives have been taken particularly in the last few years to improve the lot of the Scheduled Castes and the Scheduled Tribes. Since we got independence Pt. Jawaharlal Nehru and then Mrs. Indira Gandhi and now our Prime Minister have been trying to improve the economic and social condition of the Scheduled Castes and Scheduled Tribes. In trying to discharge a mandate of the Constitution. Poverty Alleviation Programmes which provide special attention to the Scheduled Castes and Scheduled Tribes have been expanded and intensified. First the IRDP and other programmes were improved considerably and now these have been replaced by a bigger scheme of the Jawahar Rozgar Yojana. Drinking water wells and irrigation wells have been provided for this group. The needs of housing have been met by the Indira Awas Yojana. The programme for liberation of scavengers has been given a greater impetus. The education of Scheduled Castes and Scheduled Tribes which is of crucial importance to their growth and development has received much greater attention. The number of students studying beyond the Matriculation stage has gone up to 13 lakhs. Coaching centres have been increased. A special drive is currently on for filling up the backlog which had arisen as a result of non-fulfilment of reserved seats for SC/ST. And that drive is continuing. Efforts are also being made to free them from bonded labour and to find land for cultivation. As you all know among the landless labourers about 48 per cent are from the Scheduled Castes and Scheduled Tribes.

We are witnessing today the sign of fruits of development reaching the Scheduled Castes and Scheduled Tribes. With greater spread of education and with the socio-economic condition improving the relations in society sometimes come under tension as a result of this change. Higher caste groups sometimes do not like the change in the socio-economic structure and tensions develop. The demand for justice, for equality for a human living standard, for knowledge, for education and freedom leads, in some cases, to retaliation by groups which are not enlightened enough to recognise the healthy signs of growth.

Madam, previously also the Government of India has tried to remove untouchability. In the Constitution we have abolished untouchability. But to remove it completely from the society, in 1955 the protection of Civil Rights Act was passed and again, to give it more teeth, some more clauses were added to it in 1976. Now we find that is not enough. This Act was passed specifically for the removal of untouchability and against those who are practising untouchability. The Bill which I am bringing here is especially against atrocities. For the first time, we have defined atrocities in this Bill. There are 15 types of atrocities which we have identified. I will not read it. I will mention only two or three points. The Bill defines as follows:

> 'If somebody forces a member of the Scheduled Caste or Scheduled Tribe to drink or eat any inedible or obnoxious substance; or
>
> forcibly removes clothes from the person of a member of a Scheduled Caste or a Scheduled Tribe or parades him naked or with painted face or body or does any similar act which is derogatory to human dignity; or
>
> wrongfully occupies and cultivates any land owned or allotted to or notified by any competent authority to the Scheduled Caste or Scheduled Tribe or gets the land allotted to him transferred; or
>
> wrongfully dispossesses a member of a Scheduled Caste or a Scheduled Tribe from his land or premises or interferes with the enjoyment of his rights over any land or premises or water; or
>
> compels or entices a member of a Scheduled Caste or a Scheduled Tribe to do *begar* or any other similar form of forced or bonded labour other than any compulsory services for public purposes imposed by government.'

So many other things are there. So, for the first time, we have identified and defined atrocities.

Then we have made the punishment more stringent. We have said that all these kinds of atrocities shall be punishable with imprisonment for a term which shall not be less than six months but which may extended to 5 years with fine. In the previous Act, it was only for one month and like that. We know that most of the atrocities are because of land. They insist on their minimum wages which they are denied. When they insist on the minimum wages, then these powerful people who engage them, torture them and inflict atrocities on them. Now we are witnessing today the signs of fruits of development reaching the Scheduled Castes and Scheduled Tribes. With greater spread of education and improvement in the socio-economic conditions, the relations in society sometimes come under tension as a result of this change. Higher caste groups sometimes do not like change in the socio-economic structure and tensions develop. The demand for justice, for equality, for a humane living—what I said in the Bill—for knowledge, for education and freedom leads in some cases to a retaliation by groups who are not enlightened enough to recognise the healthy signs of growth. We can say that these are especially in the rural places where atrocities or a variety of offences are committed on members of the Scheduled Castes and Scheduled Tribes. I have had occasion to tell this House regarding the recent trend, the increase of such offences against members of the Scheduled Castes and Scheduled Tribes because often the question is asked in the House. During 1988, there were a little over 15,000 offences against the Scheduled Castes and 3,300 cases in respect of Scheduled Tribes. Of these, heinous offences such as murder, rape and grievous hurt accounted for about 3,200 cases in respect of Scheduled Castes and 783 in respect of Scheduled Tribes. The nature of these offences in many States indicated that these were not isolated instances but represented a trend in the country. In cities, towns and areas where the society was generally aware about the need to bring about such changes, the upward socio-economic mobility of the Scheduled Castes and Scheduled Tribes was accepted, and tensions did not arise. But in the countryside, in the rural India, tension exists still. But in certain rural areas tradition seems to be difficult to be dislodged and from State to State it differs. In the north, because of some customs, it is more severe. And in some parts of the south also, it is something like that. The government hence thought that certain special measures would be necessary at this point of time. So, the Bill has come. The cases of such incidents were related generally to land or to continued exploitation by enforcement of traditional demeaning practices. It is regrettable that instances had been reported such as in Kerala where a member of the Scheduled Castes was forced to eat human excreta. There are reports of a bridal party being chased and the houses of this community razed to the ground merely because the bridegroom was riding a horse through a village street when the *baraat* was going on.

The efforts of government to provide land have been frustrated in many cases by forcible dispossession or illegal occupation of such land. In Madhya Pradesh recently, the government launched a special programme to see that possession or effective restoration of land is made to the members of the Scheduled Castes and Scheduled Tribes who have been given 'pattas' of the land. But we received this complaint from every State that 'pattas' are given but the possession is not given. And those who are powerful people in the villages are occupying the land and the Scheduled Castes people or the Scheduled Tribes people are not given. And non-tribal people have purchased tribal land, and in fake names they are occupying that land. So, these are some of the atrocities committed on the poor people. In some unfortunate incidents, the womenfolk of the Scheduled Castes and the Scheduled Tribes are sought to be dishonoured and assaulted with the object of teaching a lesson to that community. Even before the family members, before the parents, even young girls are molested or raped. So, this type of human acts and atrocities are committed. I am saying all this in justification of this Bill.

In tribal areas, incidents of sexual exploitation are known to have occurred where willingness of innocent tribal women is secured by exercise of authority or influence. The community is sometimes sought to be pressurised by denying them access to public places, for easing themselves, for cremation or to the source of water, etc. These are the acts of atrocities that are committed against them. Instances have come to notice about fouling of water source by dumping carcass in the vicinity of their houses. All this taken together forms a pattern which calls for more stringent legislative measures. So, we have in this Bill before the House, sought to classify most of such instances as atrocities on the Scheduled Castes and the Scheduled Tribes, perpetrated by others.

Although many of these offences could probably be covered under the normal law of the land, we are witnessing today a difference in degree which calls for a differentiation in kind in-respect of these offences. The Bill hence proposes to specify higher punishments as also laying down some minimum punishment for such offences. The Bill also provides for forfeiture of property—these are the salient features of this Act—whether movable or immovable which may have been used for the commission of an offence under this law. The dominant position of certain vested interests embolden them to continue perpetration of atrocities on the Scheduled Castes and the Scheduled Tribes. These provisions are expected to have salutary effect on such tendencies.

Prevention is better than cure and the Bill looks after the preventive measures. If an area is declared prone to atrocities—we will identify these areas—it will become the bounded duty of the law and order machinery to take all possible measures for instilling a sense of safety and security.

We are, for the first time, putting responsibility on the officers. If an officer is found wanting, we will take action... (*Interruptions*).

Shri N.E. Balaram (Kerala): We agree with the Bill, but she is not giving a real picture. I agree with the Bill without discussion.

Shri Parvathaneni Upendra (Andhra Pradesh): It is not a controversial thing. We welcome this measure.

Shri Vishvjit P. Singh (Maharashtra): With such a new-found spirit in the House is it also possible to pass the Constitutional Amendment Bills in the same manner?

Dr. Rajendra Kumari Bajpai: Schemes would be formulated under the general guidance of the Government of India to provide for such measures as also for providing prompt and adequate relief and rehabilitation in the unfortunate event of atrocities taking place.

So, this is also for the first time that we are doing it.

Then another feature is that special court is now being set-up. There is going to be a special responsibility on the public servants. That is another feature of the Bill. The Bill places a special responsibility on the public servants who are not members of SC/ST to take action to protect the interests of the Scheduled Castes and the Scheduled Tribes against atrocities being committed, and for taking preventive measures.

With these words, I move that the Bill to prevent the commission of offences of atrocities against the members of Scheduled Castes and Scheduled Tribes, to provide for special courts for the trial of such offences and for relief and rehabilitation of the victims of such offences and for matters connected therewith or incidental thereto, as passed by the Lok Sabha, be taken into consideration.

The question was proposed.

Shri Parvathaneni Upendra: Madam, while welcoming the Bill, I just want to say this. Mere legislation is not enough. There should be a political will on the part of the Union Government and the State Governments to implement it. We have already the Act relating to untouchability but, still untouchability is being practised. Therefore, all of us should see that the provisions of this Bill are implemented strictly.

The Deputy-Chairman: The question is:

"That the Bill to prevent the commission of offences of atrocities against the members of the Scheduled Castes and the Scheduled Tribes, to provide for Special Courts for the trial of such offences and for relief and rehabilitation of the victims of such offences and for matters connected therewith or incidental thereto, as passed by the Lok Sabha, be taken into consideration."

The motion was adopted.

The Deputy-Chairman: We shall now take up the clause-by-clause consideration of the Bill.

Clauses 2 to 23 were added to the Bill.

Clause 1, the Enacting Formula and the Title were added to the Bill.

Dr. Rajendra Kumari Bajpai: Madam, I move:

"That the Bill be passed."

The question was put and the motion was adopted.

What constitutes atrocity has not been defined but the offences directly or indirectly flowing from the practice of untouchability are described in detail. The inclusion of Scheduled Tribes in this Act deserves special notice. In this connection, what Dr. C. Parvathamma has stated in her book *Scheduled Castes and Tribes: A Socio-economic Survey (1984)*[2], is relevant. She opines that "Untouchability" generally does not apply to the Scheduled Tribes, who live apart in isolation. But when they come out of their habitation and develop contact with the people of plains they are equated with the "Scheduled Castes and untouchables". With the enactment of these two Acts, the prohibition of untouchability in the Constitution has been given a realistic and effective shape.

This Act specifies the atrocities which are liable to penalties under the Act. According to the Act atrocities include: forcing the eating of noxious substances, dumping waste matters on land, denudation, wrongful occupation of land, dispossession, bonded labour, intimidation during the voting, mischievous litigation, false information, public humiliation, outrage of modesty, sexual exploitation, fouling of water source, obstruction of entry to a place of public resort, eviction from habitation, mischief with explosives, destruction of buildings and suppression of evidence. These offences under the Prevention of Atrocities Act carry heavier penalties than similar offences under the Indian Penal Code. The offences of custodial rape, highway robbery and house breaking by night which carry a minimum punishment of 10 years under the Indan Penal Code are punishable with imprisonment for life and with fine under the prevention of Atrocities Act. The Act also provides for forfeiture of property, externment and collective fine.

The Scheduled Castes Prevention of Atrocities Act 1989 (PAA) came into force on January 1,1990. It is still too early to review its operation or to assess its effectiveness. The purpose of this chapter is only to look at this new Act against the background of the atrocities[3] which have been discussed in the Chapter.

(A) Objects and Reasons

Initially, the Government wanted to restore justice, liberty, equality, status, opportunity for all and fraternity by peaceful means. The statement of objects and reasons accompanying the Bill succinctly gives the rationale behind the Act. Despite various measures to improve the socio-economic condition of the Scheduled Castes and the Scheduled Tribes, they remain vulnerable. They are denied a number of civil rights. They are subjected to various offences, indignities, humiliations and harassment. They have been deprived of their life and property. Serious crimes are committed against them for various historical, social and economic reasons.

It is due to the awareness created among the Scheduled Castes and the Scheduled Tribes through spread of education, etc. that they are trying to assert their rights and this is not being taken very kindly by the others. When they assert their rights and resist practices of untouchability against them or demand statutory minimum wages or refuse to do any bonded and forced labour, the vested interests try to cow them down and terrorize them. When the Scheduled Castes and the Scheduled Tribes try to preserve their self-respect or honour of their women, they become irritants for the dominance of their might. Occupation and cultivation of even the government allotted land by the Scheduled Castes and the Scheduled Tribes is resented and more often these people become victims of attacks by the vested interests. Of late, there has been an increase in the disturbing trend of commission of certain atrocities like making the Scheduled Caste persons eat inedible substances like, human excreta, mass killings of helpless Scheduled Castes and Scheduled Tribes and rape of women belonging to these groups. Under the circumstances, the existing laws like the Protection of Civil Rights Act, 1955 and the normal provisions of the Indian Penal Code have been found to be inadequate to check these crimes. A special legislation to check and deter crimes against them committed by non-Scheduled Castes and non-Scheduled Tribes has, therefore, become necessary.

This Bill is very important. Earlier, the Protection of Civil Rights Act was passed for protecting the Civil Rights of SC and ST and removal of untouchability but they were not properly implemented and now again for the achievement of almost similar objectives, the present Act has been introduced.[4] The main objective is to check atrocities.

The Government of India has initiated many new programmes and schemes for the improvement of SC's and ST's since independence.[5] Pandit Jawaharlal Nehru and Mrs. Indira Gandhi tried to improve the economic and social condition of the Scheduled Castes and Scheduled Tribes.

The Integrated Rural Development Programme and other similar programmes helped to improve the socio-economic condition of the SC and ST considerably and now these have been replaced by bigger schemes like the "Jawahar Rojgar Yojana". Drinking water wells and irrigation wells have been provided for this group.[6] The housing schemes have been started under the Indira Awas Yojana. The programme for liberation of scavengers has been given a greater impetus. Education of Scheduled Castes and Scheduled Tribes which is of crucial importance to their growth and development has received much greater attention. Efforts are also being made to free them from bonded labour and to allot them land for cultivation. Among the landless labourers, about 48 per cent are from the Scheduled Castes and Scheduled Tribes.

The Minister of State in the Ministry of Welfare stated that the Bill to prevent the commission of offence of atrocities against the members of the Scheduled Castes and Scheduled Tribes, to provide for special court for the trial of such offences and the relief and rehabilitation of the victim of such offences and for matters connected therewith or incidental thereto, be taken into consideration.[7]

A separate Welfare Ministry was created in 1985, specially for the welfare of the weaker sections of the society. Many new initiatives have been taken particularly in the last few years to improve the status of Scheduled Castes and Scheduled Tribes, in trying to discharge the mandate of the Constitution. Poverty alleviation programmes, which provided special attention to the Scheduled Castes and Scheduled Tribes, have been expanded and intensified.[8]

A special drive is currently being made for fillingup the backlog which has arisen as a result of non-fulfilment of reserved seats for SC/ST. As we all know, about 45 per cent of the Scheduled Caste population is landless labourers and they are mostly living below poverty line. They will be freed by the Bonded Labour Act and will be rehabilitated by the grant of land and money as well.[9]

An important problem that Parliament had to face in relation to the Scheduled Castes and Scheduled Tribes was the practice of untouchability. Untouchability resulted in the creation of an inferiority complex among these classes. Parliament, thus, passed the Untouchability (Offences) Bill in 1955 in accordance with Article 17 of the Indian Constitution. Article 35 points out the law which has to be made in respect of making the various forms or aspects of untouchability an offence and they have to be passed only by Parliament.[10]

There were many laws enacted in various States of India between 1937 and 1950. To have a uniform system of laws, the Government called for the views of the State Governments in February 1950 asking whether untouchability in any form was practised in the States. The Bill declared untouchability as an offence which is punishable.[11]

The backward classes were boycotted by the villagers. Dr. Ambedkar wished that some provisions were made for removing this social boycott. The Maharashtra Government had appointed a committee for the purpose and Thakkar Bappa was its member. This committee noted that fear of open violence against the backward classes by orthodox society made no progress in achieving the object.[12]

The Untouchability (Offences) Bill of 1955 provided for punishment to deter the offender from repeating the offence and also to prevent him to adopt a criminal career. Dr. Ambedkar suggested that there should be no alternative in the punishment because the offender could pay and be free. He suggested that the Government should take security for good behaviour as there was a provision in Sections 107, 108, 109 and 110 of the Act. The Centre should administer the law and the burden of expenditure also should be borne by the Centre.[13]

In exercise of the power conferred by Article 35, Parliament enacted the Untouchability (Offence) Act (UOA), 1955 and the Untouchability (Offences) Amendment and Miscellaneous Provisions Act 1976 (Article 106 of 1976). The title of the Act is changed to the Protection of Civil Rights Act. The Act prescribed punishment which may extend to imprisonment of six months and a fine which may extend to five hundred rupees or both.[14]

The Scheduled Castes Prevention of Atrocities Act 1989 (PAA) came into force on June 30, 1990. It is still too early to review its operation or to assessits effectiveness. The purpose of this chapter is only to look at this new Act against the background of the atrocities.

The Scheduled Castes and the Scheduled Tribes (Prevention of Atrocities) Act, 1989 (No.33 to1989) short title, extent and commencement;

1. This Act may be called the Scheduled Castes and the Scheduled Tribes (Prevention of Atrocities) Act, 1989.[15]

2 It extends to the whole of India except the State of Jammu and Kashmir.

3. It shall come into force from such date as the Central Government may, by notification in the official Gazette appoint.

Definition

1. In this Act, unless the context otherwise requires:

(a) "atrocity" means an offence punishable under Section 3.

(b) "code" means the code of criminal procedure, 1973 (2 of 1974).

(c) Scheduled Castes and Scheduled Tribes shall have the meanings assigned to them respectively under Clause (24) and Clause (25) of Article 366 of the Constitution.

What Clause (3) of the Constitution (Scheduled Castes) order, 1950 contemplates is that for a person to be treated as one belonging to a Schedueld Caste within the meaning of that order, he must be one who professes either Hindu or Sikh religion.

A declaration of one's belief must necessarily mean a declaration in such a way that it would be known to those whom it may interest. Therefore, if a public declaration is made by a person that he has ceased to belong to his old religion and has accepted another religion, he will be taken as professing the other religion. In the face of such an open declaration, it would be idealto enquire further as to whether the conversion to another religion was efficacious.

The word "Profess" in the Presidential order appears to have been used in the sense of an open declaration or practice by a person of the Hindu (or the Sikh) religion. Where, therefore, a person says, on the contrary that he has ceased to be a Hindu, he cannot derive any benefit from that orders.

There would have been no need to make a mention of the Sikh religion. From the fact that a special mention is made of the Sikh religion it would follow that the word "Hindu" is used in the narrower sense of the orthodox Hindu religion which recognizes castes and contains injunctions based on caste distinction.[16]

Determination whether a caste is included in Scheduled Caste:

In order to determine whether a particular caste is a Scheduled Caste within the meaning of Article 342, one has to look at the public notification issued by the President on that behalf.

Bhaiya Lal V. Harikishan Singh (1965) 2 SCR 877: AIR 1965 SC 1557 Caste *(Chammar)* mentioned in Part X of the order it can be said to include a nonspecified caste (*Mochi*).

Parsasram V. Shivchand (1969) ISCC 20. Dohar is a sub-caste of *Chammar*.

In the present case, the notification refers to *Chammar*, *Jatav* or *Mochi*, and so in dealing with the question in dispute between the parties, the enquiry which the Election Tribunal can hold is whether or not the appellant is a *Chammar*, *Jatav* or *Mochi*. The plea that though the appellant is not a *Chammar* as such, he can claim the same status by reason of the fact that he belongs to the Dhor caste which is a sub-caste of the *Chammar* caste, cannot be accepted. It appears to us that an enquiry of this kind would not be permissible having regard to the provisions contained in Article 341 (Bhaiya Lal V. Harikishan Singh (1965) 2 SCR 877: AIR 1965 SC 1557).

(d) "Special Court" means a court of session specified as a special court in Section 41.

(e) "Special Public Prosecutor" means a Public Prosecutor specified as a special public prosecutor or an advocate referred to in Section 15.

(f) Words and expressions used but not defined in this Act and defined in the Code or the Indian Penal Code (45 of 1860) shall have the meanings assigned to them respectively in the code, or as the case may be in the Indian Penal Code.

2. Any reference in this Act to any enactment or any provision, thereof shall, in relation to an area in which such enactment or such provision is not in force, be construed as a reference to the corresponding law, if any, in force in that area.

Offences of Atrocities

Punishment for offences of atrocities[17]

1. Whoever, not being a member of a Scheduled Caste or a Scheduled Tribe:

(i) forces a member of a Scheduled Caste or a Scheduled Tribe to drink or eat any inedible or obnoxious substance;

(ii) acts with intent to cause injury, insult or annoyance to any member of a Scheduled Caste or a Scheduled Tribe by dumping excreta, waste matter, carcasses or any other obnoxious substance in his premises or neighbourhood;

(iii) forcibly removes clothes from the person of a member of a Scheduled Caste or a Scheduled Tribe or parades him naked or with painted face or body or commits any similar act which is derogatory to human dignity;

(iv) wrongfully occupies or cultivates any land owned by, or allotted to, or notified by any competent authority to be allotted to a member of a Scheduled Caste or a Scheduled Tribe or gets the land allotted to him transferred;

(v) wrongfully disposes a member of a Schedueld Caste or a Scheduled Tribe from his land or premises or interferes with the enjoyment of his rights over any land, premises or water;

(vi) compels or entices a member of a Scheduled Caste or a Scheduled Tribe to do begging or other similar kinds of forced or bonded labour than any compulsory services for public purpose imposed by Government;

(vii) Forces or intimidates a member of a Schedueld Caste or a Scheduled Tribe not to vote or to vote for a particular candidate or to vote in a manner other than provided by law;

(viii) institutes false, malicious or vexatious suit or criminal or other legal proceedings against a member of a Scheduled Caste or a Schedueld Tribe;

(ix) gives any false or frivolous information to any public servant and thereby causes such public servant to use his lawful power to the injury or annoyance of a member of a Schedueld Caste or a Scheduled Tribe;

(x) intentionally insults or intimidates with intent to humiliate a member of a Scheduled Caste or a Scheduled Tribe in any place within public view;

xi. assaults or uses force on any woman belonging to a Scheduled Caste or a Scheduled Tribe with intent to dishonour or outrage her modesty;

xii. being in a position to dominate the will of a woman belonging to a Scheduled Caste or a Scheduled Tribe and uses that position to exploit her sexually to which she would not have otherwise agreed;

xiii. corrupts or fouls the water of any spring, reservoir or any other source ordinarily used by members of the Scheduled Castes or the Scheduled Tribes so as to render it less fit for the purpose for which it is ordinarily used;

xiv. denies a member of a Scheduled Caste or a Scheduled Tribe any customary right of passage to a place of pubic resort or obstructs such member so as to prevent him from using or having access to a place of public resort to which other members of public or any section thereof have a right to use or access to;

xv. forces or causes a member of Scheduled Caste or a Scheduled Tribe to leave his house, village or other place or residence, shall be punishable with imprisonment for a term which shall not be less than six months but which may extend to five years and with fine.

2. Whoever, not being a member of a Scheduled Caste or a Scheduled Tribe:

(i) gives or fabricates false evidence intending thereby to cause or knowing it to be likely that he or she will thereby cause, any member of a Scheduled Caste or a Scheduled Tribe to be convicted of an offence which is capital by the law for the time being in force shall be punished with imprisonment for life and with fine; and if an innocent member of a Scheduled Caste or a Scheduled Tribe be convicted evidence, the person who gives or fabricates such false evidence, shall be punished with death;

(ii) gives or fabricates false evidence intending thereby to cause, or knowing it to be likely that he or she will thereby cause, any member of Scheduled Caste or a Scheduled Tribe to be convicted of an offence which is capital but punishable with imprisonment for a term of such years or upwards, shall be punished for a term which shall not be less than six months but which may extend to seven years or upwards and with fine;

(iii) commits mischief by fire or any explosive substance intending to cause or knowing it to be likely that he will thereby cause damage to any property belonging to a member of a Scheduled Caste or a Scheduled Tribe, shall be punishable with imprisonment for a term which shall not be less than six months but which may extend to seven years and with fine;

(iv) commits mischief by fire or any explosive substance intending to cause or knowing it to be likely that he will hereby cause destruction of any building which is ordinarily used as a place of worship or as a place for human dwelling or as a place for custody of the property by member of a Schedueld Caste or a Scheduled Tribe, shall be punishable with imprisonment for life and with fine;

(v) commits any offence under the Indian Penal Code (45 of 1960) punishable with imprisonment for a term of ten years or more against a person or property on the ground that such person is a member of Scheduled Caste or Scheduled Tribe or such property belonging to such member, shall be punishable with imprisonment for life and with fine;

(vi) knowingly or having reason to believe that an offence has been committed under this chapter, causes any evidence of the commission of that offence to disappear with the intention of screening the offender from legal punishment, or with that intention gives any information respecting the offence which he knows or believes to be false, shall be punishable with the punishment provided for that offence; or

(vii) being a public servent, commits any offence under this section shall be punishable with imprisonment for a term which shall not be less than one year but which may extend to the punishment provided for that offence.

3. Punishment for neglect of duties

Whoever, being a public servant but not being a member of a Scheduled Caste or as Scheduled Tribe, wilfully neglects his duties required to be performed by him under this Act, shall be punishable with imprisonment for a term which shall not be less than six months but which may extend to one year.

4. Enhanced punishment for subsequent conviction:

Whoever, having already been convicted of an offence under this chapter is convicted for the second offence or any offence subsequent to the second offence, shall be punishable with imprisonment for a term which shall not be less than one year but which may extend to the punishment provided for that offence.

5. Forfeiture of property of certain person:

(i) Where a person has been convicted of any offence punishable under this Act, the special court may in addition to awarding any punishment by order in writing, declare that any property, movable or immovable or both belonging to the person which has been used for the commission of that offence shall stand forfeited to Government.

(ii) If any person is blamed for an offence of practising untouchability, the special court may confiscate his property both movable and immovable during the period of investigation. If the trial turns into conviction, this property may be forfeited in order to compensate for the fine.

6. Presumption as to offences[18]:

In a prosecution for an offence under this Act, if it is proved that—

(a) the accused render any financial assistance to a person accused of, or reasonably suspected of committing, an offence under this Act, the special court shall presume, unless the contrary is proved, that such person had abetted the offence.

(b) a group of persons committed an offence under this Act and if it is proved that the offence committed was a sequel to any existing dispute regarding land or any other matter, it shall be presumed that the offence was committed in furtherance of the common intention or in prosecution of the common object.

7. Conferment of power[19]:

(A) That State Government may be at its best to prevent any offence against the untouchable, through the Special Court and Police Officer.

The Special Court offers the Police Officers power to investigate, assert and prosecute the offender in their specified area.

(B) All officers of police and all other officers of Government shall assist the officer referred to in sub-section (1) in the execution of the provision of this Act or any rule, scheme or order made thereunder.

(C) The provisions of the code shall, so far as may be applied to the exercise of the powers by an officer under sub-section (1).

Externment

8. Removal of a person likely to commit offence[20]:

Where the special court is satisfied, upon a complaint or a police report that a person is likely to be included in 'Scheduled Areas' or 'Tribal Area' as referred to an Article 244 of the Constitution, it may be order in writing, direct such a person to remove himself beyond the limits of such area, and not to return to that area from which he was directed to remove himself for the specified period, not exceeding two years, as may be specified in the order.

9. Procedure on failure of a person to remove himself from area and enter thereon after removal[21]:

(A) If a person to whom a direction has been issued under Section 10 to remove himself from any area;

(a) If the person banished by the special court for temporary period, returns to the specified area before the specified time, the Special Court may give order for his arrest.

(b) The Special Court can, any time, order the person to return to the specified area from which he has been banished, for a temporary period.

10. Taking measurements and photographs, etc. of persons against whom order under Section 10 is made. The Police Officer can take the measurement or photograph of a person against whom an order has been passed under Section 10.

11. Penalty for non-compliance with order under Section 10.

Any person contravening an order of the Special Court made under Section 10 shall be punishable with imprisonment for a term which may extend to one year and with fine.

12. Special Court[22] as per the chapter IV 14X22 for the purpose of providing for speedy trial, the State Government shall, with the concurrence of the Chief Justice of the High Court, by notification in the Official Gazette, specify for each district a court of session to be a Special Court to try the offences under this Act.

13. Special Public Prosecutor

For every Special Court, the State Government shall by notification in the Official Gazette, specify a Public Prosecutor or appoint an advocate who has been in practice as an advocate for not less than seven years, as a Special Public Prosecutor for the purpose of conducting cases in that court.

Miscellaneous

14. Power of State Government to impose collective fine:

The Provision of Section 10A of the Protection of Civil Rights Act, 1955 (22 of 1955) shall, so far as may be, apply for the purposes of imposition and realization of collective fine and for all other matters connected therewith under this Act.

15. Preventive action to be taken by the law and order machinery:

The District Magistrate and the Police Officer may take necessary actions to prevent any atrocities likely to be caused by the people other than Scheduled Castes and Scheduled Tribes of his jurisdiction for maintaining peace and order.

16. Duty of Government to ensure effective implementation of the Act:

The Atrocities Act enables the common man to avail himself of justice. It also provides the expenses to the victims and witnesses during investigation period. After the trial rehabilitation of the victims is done, special officers are appointed for that purpose for effective implemention. The committee is appointed by the State Government. Safety and security measures are to be taken for the victims of the atrocities. The Central Government also takes necessary steps and helps the State Government in this process for the well being of the victims.

1. The Atrocities Act enables the common man to avail himself of justice.
2. This Act offers the expenses of travelling and maintenance to the witnesses and victims during the period of investigation.
3. The victims are provided economic and social rehabilitation by this Act.
4. During the period of prosecution of investigation, this Act appoints the officers.
5. This Act declares it to befit to set different committees at the State Government level.

6. For better implementation of this Act, there is a provision of periodic survey.

7. This identification of the locality where the members of Scheduled Caste and Tribe are, is subject to the Atrocity Act.

17. Protection of action taken in good faith:

If the State or the Central Government takes certain measures in good faith, no legal action is to be taken against them.

18. Power to make rules

1. The Central Government may, by notification in the Official Gazette, make rules for carrying out the purposes of this Act.

2. Every rule made under this Act shall be laid, as soon as may be after it is made, before each House of Parliament, while it is in session for a total period of 30 days. If both Houses agree in making any modification in the rules or both Houses agree that the rule should not be made, the rule shall thereafter have effect, only in such modified form or be of no effect, as the case may be; so, however, that any such modification or annulment shall be without prejudice to the validity of anything previously done under that rule.

Steps for Enhancing Impact of the Prevention of Atrocities Act

The Scheduled Castes and the Scheduled Tribes (Prevention of Atrocities) Act, 1989 came into force on January 30, 1989 but it should be remembered that the same class of persons who perpetrated atrocities in the past would have to be tackled under the new law. These persons belong to power groups in society and especially in rural areas they would continue to have the power to influence investigation. The present study has shown that a large number of atrocity cases have been characterized by delay in visits to the scene of crime, and tardy investigation, lukewarm prosecution, protracted pendency and a high percentage of acquittals. If the same fate is not to befall atrocity cases under the PAA, special steps will have to be taken on the following lines:

(i) Publicity: A leading commentator on human rights in India has stated, "It is a sad commentary on our commitment in justice that the historic measure seeking to restore democratic human rights to the Scheduled Castes and Tirbes has virtually passed unnoticed". Widespread publicity will have to be done through all the media highlighting the offences and punishments covered by the Act.

(ii) Translation: An enactment in the English language will not be understood by the common man, especially Scheduled Castes and Tribes in the rural areas. Translation into Hindi and the regional languages should be speeded up.

(iii) Printing and distribution: A sufficiently large print order should be given and copies of the Act should be distributed so that they are available in every police station in the country.

(iv) Training: Orientation training in the provisions of the Act should be arranged for magistrates, prosecutors and police. Seminars should be arranged in which the objectives of the Act and the manner of its implemention are fully discussed.

Working of the Act

As per Section 15A (4) of the Act, the Central Government is required to place on the table of each House of Parliament every year, a report on the measures taken by itself and the State Governments to ensure that the rights accruing from the abolition of "untouchability" may be availed of by the concerned persons. The latest report pertaining to the years 1989 and 1990 states, inter alia that:

1. The problem of untouchability still continues to exist in the rural areas inspite of many efforts being taken to eradicate it.
2. The enactment of laws alone will not bring about the desired results for ameliorating the socio-economic conditions of Scheduled Castes. A new strategy having the three components of:
   (a) special component plan for Scheduled Castes by the States/ UTs and the Central Ministries.
   (b) Special Central assistance, and
   (c) State Scheduled Castes Development Corporation was involved in Sixth Plan and has been functioning since then.
3. In 1990, the number of cases registered in many States has gone down considerably, as compared to 1989. In the case of other States, however, it shows that untouchability is still practised in

many parts of the country. There is, therefore, an immediate need for gearing up and strengthening the existing machinery for effective implemention of the Act.

A statement giving details of cases under Untouchability (Offences) in pursuance of Protection of Civil Rights Act, 1955, relating to three years commencing from 1988 is given below. It will be observed that there is no significant variation over the years either in the fresh cases registered by the police or pending at the end of the year awaiting disposal. This calls for special scrutiny and initiation of the appropriate measures to bring down the occurrence of offences. Another aspect needing attention is gearing up of disposal machinery, for it is noticed that unsettled cases are mounting up.

Critique

The Protection of Civil Rights Act, 1955 and the Scheduled Castes and the Scheduled Tribes (Prevention of Atrocities) Act, 1989 are the two important legislations to deal with untouchability offences and check commission of crimes on Scheduled Castes and Scheduled Tribes. Fifty-seven Special Courts for trial of offences under the PCR Act have been set up in eight States. Similarly, for implementation of the Scheduled Castes amd Scheduled Tribes (Prevention of Atrocities) Act, the State Governments and the Union Territory Administration have specified existing district and session courts as Special Courts for trial of offences under this Act.

Exclusive Special Courts have also been set up by some States like Andhra Pradesh and Rajasthan. Monetary relief and rehabilitation assistance continue to be provided to the victims of atrocities. Many State Governments operate schemes to encourage inter caste marriages and to provide legal aid. Programmes have been developed through the media against the evil practice of untouchability. The voluntary organizations are financially assisted to propagate against the practice of untouchability. Periodic research surveys and awards to Panchayats are some of the other schemes being operated by some.

Inspite of all these, there is still a lot more to be done. This will be clear from what the Eighth Five Year Plan (1992-97) document of the Planning Commission stated. It is recorded that "untouchability stands abolished by virtue of Article 17 of the Constitution and its practice in any form is punishable. But social discrimination against Scheduled Castes still continues to linger in many parts of the country. It is a matter of concern that inspite of legal measures in the form of protection of Civil Rights Act, 1955 and the Scheduled Castes and the Scheduled Tribes (Prevention of Atrocities) Act, 1989, seven hundred and forty-eight cases of atrocities against persons belonging to Scheduled Castes and One hundred and one cases of atrocities against Scheduled Tribes were reported during the years 1986 and 1990. Of these, 3328 cases were of murder, 5,339 of rape and 4,325 of arson." The document recommends that, "In the nineties there has to be an intensification of efforts to bridge the gap in the levels of development of the Scheduled Castes, and other sections of the population so that by the turn of the century these disadvantaged sections of the population are brought on par with the rest of the society in all spheres of national endeavour."

Cases Under Protection of Civil Rights Act, 1955[24]

Sr. No.	*Categories*	*1988*	*1989*	*1990*
1.	Cases brought forward from the previous year	7401	7505	8433
2.	Fresh cases registered by the police during the year	3722	3700	3730
3.	Cases disposed of by the courts during the year ending in			
	a. Conviction	303	410	128
	b. Acquittal	1402	1463	906
4.	Cases pending at the end of the year 1990	7504	6765	8879

One of the members in the Lok Sabha stated that in a welfare state there should not be any castes and classes. Thus, the success of the Bill was to depend upon the enforcement of the law and this responsibility rested upon the police. One of the members in the Lok Sabha commented that the goal of abolition of untouchability would be realized only if the social conscience as ahole is changed.

The Deputy Minister in the Lok Sabha assured[25] that the law would be enforced properly. He informed that the penal code, the criminal laws, etc. would be made by the States to administer the provisions of the Bill. In addition, Special Courts were established for deciding whether the cases of atrocities were compoundable or not. The opposition thought the Bill to be a non-controversial one but they warned that a correct approach was necessary in implementing the Bill. It was doubtful whether the police would be serious about executing the provisions of the Atrocities Act. The Minister informed that the police were given power to arrest any person found guilty under the Atrocities Act, because the Scheduled Castes would not go and file the complaint. A resolution moved by a member of the Rajya Sabha suggested that a survey be conducted to see how far Atrocities Act had been effective in the States.[26] The member also suggested that a committe be set up for the purpose. The Minister, however, informed the House that all the States had appointed committees for the purpose and that the States were very co-operative in this regard.

The prominent defect in the implemention of the Bill was that the Home Ministry and Ministry of Welfare depended upon the States and the non-official organizations for removing atrocities. This made the progress very slow. The Minister argued on the point that this issue was a deep-rooted one and it would take a long time for social disabilities to disappear.

A Scheduled Caste member commented that the aim of the Ministry of Welfare was good but the implementation was slack, thus the policy of making Atrocities Act an offence shows no results. States on the whole were co-operative in implementing schemes for the welfare of the Scheduled Castes and Scheduled Tribes.

One of the members from Lok Sabha read the statement of objects and reasons, which says,[27] "Despite various measures to improve the socio-economic conditions of the Scheduled Castes and the Scheduled Tribes, they remain vulnerable. They are subjected to various offences, indignities, humiliations and harassment. They have, in several brutal incidents, been deprived of their life and property. Serious crimes are committed against them for various historical, social and economic reasons.

It is due to the political awareness amongst the Scheduled Castes and the Scheduled Tribes, through spread of literacy, etc. That they are trying to assert their rights and this is not being taken very kindly by the others when they try to assert their rights and resist practices of untouchability against them or demand statutory minimum wages or refuse to do any bonded and forced labour. The vested intersets try to cow them down and terrorize them. When the Scheduled Castes and the Scheduled Tribes try to perserve their self respect or the honour of their women, they become irritants for their dominance and might. Occupation and cultivation of the Government allotted land by the Scheduled Castes and the Scheduled Tribes is resented and more often these people become victims of attacks by the vested interests."

The civic, the executive and the police authorities are not really very sincere to implement these measures and go against the very object and vision of the Government. We have already enacted so many Acts but the whole question is unsolved still. The Judiciary is silent in this respect. It takes many years for a case to get settled. These poor people cannot afford to pursue the cases year after year. The result is that the offenders go scot-free, is putting the people to a lot of harassment. No doubt, this Act will give some benefit and relief to the SC and ST members. Whenever a crime, atrocity, torture, etc. is committed against the members of the SC/ST, first of all they have to go to the police station to lodge an FIR. Nothing has been mentioned in the Act about the police officers, crimes. The police officers refuse to record the FIR, and remain silent on the matter.

At the first instance, we fail to understand why the previous Bills have not proved effective. One of the members from Lok Sabha feared as to whether this Bill would also meet the same fate. The main reason is that the persons who are supposed to implement the provisions of the Bill effectively, oppose it, and are prejudiced. They do not want to protect the rights of the Scheduled Castes and Scheduled Tribes.[28] The people from whom we expect that they will protect their rights, intentionally neglect them. In such circumstances, it would be impossible to implement the provisions of the Act effectively when a person belonging to the Scheduled Castes is victimized as soon as he goes to the police station to lodge an FIR. He is rebuked and asked to go away. If at all an FIR is lodged, then some lacuna is left so that the culprits may not get any punishment. Unless, the Government checks such corrupt practices of giving shelter to the culprits by way of giving them protection in one way of the other, the Scheduled Castes and Tirbes (Prevention of Atrocities) Bill can never prove to be effective. Hence, provision should be made to penalize the officials who indulge in such practices. The Bill would not be useful if it gives protection to such people in any way. The officials make it a point to exploit the person if he happens to belong to Scheduled Caste. Therefore, the Government should pay attention to it. At some places, the State

Governments follow the policy of suppressing the incidents of atrocities committed on the people belonging to Scheduled Castes and Scheduled Tribes.[29]

Our ideology is clear and the intention of our Government is also good, but the implementation of these laws is the responsibility of the State Governments and they do not fulfil it. We enact the laws, but they are rarely implemented effectively. The fact was also corroborated by the Hon. Member of Lok Sabha that the laws for the weaker sections are not properly implemented. Uplifting the status of Harijans and tribals is the responsibility of the Central Government. So monitoring cells should be set up at the district level instead of State level to keep a close watch on the atrocities in various areas on different sections for the continuous flow of information. The Commissioner of Scheduled Castes and Scheduled Tribes provides all the necessary information to the Government.[30]

Several laws have been enacted and forwarded to the State for implemention but before reaching the district level, these laws become handicapped. The provisions to prevent atrocities have been made in the Bill and they are good too. But if we look at the already existing provisions made in the Constitution or in the Indian Penal Code, we shall find that in a case of atrocities on Harijans, chargesheet has to be produced in the court within a maximum period of 90 days. But we have seen that police officers take one year or more to produce chargesheet in the courts, as a result of which the cases are dismissed in the absence of proof or final reports. The Bill should also ensure that chargesheets relating to incidents of atrocities committed on the Harijans should be produced in the courts within a maximum period of 90 days.[31] If this is done, the cases pertaining to atrocities will definitely be on the decrease.

More courts should be set up at places where the incidents of atrocities are more and only then justice will be rendered in the real sense and the provisions of this Bill be implemented properly. This type of Bill which is necessary at the end of the 20th century, is very regrettable. The so called high caste people and the land owners are the main culprits for atrocities on Scheduled Castes and Scheduled Tribes.

It is a pity that despite several measures taken by the Government, all these facilities have not reached the rural areas at the grass-root level. We must find out the reasons for this. Besides enacting this legislation we must also consider the effective implemention of measures taken for uplifting their status because atrocities are closely interrelated to it.

There are some good provisions in this Bill. But mere passing of the Bill and making an Act will not be able to stop atrocities on Scheduled Castes and Scheduled Tribes. We have to find out the root cause for the atrocities, which are being perpetuated on them. If we make a proper analysis of it, we will see that social, economic and educational backwardness are the main reasons as to why atrocities are being perpetuated on them.[32] The entire Scheduled Castes and Scheduled Tribes population in the country is not educated. Due to their illiteracy they are not well informed. Since the economic condition of these people is very weak, they are not able to get respectable status in the society. Of course, our Government has launched several schemes for uplifting the status of the SC/ST. The Government wants to enhance their status in the society by conferring many economic benefits through various schemes. The Government must see whether the schemes launched for the welfare of SC/ST are effectively implemented or not and funds earmarked under these schemes are properly utilized or not.

Today it is a challenge to our politicians, the educated and the youth of our society. If we could not generate a feeling of brotherhood[33] in the society and enforce these laws, we would not be able to provide economic, social and legal protection to the Harijans and Adivasis.

In this chapter, the Atrocity Act has been dealt with thoughtfully and effectively. The focal point in this chapter is on the provisions and plans for the welfare of the Scheduled Castes by the Central Government.

Actual cases of PCR and Atrocities Act which took place in Karjat Taluka will be explained and analyzed in short in the further chapters.

References

1. Received the assent of the President on Sept. 11, 1989 and published in the *Gazette of India,* Extra Part II, Section 1 SI.NO. 39, dated Sept 12, 1989.
2. Dr. Menon P. S. K. "Abolition of Untouchability and Removal of Social Disabilities" *Yojana* Vol. 37 No. 23, published by Director, Publication Division, Patiala House, New Delhi p. 21.1993.
3. Report of National Commission for Scheduled Castes and Scheduled Tribes, Atrocities on Schedued Caste\Scheduled Tribe. Causes and Remedies, published by Government of India, 1990, p. 1-87.
4. Lok Sabha Debates Vol. LI. No. 21 Wed. August 16, 1989, p. 60.
5. *Ibid.,* Col. no. 57.
6. *Ibid.,* No. 20 Co. no. 98
7. Rajya Sabha Debates Vol. CLI No. 22 Co. No. 239, August 18, 1989.
8. *Ibid.,* Co. No. 246, 110 Ct. 241.
9. *Ibid.,* Co. No. 257, 23 Aug. 1989.

10. Lok Sabha Debates Vol. No. 17, Co. No. 311, August 19, 1989.
11. *Ibid.,* 20, Co. No. 111, August 14, 1989.
12. Rajya Sabha Debates Vol. 13, Co. No. 253, August 3, 1989.
13. *Ibid.,* Col. No. 266
14. Lok Sabha Debates Vol. No. 20, Co. No. 69 to 75, August 14, 1989.
15. Report of National Commission, Goverment of India, April 1, 1990, p. 1.
16. Punjabrao V. D. P. Meshram (1965) ISCR 849, ISR 1965 SC 1179, 1184, Eastern Book Company, Lucknow, 1993, p. 2.
17. The Scheduled Castes and the Scheduled Tribes (Prevention of Atrocities) Act,1989, S. K. Awasthi, Premier Publishing Company; Nagpur 1992, pp. 153-156.
18. *Ibid.*, p. 356.
19. Scheduled Castes and Scheduled Tribes (Prevention of Atrocities) Act, 1989, Eastern Book Company. Lucknow, 1993, p. 6.
20. *Ibid.,* p. 7
21. *Ibid.*, p. 7
22. *Ibid.*, p. 327.
23 Report of the National Commission, Government of India, April 1990, p. 36.
24. Abolition of Untouchability and Removal of Social Disabilities, An Appraisal, *Yojana,* New Delhi, 1993, p. 28.
25. Rajya Sabha Debates Vol No. 13, Co. No. 257, August 3, 1989.
26. *Ibid.,* Vol. No. 23 11 Co. No. 244, October 1989.
27. *Ibid.,* Vol. No. 19 Co. No. 284 to 286, 1989.
28. *Ibid.,* Vol. No. 21 Co. No. 84-89, August 16, 1989.
29. Lok Sabha Debates Vol. No. 20, Co. No. 55 to 80, August 16, 1989.
30. *Ibid.,* Vol. No. 20. Col. No. 79 to 85.
31. *Ibid.,* Co. No. 107 to 110.
32. *Ibid.,* 21 Co. No. 55 to 61.
33. *Ibid.,* 21 Co. No. 74 to 78.

6

Cases Under Protection of Civil Rights Act 1976 and Prevention of Atrocities Act, 1989

In India, the Hindu society finds itself stratified permanently. The caste has rigidly divided the Hindus into various birth-based categories. One has to remain confined to the caste in which one is born and accept its advantages and disadvantages. The untouchables live on the fringe of society. They are denied social and economic justice by the people from the so called "upper class". They suffer from numerous stigmas, social and economic, which are attached by birth itself.

In order to confront such a situation, the framers of the Indian Constitution have made certain provisions which seem to be inadequate to grant social and economic justice to the depressed and oppressed people. Let us study the nature of injustice done to the people in the villages with reference to some of the cases which took place in Karjat Taluka of Ahmednagar District, taking into consideration the implementation of Protection of Civil Rights Act of 1976 and Atrocities Act of 1989.

The cases selected here indicate whether the untouchables were able to get due justice or not. These cases reveal the discrimination meted out to the lower caste people by the caste Hindus. The study shows that the Hindu society is not a homogeneous society. It is because of this nature of society that the quarrels and conflicts take place in the villages.

1. An incident took place in Kombhali, Karjat Taluka, Ahmednagar District, in which a higher caste Hindu, who was a Sarpanch, abused a lower caste villager. The Sarpanch demanded Rs. 300 for building a channel

in the farm. The lower caste villager refused to pay the money. The quarrel led them to the court on the ground of abuse, in the name of caste.

The charge was made against the accused under Section 7 (1) (d) (c) of Protection of Civil Rights Act, 1976 and under Section 323, 504, 506 Indian Penal Code.[1]

After the necessary legal formalities, the Judge (the Judicial Magistrate First Class Karjat) passed the order on May 6, 1991 with the effect that, the basic complaint was false and that the higher caste person had never demanded the said amount from the lower caste person. Therefore, there was no question of his abusing the aggrieved party; consequently, his bail bond was cancelled and he was set free.

The Judge was of the opinion that the intention of the Sarpanch was not of abusing the lower caste villager. So after hearing the case, the accused Sarpanch was acquitted. This case shows that lower caste villagers lodge false complaints if their interests are not protected.

The Article that makes an implemention of non-discrimination of law, clearly states, "All are equal before law and entitled without any discrimination to equal protection of the law. The violation of the law will result in punishment as offered by the law." The Article further says that the law shall prohibit any discrimination and guarantee equal and effective protection against any injustice on any ground. According to this provision every citizen can enjoy the rights given to him by the Constitution.[2]

Hence, every person is equal before the law. No one is superior or inferior. With reference to this, the atrocities committed on the backward people in Karjat Taluka of Ahmednagar District make one aware of the opinions expressed by some of the scholars in the field and the senior members of Parliament. They are worthwhile to be considered in the light of the prevention of Atrocities Act. When the Bill was being introduced in Parliament, there were mixed reactions amongst its members about the passing and implemention of this Act against the Indian social background.

Parliament witnessed hot discussions when the Bill was being passed. The question was constantly being raised in the house that there was increase in such offences against members of Scheduled Castes Scheduled Tribes. Sometimes, Hon. Members were also agitated on this point.[3]

2. There was another significant case which took place in the village called Alsunde. A lower caste person complained about the absence of

the street lights in the Harijanwada, whereupon a high caste person abused him. Consequently, the lower caste person lodged a complaint. This complaint was filed against the accused (a higher caste Hindu) under Section 7 (1) (d) of Protection of Civil Rights Act, 1976.

After hearing the entire case, the Additional Session Judge, Ahmednagar, acquitted the higher caste person, for there was no intention on the part of the a higher caste person to insult the lower caste villager on the grounds of untouchability.[4]

It is quite clear that the above complaint was based on local level issue. The Judge also remarked that all complaints do not come within the ambit of the law of untouchability. Constitutionally, racial and religious discrimination is prohibited by Article 19.[5] Accordingly, every villager irrespective of his caste, creed or religion has a right to demand civil facilities in his village. But sometimes incidents take place due to conflicts and misunderstanding among villagers. These create problems and additional cases are lodged in the courts.

The aims and objectives of this Bill are to give deterrent punishment to the accused persons who are involved in the case of atrocities on Scheduled Castes and Scheduled Tribes. There are general Acts like IPC and Civil Rights Act, but it seems that they have "not been properly implemented and that is why the present Bill had been brought. While the Bill was being brought, it was necessary to define atrocity. Here the word "atrocity" has not been defined exactly and fully and only certain offences have been quoted, i.e, taking possession of land forcibly, removing clothes of Scheduled Castes and Scheduled Tribes, etc. This Bill also provides an enhanced punishment, i.e, more punishment to those who are habitual offenders and who committed offences more than once. One of the senior parliamentarians said in his speech:

> "I think it is necessary to define the word "atrocity" here fully if not today at least after some time".[6]

3. A similar and interesting incident like the above ones took place in the village called Nimbodi, Karjat Taluka, Ahmednagar District. The higher caste persons approached the lower caste persons for the share in the agricultural produce. But the party refused to comply with the request of the higher caste persons. Being provoked by this, they turned down their request and indulged in abusing him. The result was that the lower caste persons lodged a complaint against the higher caste persons at the police

station. The chargesheet was filed against the accused under Section 7 (1) (d) of Protection of Civil Rights Act, 1976, and under Section 506 Indian Penal Code.

After hearing the case, witnesses and facts, the Judicial Magistrate, First Class Karjat passed the order on January 15, 1983. Accordingly, the accused persons of higher caste were acquitted of the offence punishable under Section 7 (1) (d) of Protection of Civil Rights Act and Section 504 of Indian Penal Code and their bail bond was cancelled.[7]

The Judge decided that such an incident never occurred. In fact, the Judge inevitably acquitted the higher caste persons. The Judge expressed quite clearly that the case before the court, was concerned with a dispute on the share of crops and hence it had no concern with the law of untouchability. The motive of the higher caste persons was purely pecuniary. Therefore, the question of untouchability was irrelevant and beyond consideration. The question of abusing the lower caste people is to be seen in the light of the UNESCO Declaration of Human Rights (Article 9). It clearly mentions equality of opportunity to all, absence of any racial discrimination under all circumstances and also a sense of human dignity. This will assure an era of human brotherhood.[8]

The M.P. wanted to know from Dr. Rajendra Kumari Bajapaye, the then Law Minister, as to what would be the future of the passing of this Bill. In reply to the questions raised by the M.P. she said:

> "The Bill that is going to be passed by the House is a good step in this direction. I am hopeful that the Bill will be proved much helpful in future also".[9]

4. There was another significant case which took place in the village called Babhulgaon in Karjat Taluka, Ahmednagar District where a lower caste person demanded some loan from the Chairman of the Co-operative Society who was a higher caste Hindu. The Chairman explained that a permission had to be sought from the District Co-operative Bank. A quarrel took place between them in which the higher caste person abused the lower caste villagers. Therefore, the villagers lodged a complaint against the Chairman and the peon of the Co-operative Society.

The charge was framed by Judicial Magistrate (First Class Karjat), against the accused on the ground of untouchability, punishable under Section 7 (d) of Protection of Civil Rights Act. The Judicial Magistrate giving his judgement pointed out that the bail bond was cancelled and the accused were set free because this case did not stand on the grounds of untouchability. Therefore, the complaint stood false. It was more a legal matter than the matter of untouchability. Therefore, it was not an offence under Section 7 (1) (d) of the Act on the grounds of untouchability.

In this case also one can observe that the Untouchability Act was misused by the person belonging to the lower caste people. However, the Chairman and the peon were acquitted. One needs to look at this case from the point of view of the Universal Declaration of Human Rights (Article 9) which forbids any type of discriminatory measures and emphasises various democratic values.

In many cases lower caste villagers are disallowed to enter a village temple. Complaints are lodged by the lower caste people. After recording the complaint, verification process was issued under Section 7(d) of Protection of Civil Rights Act and Sections 323, 506 (2) of Indian Penal Code, a charge was lodged against the high caste Hindus. The Judge did not find the witness and acquitted higher caste villagers.[10]

According to the Declaration of Human Rights, religious separation is not allowed. This means everybody can worship according to the provisions of the Constitution. The only precaution to be taken is the observance of the prevailing local practices.[11] In this context, it is everywhere observed that every normal person can have access to religious temples.

A special provision has been incorporated in the Bill. The responsibilities imposed upon the people in the Bill and administrative set up is of much help in the implementation of the Atrocities Act. If they show no concern for doing their duties in this regard, they would be entitled to punishment. Clause 4 of the Bill very categorically says, "Punishment for neglect of duty". The Government had gone a step further and provided more protection to the victims of this act. In his speech the Minister says:

"Whoever being a public servant but not being a member of Scheduled Castes or Scheduled Tribes wilfully neglects his duties required to be performed by him under the Act shall be punishable with imprisonement".[12]

5. There is one more peculiar case which took place on April 21, 1982, in the village Babhulgaon (Khalsa) Karjat Taluka, Ahemednagar District, in which a higher caste Hindu abused a lower caste person and denied him an entry into the temple of God Bhairvanath in the village. The lower caste person was going to perform rituals in front of the God Bhairvanath. He, along with other villagers, went into the temple for worship. On seeing this person in the temple, a higher caste Hindu came there and tried to drive

him out of the temple. The quarrel which took place led a higher caste Hindu threating to kill the lower caste. He insulted the lower caste person in the name of his caste and also abused him. Thereupon the lower caste person lodged a complaint at the Police Station. The matter reached the Court. After verification, the case was registered under Section 7 (A) (D) of Protection of Civil Rights Act and Section 323, 506 (2) of Indian Penal Code. After hearing the case, witnesses and facts the Judicial Magistrate, First Class Karjat, passed the following order:

All the accused persons of Babhulgaon (Khalsa), who are higher caste, are acquitted of the offence punishable under Section 7 (1) (D) of Protection of Civil Rights Act, and they are also acquitted of offence punishable under Sections 323, 506 (2) Indian Penal code. Their bail bond stands cancelled. They are set at liberty vide Section 428 of the Criminal Procedure Code.[13]

Explaining the judgement, the Judge pointed out that no such incident had taken place in the village. The Judge further said that the high caste Hindu person who was charged of abusing the lower caste person on the grounds of untouchability was seriously ill and was in hospital for treatment at the time of the crime. Thirdly, the police head constable was present in the temple at the time of the village fair. The police had written in his daily notebook that no such incident had taken place in the said village.

The village priest (Gurav) who was an eye witness to the incident, also strongly denied that no such incident had occurred. The village priest submitted that the entry into the temple was open to all, irrespective of caste, creed and religion. After hearing all the witnesses, including the nephew of the lower caste person, the Judge was of the opinion that the entry to the temple was allowed to the lower caste people also. The nephew from the complainant submitted that before this case took place, he used to recite the hymns of *Bhagwat Gita* and *Ramayana* in the temple of Lord Bhairvanath.

It is important to note that temple entry is allowed to all sections of society irrespective of caste and religion under Section 25 of the Indian Constitution. The Constitution emphatically stresses that all are equal before law and Article 19 grants equal freedom to all citizens. Nowadays nobody denies entry to the untouchables into public temples in the villages. If anybody obstructs this, it is a punishable crime according to the Indian Penal Code.[14]

It is acknowledged that the whole purpose of this Bill is to focus on atrocities committed by persons other than SC/ST on members of Scheduled Castes and Scheduled Tribes. Such atrocities are prepetuated by a group against another or by an individual against another. We come to an understanding that there are some good provisions in the present Bill which need to be highlighted. Mere passing of the Bill and making the Act is not enough to stop or prevent anyone from committing atrocities on backward classes. This is a good Bill in so far as the prevention of atrocities are concerned. But some of the members showed their deep concern and lamented about the Act. One of the Hon. Members stated:

> "I feel extremely sorry that this type of Bill is necessary at the end of the 20th century. It is very regrettable that the so-called high caste people and the land owners are the main culprits for committing the atrocities on Scheduled Castes and Scheduled Tribes".[15]

In order to arrive at a certain understanding, we need to look into more cases. Here is a similar case in point in which a lower caste person lodged a complaint against a person from a higher caste. The incident, in short, is as follows. In the same village (Babhulgaon), the villagers arranged a community meal for the teachers of the primary school. At the time of lunch higher caste persons abused lower caste villager. Thereupon, the lower caste villagers filed a case against the higher castes. The matter was sent to the police station.[16] Both the parties arrived at a compromise when the higher caste persons apologized. The accused was really guilty but his intention was not to harm or insult the lower caste persons on the grounds of untouchability.

It is observed that every insult of a lower caste is not on the grounds of untouchability. For any offence, the intention behind the insult is to be observed. However, in this case the lower caste person was denied the opportinity to take his meal alongwith the higher caste Hindus. In connection with such type of cases, it is commonly observed that the Harijans are discriminated on social occasions and at public places. The lower caste people are not allowed to enjoy equal status.[17] It is a very sad and pitiable situation that inspite of the constitutional protection of SC and ST people, the country has been unable to curb the atrocities on the backward class people.

One of the MPs brought to the notice of the House that mostly atrocities on Harijans are committed in predominently Hindu villages in Bihar.

He opined that not a single case of atrocity on Harijans has been reported from any village in Bihar inhabited by Muslims. He said, "If the Government is not able to check atrocities on Harijans, they should be rehabilitated around the Muslim villages, so that they would feel safe and secure" [18] Several laws have been enacted and forwarded to the States for implementation but before reaching the district level, these laws get crippled and weakened by certain forces. The provisions to prevent atrocities have been made in the Bill and they are good too. But if we look at the already existing provisions made in the Constitution or in the Indian Penal Code, the cases of atrocities are delayed and finally some cases are dimissed.

6. There was another incident that took place in village Babhulgaon, Karjat Taluka, Ahmednagar District in which a lower caste villager secured a loan for construction of a well in his agricultural land. According to a custom prevalent in the village, the party concerned carried the water from the new well to the local deites, namely, Hanuman and Bhairvana as the offerings. But the higher caste people refused an entry to these temples, hence, the party decided to file a complaint at the police station.[19]

The aggrieved person approached various authorities including the Home Minister for seeking justice. The Head Constable visited the concerned village, convened a meeting of the villagers and later the complaint was presented at the villagers meeting and the complainant offered his apologies for what had happened; and therefore, the local police authorities closed the case. It is observed here in this case that the lower caste person misused the Protection of Civil Rights Act which says that no villager should be discriminated on the basis of caste and suffer injustice.[20]

In the light of the above observations one of the M.P.s commented.

> "I would like to state that the provision dealing with the production of chargesheet within 90 days should be strictly implemented. Besides, the Bill should also ensure that chargesheet relating to incidents of atrocities committed on the Harijans should be produced in the courts within a maximum period of 90 days."[21]

It is absolutely necessary to restrict the period to minimum days so that justice may not be delayed. It is said that justice delayed is justice denied.

Atrocities committed on the Scheduled Castes and Scheduled Tribes can be checked only by ensuring their economic development. During the freedom struggle, it was Gandhiji who started a social revolution followed by Dr. B.R. Ambedkar to abolish the practice of untouchability. Practically, he gave them the status of God. But what is the plight of the depressed classes today? Political awareness has been created by the Government as far as the Acts of prevention of atrocities are concerned, but it should be followed by economic development of the Scheduled Castes and Scheduled Tribes. Social and political justice is inadequate if it is not followed by economic justice. Economic factor is also responsible for the atrocities committed on the backward class people. Feudal elements continue to hold these people as bonded labourers. Feudal system can be abolished if the economic status of these people is improved and by bringing them to the level of the upper caste people.

Economic opportunities could be given by way of providing employment to the backward class people in the bureaucratic set up where the cases of the atrocities are being brought.

There is a different case for the purpose of making it clear that discriminatory treatment is not given to the lower caste person not only on social occasions but in their daily life. It so happened that a lower caste person went to purchase oilcake at the shop of a higher caste person at Mirajgaon, Karjat Taluka, Ahmednagar District and inquired the rates of oilcake. Thereupon, the owner of the shop got annoyed and a quarrel took place. The lower caste person lodged a complaint against the owner, who exploited the Untouchability Act. In this case also the higher caste person was acquitted. In his remark the Judge declared that the complaint was false and the person who complained was a Buddhist and the provisions of the Untouchability Act are not applicable to such persons according to Section 12 of the Protection of Civil Rights Act. It appears that the case was filed by the lower caste person for the purpose of blackmail.[22]

Nobody dare commit atrocities on these people if they are given employment opportunities in different fields. It is being observed that educated people belonging to these neglected sections of society do have the opportunities of becoming doctors, teachers and engineers. But they are forbidden even to draw water from the well in their own native place. However, it is said that even the barbers of their areas do not meet them even if their economic condition has improved.

8. One more case took place in the village of Kolwadi, Karjat Taluka

which was politically motivated. In this case one lower caste person went to attend a public meal. He was denied the use of leaf-dish by the higher caste person. A complaint was lodged by the lower caste person against the higher caste person. According to the provision the matter went to the Court. The Court gave the verdict that the incident took place due to the political rivalry between two groups in the village, and so the lower caste person was forced to lodge a complaint. Such incidents take place on account of political motives and the vested interest of the various political groups in the villages.[13]

9. The above cases are related to the lower caste people. Now, we will study a case which is totally different from the earlier ones and is connected with a woman from a village Nimgaon Gangarda, Karjat Taluka, Ahmednagar District. The lady lodged a complaint against a male neighbour for having abused her in the name of lower caste. The matter went to the Court according to the Protection of Civil Right Act. The Judge passed an order saying that the lady did not belong to the lower caste because she had married a high caste Hindu and; thus the case did not come under the provisions of Protection of Civil Rights Act. It is very necessary to the debate which took place in the Lok Sabha as it aimed at pointing out the nature of intercaste marriages and the treatment given to the newly married couples by the family members in the society. A careful study of this case reveals the nature of intercaste marriages in India.[24]

It is strongly felt that improvement in the economic status does not bring the desired changes in the minds of the upper caste Hindus. What is important is that they should go in for intercaste marriages if they want to do away with the caste system. Mahatma Gandhi had clearly stated that he would give his blessings to couples where one of the partners is a Harijan and the other one is non-Harijan. But the fact today is that a person from a priviledged class marrying a Harijan girl incurs the anger of his family and does not get protection from any corner. To support the cause of intercaste marriages, the researcher feels that some provision should be made where the top priority is given to the intercaste mariages giving a special protection to those who go in for intercaste marriages. The aim here is to abolish the stigma of untouchability.[25]

The aims and objects of the prevention of atrocities Bills are to give deterrent punishment to the accused persons who are involved in the cases of atrocities on Scheduled Castes and Scheduled Tribes. There are several general Acts like IPC, Civil Rights Act, but they are inadequate to fulfil the aims of the Bills prevention on atrocities.

10. On January 1, 1981, an incident took place in the village Babulgaon Dumala, Karjat Taluka, Ahmednagar District in which a quarrel took place between a lower caste and a higher caste person because of political differences, which led the lower caste person being abused in the name of caste by the higher caste person. The matter went to court and the higher caste person was set free.[26]

Such cases happen because of the rival groups in the villages that instigate the complainant for some political gains.

11. There is a different case in point which took place at Koregaon, Karjat Taluka, Ahmednagar District in which a lower caste milkman was not given proper treatment by the high caste Hindu while purchasing the milk. The lower caste person was abused and beaten. The case went to court and the Magistrate of Karjat, after examining the witnesses and hearing the case and the facts, acquitted the higher caste person on the grounds of bogus filing of the case.

From the above case, one can gather that false cases do not yield desirable results in favour of the lower caste complainants.[27]

12. Now let us look at the attitude of the higher caste people towards the lower caste people. An incident took place in Karjat Taluka, Ahmednagar District in which a lower caste person was abused by a higher caste person on account of some love affair. The girl whom the lower caste person loved belonged to the higher caste. The matter went to court and the Judge on hearing the case and witnesses, acquitted the higher caste person.[28]

Thus, it is observed that the lower caste people do not get sufficient proofs and witnesses in the rural areas.

13. One more case on a different issue is here for the purpose of study. An incident took place in Chilawadi, Karjat Taluka, Ahmednagar District in which a lower caste person was abused by the higher caste person when he asked for the correct decision of the wrestling match which was being held on account of the village fair. The case went to court. Due to the lack of insufficient eye witnesses, the higher caste person was set free by the Judge.[29]

From the above case it is learnt that the lower caste people in rural areas do not get eyewitnesses because of the suppression from the higher caste Hindus.

14. A case from Mirajgaon, Karjat Taluka, Ahmednagar District reveals the the kind of relations the lower caste people and high caste Hindus have in the rural area. In this incident a lower caste person picked up a quarrel with a higher caste person because the latter was building a house on the land owned by the lower caste person. The matter went to the District Court and is still pending.[30]

The above case indicates the delay in the decision of the Court due to some unknown reasons.

15. There is another case of land issue which took place in Bhairobawadi, Karjat Taluka, Ahmednagar District in 1984. In this case a lower caste person was abused and insulted in the name of caste by a higher caste Hindu farmer on account of the right of ownership over the land.

The lower caste person tilled the land of the higher caste person on contract basis. But later on he refused to disclaim the ownership of the land. The matter went to court at Karjat and the higher caste person was acquitted and his bail bond was cancelled.[32]

16. A similar case of land issue took place in Kopardi, Karjat Taluka, Ahmednagar District, on November 2, 1983 in which a lower caste person was abused and insulted in the name of caste over the nature of the boundary of the land they possessed. The matter went to the court and the higher caste person was set free on the grounds of lack of witnesses.[32]

In both the above cases, lack of eyewitnesses led to the acquittal.

17. An incident took place in the village Babhulagon Dumala, Karjat Taluka, Ahmednager District on October 28, 1987. In this case a lower caste person was forbidden to take the road which went through the farm of a higher caste Hindu. The lower caste person was abused and insulted in the name of caste by the higher caste person. The lower caste person lodged a complaint and the matter went to court at Karjat. On hearing the case and witnesses, the Judge acquitted the higher caste Hindu.[33]

18. There is a similar case in point in which a lower caste person from the village Therwadi, Karjat Taluka, Ahmednagar District, was abused by a Hindu in the name of caste. The quarrel took place over the rights of ownership of the land which was tilled by the lower caste person, and was owned by him on rent. The matter went to the Court and the higher caste

Hindu was set free on the grounds that the case was admitted falsely. This case took place in the year 1990.[34]

19. There are some cases which are related to the Atrocity Act and which took place in the same taluka. An incident took place in the village Mirajgaon, Karjat Taluka, Ahmednagar District in the year 1993, in which a lower caste person was abused and harassed by a higher caste person in the name of caste. The quarrel took place during the Gram Panchayat meeting which led both the parties to the High Court. The decision is still awaited.[35]

20. A similar incident is here for the purpose of study. The incident took place in Karjat Taluka, Ahmednagar District in 1994. A brother of an M. L. A. who belonged to the lower caste was abused by the members of higher caste of the Shiv Sena party. Thereupon, a complaint was lodged by the brother of the M. L. A. The matter went to the High Court and is still pending.[36]

21. One peculiar case of atrocities was filed by a lower caste person of the Village Shinde, Karjat Taluka, Ahmednagar District, on the grounds that the right to the post of Sarpanch was denied to a low caste person. In his complaint he made a mention that the high caste people stoned him in front of his house and beat him black and blue and also abused him in the name of his caste and even went to the extent of threatening to murder him. The above said complaint was lodged at the Karjat police station on May 29, 1991. The result of the case is still awaited.[37]

22. There is one more case for the purpose of study. It took place in Takali Khandeshwari, Karjat Taluka, Ahmednagar Distirct, in which a lower caste person filed a case against a higher caste person on the ground that the latter did not allow him to send the copying material to his ward who was taking annual examination. The quarrel took place which led the lower caste person to file a false atrocity case under Sections 110, 107 (2) 143, 149 (3) 12A. The case remains pending in the High Court till today.[38]

23. Let us study a similar case of lodging a complaint of atrocities in Patewadi, Karjat Taluka, Ahmednagar District, in which a lower caste person filed a case against a higher caste person on the ground that the latter did not allow him to take the funeral procession through the temple gates of the village. The decision of the Court is still awaited.[39]

24. There is another case of atrocities which took place in the village

Malthan, Karjat Taluka, Ahmednagar District, in which a lower caste person filed a case against a higher caste person over the dispute of possession of land. The case is still pending in the Court of law.[40]

25. The final case took place in the village Khandvi, Karjat Taluka, Ahmednagar District. The complainant claimed that he was abused and harassed in the name of caste by the upper caste person. In his complaint he said that the higher caste people had always insulted him in the name of caste, creating problems for him in the village unnecesarily. The case is still pending in the court.[41]

Finally we come to an understanding that serious crimes with regard to atrocities have been committed against the Scheduled Castes and Scheduled Tribe people for various historical, social and economical reasons. Some of the cases have taken place on the grounds of historical reasons. It is because of the political awareness created amongst the Scheduled Caste/Tribe people through spread of literacy, that they are trying to assert their rights and this is not taken very kindly by others. It is found that when these supressed people assert their rights against the practices of untouchability, the vested interests of the upper class people try to cow them down and create terrorism in the society to which they belong. When they try to preserve their self respect or the honour of their women, they take revenge on the upper caste people and lodge false complaints of atrocities and bring the matter to the courts which lead to dismissal or withdrawal of cases.

One point which emerges out of this and which should be taken into consideration is that the executive, the police or the bureaucrats are not really very sincere in implementing the preventive measures taken by the Government. The cases do not really stand before the courts and the acquitted or the accused are set free. In this context one of the senior members of Parliament observed, "We have already enacted so many Acts but the question remains that why the Judiciary is silent in this respect. It takes years and years for a case to get settled".[42] He further lamented and questioned, "Do you think these poor people can afford to pursue the cases for years and years?"

In the light of the above remarks we are led to think that it is a pity that despite several measures taken by the Government, all these provisions and facilites do not reach the rural areas where these people reside. Therefore, it is the need of the hour to find out the real reasons and rediscover the entire process of the implementation of PCR Act and the Atrocities

Act. The researcher feels that besides enacting this legislation we must also consider the effective implementation of measures taken for their upliftment. Dr. B. R. Ambedkar had also suggested the reservation for improving their social lot because these people are subjected to social discrimination and segregation for thousands of years. The reservation will provide them a base to create their own employment and to improve their economic condition. The Harijans and Adivasis are trying to assert their rights in getting their employments in various fields, i. e, education, agriculture, industry, administration, etc. But the question remains unanswered as to how we are going to curb the atrocities committed on the Dalits in the remote, rural parts of the country where the economic status of these people is below poverty line and where people lead hand to mouth existance.

Dr. B. R. Ambedkar was unhappy over the plight of the downtrodden and people living in poor conditions. Even today poverty exists in the society and the Adivasis still live in deplorable conditions as their forefathers had lived thouands of years ago.

Of course, there are many reasons behind atrocities committed on Harijans and Tribals. It is due to the improvement in the social set up during these 50 years of Independence, that these people have arisen, awakened and have started resisting oppression. In urban areas, these people do not find it difficult in getting justice with regard to cases of atrocities because they are well organized and united. But in the rural parts of the country we experience that the people are disorganized and they lack unity which prevents them from getting early justice.

Till now much has been said about the PCR Act and the Atrocities Act and how they are being implemented. Now we shall turn to specific solutions which can be offered for the total eradication of untouchability and establishing an ideal society where there will be no scope for any kind of opposition, depression or segregation. However, it is a very difficult task to be achieved. But we must not leave any stone unturned while marching towards a progressive, united India.

After carefully examing the cases of PCR Acts and atrocities commited on some of the Scheduled Caste people in Karjat Taluka of Ahmednagar District; it has been found that the above Acts were misused by the upper caste people forcing the lower caste people to lodge false complaints. Sometimes, the lower caste people themselves are responsible for filing false cases against the higher caste people. Here, one can notice that both the Acts were unsuccessful in fulfilling the intentions for which they were enacted. The provisions of these Acts are for the protection of the civil rights of the downtrodden but the very purpose of implementing these Acts seems to have been unsolved. The present study reveals that the Scheduled Castes and Scheduled Tribes have not been beneifitted by the steps taken by the Government

One of the MPs remarked, "Our ideology is clear and the intention of our Government is also good, but the implemention of these laws is the responsibility of the State Governments and they do not fulfil it. We enact the laws, but they are rarely implemented effectively."[43]

The above remarks make it clear that the laws are inadequate for uplifting the downtrodden people to the level of higher caste people. The rift between the lower caste and higher caste people is to be removed and steps should be taken to bring these classes together with a common culture. India has a fine legacy of cultural values. But the question is that whether we should preserve these values or not. Therefore, it is very necessary to see that there is no misuse of the PCR and the Atrocities Act by the upper caste as well as the lower caste people. The State Governments should take strong measures for the successful and proper implementation of the Acts. Governmental machinery is not taking the Acts seriously and therefore the FIRs are not properly registered causing the failure of the cases. The respective police stations do not give sufficient protection to the poor Scheduled Caste people in the rural parts of our country in general and Maharashtra in particular.

Conclusion

After having studied the cases which took place in Karjat Taluka of Ahmednagar District, in the light of the PCR Act and the Atrocities Act, it is necessary to draw a conclusion notwithstanding the verdict passed by the respective judges after the hearing of each one of the cases selected for the purpose of the study. It is keenly observed that the verdict passed by the judges in these cases is based on the facts, witnesses and the nature of the Acts applicable to the cases. The results of most of these cases show that the higher caste Hindus, who were the accused, were either acquitted by the court or the cases were withdrawn. The question remains as to why the untouchables or the Dalits tend to lodge complaints against the higher caste Hindus. Do they think that the higher caste Hindus are the most cruel and barbaric people in the world? Why do the Dalits feel alienated from the mainstream of Hindu society. Today, the Dalits, comprising of 20 per cent of the country's population, refuse to be called Hindus. Why? The Hindu society has always deprived the Dalits of their rights, ill treated, segregated and ostracized them. According to Varnashram dharama, they are to be placed in the lowest strata of Hindu society. Due to these and other reasons they prefer to keep themselves in isolation from the Hindu society.

The following conclusions can be drawn in the light of the above questions and in relation to the use of the PCR Act and the Atrocities Act in Karjat Taluka:

1. In most of the cases which have been studied so far, it is observed that the acused is set free by the Judge concerned. If we go to the root of the problem, we feel that due to lack of enough evidence and eyewitnesses in the villages, the higher caste Hindu is benefitted. The untouchables or the Dalits involved in these cases do not produce evidences and witnesses before the court. Despsite the crime committed by the upper caste Hindus, people in the villages are unable to open their mouths before the police and the Judge. The fear in their minds does not allow them to speak the truth. The untouchables are afraid of the police. The people who witness the incident of a higher caste Hindus abusing a Dalit, do not come forward and stand in the witness box for the Judge to give the verdict. Therefore, most of the cases were either withdrawn or the accused were set free.

2. The second genuine reason is "poverty". The lower caste people are not economically well off. They have to toil from dawn to dusk for earning their livelihood. Most of their time is spent in collecting food and other requirements. Therefore, the untouchables who complain against the higher caste persons are unable to handle the case. Infact, they are unable to produce evidence in the court of law. On the other hand the upper caste person who are accused are considerably rich. The poor people fall a prey to the rich man's offer of bribe money and speak against the untouchables.

3. It is obseved that some cases are politically motivated. There are so many people belonging to different political parties. The Dalits also join hands with these political parties. It is due to rivalry, that the upper caste Hindus or landlords, instigate the poor untouchables to lodge a complaint against their high caste Hindu using the PCR Act and the Atrocities Act with the intention of giving a lesson to the members of the rival political party. However, these cases are either withdrawn or remain pending for many years.

4. The untouchables or the Dalits do not have sufficient knowledge of the Acts on the basis of which they lodge complaints. Many of the Dalit villagers are not educated enough to understand and realize the pros and cons of the situation. They only know that law is behind them. It is communicated to them that the Government is with them and they can lodge a complaint against a higher caste Hindu who abuses them in the name of their caste. They do not know how to lodge a complaint. They take the help of the upper caste person who knows how to lodge a complaint. Nobody gives them the knowledge of the said matter.

5. It has been categorically said that there exists casteism within the castes in the villages, where the Dalits among the Dalits exercise superiority over the weaker, backward caste people or show that they are superior to the people of upper caste. There is a tendency to provoke the more backward among the backwards and to lodge a complaint of atrocities against the persons from upper class category.

6. One of the observations is that there have been some lower caste people or higher caste people who instigate some of the lower caste people and force them to lodgc a complaint in the name of caste against the person from the so-called established class. The vested interest of these people can be of any kind. For example, in order to take revenge on others these cases of atrocities are lodged. Some cases are being lodged on the grounds of establishing superiority over other's success. Earning money is also one of the purposes of lodging the complaints which are false in nature. After studying the cases, one is led to realize that some of them are lodged on the basis of rivalry between the groups in the villages, trying to pull down one another and drawing the attention of the entire village community. It also has been noticed that due to conflict or strife between two political parties, some cases of atrocities have taken place in the villages of Karjat Taluka of Ahmednagar District. The cases taken for the purpose of study also indicate that there has been a selfish motive behind each one of them and, therefore, all those cases were acquitted by the respective judges and the accused were set free. Some cases reveal that there has been a revenge motive in the social groups involved in them. Some people in the villages who are unemployed, unnecessarily try to create disturbances in the society causing disharmony, leading the backward class people to file a case of atrocities in the court. In other words, there has been a tendency in some of the villagers to provoke quarrels between the backward class people and the upper caste people.

References

1. State v/s Sankar Kondiba Gorkhe, Vittal Sankar Gangarde case No. 157/79 January 16, 1979 order 6/5/1991.
2. Human Rights in International Law. Legal and Police Issues Edited by Theodor Neron. Clarendon Press, Oxford, reprinted 1988, pp. 1-566.
3. Vol. L 11 No 20 "Lok Sabha Debates". Monday August 14, 1989, Col No 1 to176. 1989, published under Rules 379 to 382 of the Rules of Procedure and Conduct. Business in Lok Sabha (Sixth Edition) and Printed by S. Narayan & Sons, Delhi 6, p. 59 (Shri Somnath Rathi).
4. State v/s Nilkanth Balasahedb Saluhkhe, Alsande 30/7/1979 case No. 277 1979, order 27/12/1984.
5. *Human Rights in the Modern World,* R. S. Agarwal, Chetana Publications, New Delhi, 1978, First Edition, January 1979, p. 85.
6. Sh. Pardhani (Navrangpura) Lok Sabha Debates 1989. Vol. L 1 No. 21 Column No 1 to 180, August 16, 1989, p. 83.
7. State v/s Kashinath Balbhim Udamle, Sabaji Nana Garde 20/8/1981 order on 15/1/1983.
8. International Documents on Human Rights, Satish Chandra— Forwarded by T.V.G. Krishnamurty—Mittal Publication, New Delhi, India, First Edition, 1990, page x/r. 166.
9. Dr. Rajendra Kumari Bajpai, Home Minister, Lok Sabha Debates. Vol. No 21 Col No 1 to 180. August 16, p. 87.
10. State (Pandurang Udmal) v/s J.B. Labde and D. T. Amte on 5/2/1981, case No. 265/1981 order 11/3/1983.
11. International Document on Human Rights. Satish Chandra—Foreword by T.V.G. Krishnamaury—Mittal Publication, New Delhi, India, First Edition, 1990, pp. 159-60.
12. Dr. Rajendra Kumari Bajpai, Minister of State of the Ministry of Welfare, Lok Sabha Debate Vol. No. 21 Col No. 1 to 180, August 16, 1989, p. 89.
13. State (Rangnath Shivram Udmale) v/s Dattatray Narsingrao Purne, on 21/4/1982 case No. 54/1982 order on 16/11/1983.
14. *Ibid* Human Rights, p. 67-68.
15. *Ibid* Vol. L I No. 21 Col No. 1 to 180, August 16, p. 27 (Dr. Phulrenu Guba Contai).
16. Shri Baban Dingra Zodges application about abusing him to Police Station on 22/2/1982.
17. Bombay Criminal Report 1980—Laxman Jayaram Shant. Pettitioner v/s The State of Maharashtra Criminal Revision Application No. 38 of 1980 decided on 17/4/1980.

18. Sh. Bapula Malavya. "Lok Sabha" Debates Vol. No. L. II No. 20 Monday August 14, 1989, New Delhi, 1989, p. 86.

19. Shri Pandurang Dingra Zodge's application about (denial of temple entry) Ahmednagar on 20/2/1984.

20. International Documents on Human Rights, Satish Chandra, forwarded by T.V.G. Krishnamurty, Mittal Publication, New Delhi, India, First Edition, 1990, pp. 166-67.

21. Dr. Phulrenu Guha (Conti), Lok Sabha Debates Vol. No. 21 Col No. 1 to 180 August 16, 1989, p. 27.

22. State v/s Kantilal Lodha, Mirajagaon 8/6/1988. Case No. 263/1988 (Pending in the High Court).

23. State v/s Sampat Sahadu Wagh and others, Kolwadi on 26/10/1988 case No. 462/1988 order February 14, 1990.

24. State v/s Ashok Gopalrao Palshikar, Nimgan Gangurda 14/12/1988 case No. 516/1988 order 11/2/1993.

25. Sh. Rampyare Panika, Lok Sabha Debates, Vol. No. 21, Col No. 1 to 180. August 16 1989, p. 39.

26. State v/s Ramchandra Digambar Kharde. Babhulgaon order on 11/1/1981 case No. 180/1981 order 7/9/1982 case no.11.

27. State (Soma Yamaji Adsul) v/s Vasant Baskar Murkute A/P Koregan 18/5/1985 case No. 98/1985 order 20/6/1986.

28. State v/s Shripati Rama Kadam A/P Mahjilgaon on 25/10/1988 case No/455/1988, order 19/11/1992.

29. State (Maruti Bhagwan Sonawane) v/s Babasaheb Rambhau Admane A/P Chhilwadi T. Karjat on 30/5/1985 Case No. 42/1985 order 7/5/1991.

30. State v/s Suraji Dattatray Deshmukh at post Mirajgaon Karjat Taluka, on 1/2/1990 case No. 84/1990. (Pending in the High Court.)

31. State (Pandurang Yashwant Gaikawad) v/s Devram Bhaurao Yadav at post Bhairobawadi Karjat Taluka, on 21/11/83 case No. 131/1983, order acquitted 1987.

32. State (Uttam Dasharath Shinde) v/s Bhimrao Babaji Sudrik and other on 2/11/1983 case No. 122/1983 order on 1/2/1984.

33. State (Ashok Babaji Chavan) v/s Gulab Bapurao Kharade at post Babhulgaon (Dumala) Karjat Taluka on 28/10/1987 order 8/12/1991.

34. State v/s Indar Bhikaji Thorat and others A/P Thersadi case on 14/8/1990 case No. 145/1990 order on 15/12/1992.

35. State v/s Dhayndeo Ganpat Khetmalas at post Mirajgoan Karjat Taluka, on

23/9/1993 case No. 154/1993 still pending matter within High Court.

36. State v/s Ramdas Shivji Raut at Karjat Taluka, on 15/10/95. Matter in the high court still pending.

37. State v/s Sarjerao Shinde At. Shinde - case No.85/1991 29/5/1991 still pending in the High Court.

38. State v/s Doobe Patil. G. D at Takkli Khandeshwari. Matter in the High Court.

39. State (Ratan Rajguru) v/s Sukhdev Uttam Disale at post Patewadi, Karjat Taluka, Matter in the High Court.

40. State (Nana Ganpat Wagmare) v/s Vishwanath Bhise A/P Malthaan, Chondi. Matter in the High Court.

41. State v/s Tapkir Bhanudas Bajirao A/P Khandvi. Matter in the High Court.

42. Sh. Ramratan Ram (Hajipur) Lok Sabha Debates, Vol No. 20, Col No. 1 to 176, August 14, 1989, p. 66.

43. Sh. Somnath Rath, Lok Sabha Debates, Vol. No. 20 Col No. 1 to 176. August 14, 1989, p. 56

7

Conclusion and Suggestions

The careful study of the cases under Protection of Civil Rights Act and Atrocities Act which were implemented in Karjat Taluka of Ahmednagar District reveals that despite civil rights granted to the Scheduled Caste people, some cases have been investigated and some have been dismissed. The policy of protective discrimination in general and the Protection of Civil Rights Act and Atrocities Act in particular were aimed at giving special treatment and special protection to the Scheduled Castes who are socially, economically and politically very weak. The national policy is very in necessary of the integration of the Scheduled Caste in the mainstream of the Indian society.

Only making the policies and enacting laws is not going to help in improving the socio-economic conditions of these people. The process of integration of these people is insufficient and needs to be given a different dimension by bringing the higher and lower caste people together. There should be some kind of binding force which should really bring all the castes of the Hindu society together.

As far as Maharashtra is concerned, as described in earlier chapters, it has a fine legacy of social reform movement of stalwarts like Mahatma Phule, Agarkar, Shahu Maharaj of Kolhapur, Lokmanya Tilak, Maharshi Karve, Vitthal Ramji Shinde and Dr. B. R. Ambedkar. This reform movement had been continuing for nearly 150 years. But the desired effects of this movement were not experienced by the Scheduled Caste people in the true sense of the term. It was because of this legacy and the government's policy of protective discrimination that the caste Hindus have become aware of the rights of the Scheduled Castes in rural areas. But many of the Scheduled Caste people in Maharashtra today still are unaware of the rights which are included in the Indian Constitution and the Protection of the Civil Rights Act and the Atrocities Act. It is due to lack of awareness and knowledge about the laws that the Hindu society, specially the Scheduled Castes, have become handicapped. Secondly, even now many known and unknown social reformers of different abilities are working to stop and condemn the social segregation or discrimination. They have been struggling for the cause of social justice in urban and rural areas. In urban areas, the cases of atrocities are less as compared to the cases which take place in rural areas. The main reason of the increasing number of cases of atrocities in rural area is the vested interest of the rival groups or individuals. Thirdly, the cases take place for the purpose of domination over one another in villages. A number of youths are unemployed. They tend to create disturbances and disharmony in the village community. The real nature of the cases never come to the surface level and confusion is created. Sometimes the police authorities do not ensure the safety and security of the Scheduled Caste people in villages.

It has already been mentioned in earlier chapters that a responsive police administration is the prerequisite for ensuring that the Scheduled Caste victims get redress under the laws meant for the purpose. It is an acknowledged fact that the Scheduled Caste victims usually approach the police station in fear and trepidation. The study has been done to manifest that there are instances of failure to register heinous offences, delayed visits to the scene of the crime, delays in filing chargesheets and failure to invoke the relevant provisions of the law. The cases which have been studied show that the attitude of the higher castes has ranged from apathy to hostility to downright brutality. The researcher opines that delayed investigation, faulty and delayed chargesheets, lukewarm prosecution and protracted proceedings—all have contributed to a high percentage of acquittals in the cases under the Atrocity Act. Unless special steps are taken, the fate of the cases registered under the Protection of Civil Rights Act and the Atrocities Act will remain unchanged. One feels that the harassment of the Scheduled Castes can be stopped by bringing revolutionary changes in the judicial and administrative set-up. The system should genuinely assess the registration, effective prosecution and quick disposal of cases under the Atrocity Act.

Now let us think about the changes which can be brought about for creating a healthy society in general. The study shows that the Government is right in legislating the useful and necessary laws. But the same laws can be/are used to disturb social peace. Thus, the laws that should help in creating social peace are pursued in wrong spirit to destroy the peace and harmony. That is solely because the society is uneducated, backward and illiterate. Petty desires dominate the minds of the mischief mongers in the rural areas. They misuse the backward and downtrodden people for some selfish aims, gains and power politics. The Scheduled Caste people also become a "willing" prey in the hands of such mischief mongers. They are economically weak, socially backward and politically unaware. Selfishness and narrrowmindedness make such victims play into the hands of the power seekers and as a result a good law is misused.

This can be changed by the spread of literacy among the large population of the backward people. Political awareness, employment opportunities and the status of equality and dignity can slowly change the whole situation. Education of the masses is the only solution to this great problem. The careful perusal of the cases in the present investigation and their analysis show that social, economical and educational backwardness are the main reasons why atrocities are being perpetuated on the Scheduled Castes in the rural areas. The entire SC/ST population in the country is not fully educated. It is due to the literacy programmes that they are able to know many things about the laws and also what has been going on in the country. The Government is launching several schemes to uplift the status of these people. The Government wants to enhance their status in the society by conferring many educational and economic benefits on them through various schemes. Here, it would be in the fitness of things to suggest that launching schemes for improving the status of these people is not going to help in solving their problems. The need of the hour is to make the people literate and educate them in such a way that discrimination can have no scope in the Hindu society.

The feeling of brotherhood must be generated in the minds of different communities for breaking the vicious circle of casteism. Slogans and proclamations are not enough to create a harmonious community. In other words, only saying that "We are all brothers and sisters" is not going to help us establish social justice. What is preached must be practised. It means action and thought must go hand in hand. A powerful reason behind inequality is the caste system itself. Therefore, our main concern should be to abolish the stigma of caste system.

One more valuable suggestion would be that we must restructure the Hindu society by bringing different castes together, keeping the sole aim of creating a united India. The spirit of patriotism should be the prime objective before all of us and this is possible only through proper education, and a common educational pattern. The difference between Bharat and India must come to an end at any cost.

The author is led to suggest one more thing that intercaste marriages could be one of the solutions which can be offered to abolish the caste system completely. A number of youths should come forward and go in for intercaste marriages. This will give rise to a new social order where caste will have no scope to exist. The existing incentives given by the Government are inadequate. More incentives should be given and the knowledge of the schemes with regard to the intercaste marriages should be made available and known to the masses. The younger generation should be encouraged by the Government by way of providing employment opportunities to those who go in for intercaste marriages.

Finally, the author strongly feels that more stress should be put on implementing a common civil code so as to enable social justice for all. This will certainly help to stop discriminating people on the basis of caste, religion, language, and the States in which they live. The code should be applicable to all those who are living in India. The people of other religions should give their wholehearted support to the common civil code for holding the values imbibed in them. If the above suggested measures are adopted by every individual in the society, the spirit of equality will prevail and we can make India more strong and united. We will really have realized the dream of Rabindranath Tagore as stated in the following lines:

> "And into that heaven of freedom my Father,
> Let my country awake."

Bibliography

Books

1. Ambedkar B.R. *States and Minorities,* C. Murthy for Thacker: Bombay, 1947.
2. Ambedkar B. R. *Who were the Shudras?* Thacker and Co: Bombay 1970.
3. Ambedkar B. R. *Annihilation of Caste,* The Bharat Bhushan Press: Bombay, 1945.
4. Ambedkar B. R. *What Congress and Gandhi have done to the untouchables,* Thacker and Co: Bombay (2nd edition).
5. Asmitardarsh (ed).Pantavane, Ganagadhar, Aurangabad.
6. Beteille, Andre *Caste: Old new,* Asia Publishing House: Bombay, 1969.
7. Beteille, Andre *Inequality and Social Change,* Oxford University Press: Delhi, 1972.
8. Galanter, Marc *Competing Equalities Law and the Backward Classes in India,* Oxford University Press: Bombay, 1984.
9. Ghurye, G. S. *Class and Occupation,* Popular Book Dept: Bombay, 1961.
10. Hutton J. H. *Caste in India* (4th edition), Oxford University Press: Bombay, 1969.
11. Kamble, J. R. *Rise and Awakening of Depressed Classes in India,* National: New Delhi, 1979.
12. Kamble, N. D. *Deprived Castes and Their Struggle for Equality,* Ashish Publishing House: New Delhi, 1983.
13. Kamble. N. D. *The Scheduled Castes,* Ashish Publishing House: New Delhi, 1982.
14. Kane P. V. *History of Hindu Dharmashastras,* Vol. II Part I, Bhandarkar Oriental Research Institute, Poona, 1974.

15. Karve Irawati *Hindu Society: An Interpretation* (2nd edition), Deccan College Post Graduate and Research Institute, Poona, 1968.

16. Keer Dhananjaya *Dr. Ambedkar Life and Mission* (2nd edition). Popular Prakashan: Bombay, 1954.

17. Kharirmode, C. B. *Bhimrao Ramji Ambedkar* Vol. I, Y.B. Ambedkar. 1952, Vol.II, Bandhajan, Panchayat Samiti: Bombay 1958 Vol, III Pratap Prakashan: Bombay 1964 Vols. IV and V.

18. Dr. Ambedkar Education Society Bombay 1966. (1968) (in Marathi).

19. Kharat Shankarrao (ed) *Ambedkar B. R.* (Marathi). Indrayani Sahitya: Pune, 1987.

20. Kothari Rajni (ed). *Caste in Indian Politics* (2nd ed.), Orient Longman, Ltd: New Delhi, 1973.

21. Mahar Migh J. (ed). *The Untouchable in Contemporary India* Arizona, The university of Arizona Press: Tueson (U.S.A), 1977.

22. Mate S. M. *Problem of the Untouchable* (Marathi), S. R. Date: Pune, 1933.

23. Majumdar, D. N. *Caste and Communication in an Indian Village,* Asia Publishing House: Bombay, 1958.

24. Omvedt, Gail *Cultural Revolt in a Colonial Society,* Bombay Scientific Socialist Education Trust, 1976.

25. Pandit, Nalini *The Problem of Scheduled Castes after Independence* (Marathi), Sadhana Prakashan: Pune, 1974.

26. Pantavane *Gangadhar Patrakar. Dr. Babasaheb Ambedkar* (Marathi), Abhijit Publication: Nagpur, 1987.

27. Patwardhan Sunanda. *Changing Religious Behaviou and Tradition of Scheduled Caste,* Bull. ether D. C. R. 28 (1-2).

28. Purogami Satyashodhak, (ed). Adhav Baba, Pune, 1967-68.

29. P. C. R. Act Castes in village Bhabhulgaon (Khalasa) 1979 to 1985. Documents acquired from the Taluka court, Karjat.

30. Reports of Commissioner for Scheduled Castes and Scheduled Tribes, Manager of Publications, Government of India, Delhi, 1956 to 1977.

31. Report of the Committee on Untouchability, Economic and Concerned Documents, (Chairmam L. Elayaperumal).

(Delhi: Department of Social Welfare 1969).

32. Sadhana (ed) Thatte Yadunath, Pune

33. Shah Ghanshyam *Studies on politics of Scheduled Castes and Scheduled Tribes,* mimeography (New Delhi, 1971).

34. Shinde, V. R. *Problem of the Indian Untouchables* (2nd ed), Bombay: Government of Maharashtra, 1978.

35. Srinivas M. N. *Caste in Modern India and Other Essays,* Asia Publishing House: New York, 1962.

36. Vatkar Namdeo *Bharatatil Jatibhed anityavar upaya* (Marathi), IInd (ed), Ajab Prakashan: Kolhapur, 1972.

Articles

Many books have been written on various legislations passed on the subject. Related literature can be enumerated as follows:

1. "Who were the Shudras?" Dr. Ambedkar B. R., Thacker and Co., Bombay, 1970.
2. "States and Minorities" Dr. Ambedkar B. R., C. Murthy Thacker, Bombay, 1947.
3. "Annihilation of Caste" Dr. Ambedkar B. R., The Bharat Bhushan Press, Bombay, 1945.
4. "Rise and Awakening of Depressed Classes in India" Kamble, J. R., National, New Delhi, 1979.
5. "The Scheduled Castes" Kamble, N. D., Ashish Publishing House, New Delhi, 1982.
6. "Competing Equalities, Law and the Backward Classes in India" Galanter More, Oxford University Press, Bombay, 1984.
7. "The Untouchables in Contemporary India" Mhar Mich J.(ed) Arizona Press, Tueson (U. S. A.), 1977.
8. "Dr. Babasaheb Ambedkaranche Dharmantar" (Marathi) Kharat Shankarrao, Thokal Prakasha, Pune, 1966.
9. "Dr. Babasaheb Ambedkaranchi Patre" (Marathi) Thokal Prakashan, Pune, 1961.
10. "Hindu Society: An Interpretation" Karve, Irawati, Deccan College Post Graduate and Research Institute (Revised Ed.), Pune, 1968.
11. "Problems of the Indian Untouchables" Shinde V. R. Government of Maharashtra, Bombay, 2nd. Ed. 1976.
12. "Scheduled Castes and Scheduled Tribes Commission Report" Government of India, Delhi, 1975-77.
13. "Atrocities on Scheduled Castes and Tribes: Causes and Remedies" Report of National Commission for SC/ST, April 1989-1990.

14. "Lok Sabha Debates" Lok Sabha Secretariat, New Delhi, 1975- 1992.
15. "Rajya Sabha Debates" Rajya Sabha Secretariat, New Delhi, 1975-1992.
16. "Reservations for Backward Classes" Mandal Commission Report, Central Govt, Delhi, 1980.
17. "The Protection of Civil Rights Act" Central Govt. Publication, Delhi, 1955, 1976.
18. "Maharashtra Assembly/Vidhan Sabha/Vidhan Parishad Debates, Maharashta Government Secretariat (1975-1992)."
19. "Scheduled Castes and Scheduled Tribes (Prevention of Atrocities) Act, 1989. Central Government Publication, Delhi, 1990."
20. "P. C. R. and Atrocities cases in Karjat Taluka" Court Judgements.
21. "Human Rights: Arnold C. Edward Arnold, London, 1978."
22. "Human Rights Critique" Bastra. T. S. Metropolition, New Delhi, 1979.
23. "Human Rights in the Modern World" Agarwal, R. S. Chetana Pub, New Delhi.
24. "Human Rights: From rhetoric to reality" Campbell, Tom and others Ets, Basil Block Well, Oxford, 1986.
25. Patrakar Dr. Babasaheb Ambedkar, Dr. Gangadhar Pantawane, Abhijit Prakashan, Nagpur, 1987.
26. Dr. Babasaheb Ambedkar, Gaourav Grantha, Sampadak Daya Pawar (Nimantrak) Prof. Keshav Meshram, Kalaynkar wa Itar Maharashtra Sahitya ani Sanskriti Mandal, Mumbai, 1993.
27. Source Material on Dr. Babasaheb Ambedkar and the Movement of Untouchables Volume II published by Vasnat Muun (Marathi), Education Department, Government of Maharashtra, Bombay 1990.
28. India 1991, A Reference Annual, Edited and Complied by, Research and Reference Division, Ministry of Information and Broad- casting, Government of India, 1991.
29. Nirmal Kumar Bose, "Who are the Backward Classes Men in India? Vol. 34, 402 April (1954 P. 98).
30. Lok Sabha Debates Vol. No. 50, Tuesday, May 23, 1972/Jyaistha Z 1984 (Saka) Columns 155 to 249, Lok Sabha Secretariat, New Delhi, 1972.
31. Bombay Criminal Report 1980—page No. 610. Laxman Jayram Shant Petitioner v/s The State of Maharashtra Criminal revision Application No. 38 of 1980 decided on 17/04/1980.
32. The Protection of Civil Rights Act, 1955 (Act 22 of 1955) N. R. Bhalerao, Law Book Sellers and Publishers, Pune, 1978.

33. The Protection of Civil Rights Act S. C. R. C. Office, Supreme Court Rev. Cases, Anand Bunglow, Patel Colony, College Road, Nasik Page 1 to 15.
34. The Protection of Civil Rights Act, 1955 (Formerly known as Untouchability (Offences) Act, 1955) (Act No. 22 of 1955) Published by Govt. of India, Shimla New Delhi, 1992, Page 1 to 10.
35. The Scheduled Castes and the Scheduled Tribes (Prevention of Atrocities) Act, 1989 by S. K. Awasthi, Premier Publishing Company, Banglore Ed., 1992.
36. Scheduled Castes and Scheduled Tribes (Prevention of Atrocities) Act, 1989, Eastern Book Company, Fourth Ed, (Report of the Commissioner for 1993).
37. Reservations for Backward Classes, Mandal Commission Report of the Backward Classes Commission. Printed by Akalank Kumar Publications, Delhi, 1980.
38. Report of National Commissioner for Scheduled Castes & Tribes, Causes & Remedies, April 1990—Page 1 to 87.
39. Report of the Commissioner for Scheduled Castes and Scheduled Tribes, 1975, 76 and 1976, 77 (Twenty, Fourth Report), New Delhi, 1976.
40. Report of the Commissioner for Scheduled Castes and Scheduled Tribes, 1975 to 76 and 1976, 1977, New Delhi, 1977.

Newspapers

The Daily Newspapers (English & Marathi)

1. *The Times of India,* Editor Gautam Adhikari, Published by Bennet Coleman & Company Ltd. by K. N. Amrjam, Mumbai.
2. *The Indian Express,* Editor Shekhar Gupta, Published by George Verguese, Pune.
3. *Maharashtra Times,* Editor Kumar Ketkar, Published by Bennet Coloman & Company, Mumbai.
4. *Loksatta,* Editor Arun Tikekar, Published by George Verghess for Indian Express Newspapers, Mumbai.
5. *Sakal,* Editor Vijay Kuvlekar, Published by Pratap Pawar, Pune.
6. *Tarun Bharat,* Editor Laxuman Trimbak Joshi, Published by Rajendra V. Sonawane, Jansampada Ltd. Kesri Mudranalay, Pune.
7. *Kesri,* Editor Arvind V. Gokhle, Published by Dr. Deepak Jayant Tilak, Pune.
8. *Samna,* Editor Bal Thackrey, Published by Subhash Desai, Aaj Ka Anand, Sagar Plaza, Pune.

Index